MEDS
Most Effective Discipleship Seeds

ENGRAFTING GOD'S WORD ON YOUR HEART
THROUGH THE ENJOYMENT OF FELLOWSHIP

D.S. FOSTER

Book 1 – Year One

Little Child to Young Man Level

Charleston, SC
www.PalmettoPublishing.com

Most Effective Discipleship Seeds (MEDS)
Copyright © 2021 by D.S. Foster

All rights reserved
Any part of this book may be photocopied by a church, small group, or individual if used to build up believers in Christ and expand the Kingdom of God. Any reproduction for monetary profit or any other purpose is prohibited.

ISBN-13: 978-1-64990-268-9
ISBN-10: 1-64990-268-9

Dedication

To both my natural and spiritual families who have consistently exemplified God's immeasurable love for me and continue to stand with me in service *(ministry)* to others.

Acknowledgements

I acknowledge as my center and top enjoyment, the Lord Jesus Christ,
Who has answered my two greatest prayers.
First, my prayer for genuine inner peace,
Which He answered abundantly by revealing Himself to me
As the Real Peace, and second…
My prayer to be effective in spiritual ministry *(service)*
Which he answered generously by His gift of
Most Effective Discipleship Seeds *(MEDS)* to the church through me and
Through the spirit led help of many brothers.

I want to thank Doug Melven, George Bursler, Mark Woodbeck,
Michael Filipiak, Wesley Vande Streck, Cameron Idol,
Tom LaForest, Mitchell Brindisi, John Shank, and
Many others for their dedication and persistent mutual fellowship in
Most Effective Discipleship Seeds *(MEDS)*, in
Proving and testifying to the effectiveness of this Christ centered Discipleship.

Finally, special thanks to George Crear III, and others for their enduring and patient work in proofreading, editing, and their invaluable suggestions in formatting the original manuscripts of this book. It is difficult to imagine how this book could have ever been completed without their help and encouragement.

Gender Designation

Whenever the pronoun "Him" or "He" is capitalized *(except at the beginning of a sentence)* it refers to deity *(Father, Son or Holy Spirit)*.

Otherwise, all other references in this book to "him" or "his" are intended to mean all people without respect to gender

Most Effective Discipleship Seeds *(MEDS)*

DEFINITION OF SEEDS

SEEDS are units of spiritual revelation of Bible truth that progressively increases the Presence and Power of Jesus Christ in the experience of the believers, in direct proportion to their heart mastery of them.

Most Effective Discipleship Seeds *(MEDS)*
MISSION STATEMENT

To significantly aid multitudes of believers to conceptually engraft God's Word on their hearts for the purpose of developing a stronger, more intimate relationship with Jesus Christ and to help each believer to uncover their own unique ability to "Pay It Forward" in this lifestyle. All glory to God!

(Book 1: Covers Year One of Phase I and the Galatians Phase)*

SCRIPTURAL DIVISIONS OF PHASE ONE
1 John 2:12-14, Mark 4:8, 4:26-28 Song of Solomon 2:16, 6:3, 7:10

Book One*
Level: Little Child to Young Man Year
Content: Year 1 of Phase I and Galatians Phase
Little Children..."you know the Father"
"your sins are forgiven"
"bear fruit: some 30 fold"
"my beloved is mine"
"First the blade"

Book Two**
Level: Young Man to Father Year
Content: Year 2 of Phase I, Phase II *(Spirit Empowered Control of Body)*,
John Phase, Romans Phase
Young Men... "You are strong "the Word of God abides in you"
"you have overcome the wicked one"
"bear fruit: ...some sixty fold"
"I am my Beloved's
"Then the head"

Book Three**
Level: Father to Master Craftsman
Content: Year 3 of Phase I, Phase III *(Christlikeness Phase)*, Ephesians
Phase, Hebrews Phase
Philemon Phase, James Phase, 1st, 2nd, and 3rd John Phase
Fathers... "you have known Him Who is from the beginning"
"some sixty, some one hundred fold"
"His desire is for me"
"then the full grain in the head"

* See Appendix #5 for Overview of Seeds and Scriptures for Book/Year/Level 1
** See Appendix #4 for for Overview of Five Years/Levels of Discipleship

Most Effective Discipleship Seeds *(MEDS)*
Book and Year One
(Year One of Phase I and Galatians Phase)
Little Child to Young Man Level

TABLE OF CONTENTS

Most Effective Discipleship Seeds (MEDS)
Book and Year One
(Year One of Phase I and Galatians Phase)
Little Child to Young Man Level

Dedication	i
Acknowledgments	ii
Gender Designation Statement	iii
Index of the 15 Appendixes	xv
Preface	xviii
Introduction	xix
History and Testimonies	xxi
History	xxi
Testimonies	xxi
Five Christ-Centered Philosophies of MEDS	xxv
Mutuality and Cooperation	xxv
Inward Transformation	xxv
Conceptual Learning	xxvi
Enjoyment of fellowship	xxvi
All Become Equipped to Teach	xxvi
Structure of MEDS	xxviii
Process of MEDS	xxviii
Results of MEDS	xxix
How to Use This Book	xxxi
Outline Formats - Simple Outline and Sample Fellowship	xxxiii
Further Explanations	xxxiii
Seed Numbering System xxxiii	
Gender Designation xxxiv	

PART ONE

Year One of Phase One

Little Child to Young Man (Spiritual) Level

Chapter and POD 1 - FACC

Seed 111 **F**AITH RIGHTEOUSNESS
Sample Format 1
Further Information 5

Seed 211 **A**SSURANCE
Sample Format 7
Further Information 9

Seed 311 **C**LEARANCE
Sample Format 10
Further Information 12

Seed 411 **C**ONSECRATION
Sample Format 14
Further Information 16

OVERVIEW OF THE FIRST POD 17
Epilogue for Chapter 1 18

Special Implorer Seed Floater
Seed 000 SHARED INITIATIVE AND SHARED LEADERSHIP (*SISL*)
Explanation of Use and Seed Outline 19

Chapter and POD 2 - BDSR

Seed 121 **B**IBLE RELIABILITY
Sample Format 22
Further Information 25

Seed 221 **D**EITY OF CHRIST
Sample Format 28
Further Information 30

Seed 321 **S**PIRIT, SOUL, AND BODY
Sample Format 32
Further Information 34

Seed 421 **R**IGHTLY DIVIDING THE WORD
Sample Format   36
Further Information   38

OVERVIEW OF THE SECOND POD   42
Epilogue for Chapter 2   43

Chapter and POD 3 - 3B2K

Seed 131 **3** ASPECTS OF SALVATION
Sample Format   44
Further Information   46

Seed 231 **B**OOKS OF THE NEW TESTAMENT
Sample Format   48
Further Information   50

Seed 331 **2** OR 3 WITNESSES
Sample Format   52
Further Information   54

Seed 431 **K**ENOSIS
Sample Format   55
Further Information   57

OVERVIEW OF THE THIRD POD   58
Epilogue for Chapter 3   59

Chapter and POD 4 - 4PK3K

Seed 141 **4** LAWS, 4 *LIFES*, SOSL
Sample Format   60
Further Information   64

Seed 241 **P**RIDE VS. GODLY HUMILITY
Sample Format   67
Further Information   70

Seed 341 **K**INGDOM OF GOD
Sample Format   72
Further Information   74

Seed 441 3 KINDS OF LOVE
Sample Format   75
Further Information   77

Seed 541 **K**INGDOM QUALIFIED
Sample Format — 79
Further Information — 81

OVERVIEW OF THE FOURTH POD — 82
Epilogue for Chapter 4 — 84

Chapter and POD 5 – 5PPT

Seed 151 **5** ASPECTS OF OBEDIENCE
Sample Format — 85
Further Information — 89

Seed 251 **P**OWER OF THE TONGUE
Sample Format — 91
Further Information — 94

Seed 351 **P**RAISE AND WORSHIP
Sample Format — 96
Further Information — 98

Seed 451 **T**OTALLY EQUIPPED
Sample Format — 100
Further Information — 102

OVERVIEW OF THE FIFTH POD — 103
Epilogue for Chapter 5 — 105

Chapter and POD 6 – 6DSP

Seed 161 **6** ELEMENTARY PRINCIPLES OF CHRIST
Sample Format — 106
Further Information — 110

Seed 261 **D**OCTRINE OF CHRIST
Sample Format — 116
Further Information — 118

Seed 361 **S**ENSE OF WORTHINESS
Sample Format — 119
Further Information — 122

Seed 461 **P**RAYER
Sample Format — 124
Further Information — 126

OVERVIEW OF THE SIXTH POD — 127
Epilogue for Chapter 6 — 129

Chapter and POD 7 – 7WFSF

Seed 171 **7** BAPTISMS OF THE NEW TESTAMENT
Sample Format — 131
Further Information — 136

Seed 271 **W**ITNESSING
Sample Format — 150
Further Information — 152

Seed 371 **F**OUNDATIONAL MINISTRIES
Sample Format — 158
Further Information — 161

Seed 471 **S**OWING AND REAPING
Sample Format — 164
Further Information — 166

Seed 571 **F**AITH ADDITIVES
Sample Format — 168
Further Information — 172

OVERVIEW OF THE SEVENTH POD — 174
Epilogue for Chapter 7 — 177

PART TWO

Galatians Phase
Chapter and POD 1 - DNRP — 181
Chapter and POD 2 - SRNM/CF — 182
Chapter and POD 3 – PSLC/BRF.IFLCA.GAA — 184
Chapter and POD 4 - …. /HFSS.BE.ZL - TBCC — 187
Chapter and POD 5 – SFCI/F.HPLL.OLW.FB — 190
Chapter and POD 6 – BGGG/OSN — 193

INDEX OF APPENDIXES

1. Invitation Letter to Participate in Most Effective Discipleship Seeds (MEDS) — A1
2. MEDS Synopsis — A2
3. Overview of Phase I - 100 seeds (Core Curriculum of 1st Three Years) — A3
4. Overview of MEDS - 5 Years / 5 Levels / 5 Books — A4
5. Year / Level / Book 1 Little Child to Young Man — A5
   Contents: Seeds of 1st Year of Phase I and Galatians Phase
6. Year / Level / Book 2 Young Man to Father — A6
   Contents: Seeds of 2nd Year of Phase I, Phase II Spirit-Empowered Temperance, Romans Phase, John Phase
7. Year / Level / Book 3 Father to Master Craftsman — A7
   Contents: Seeds of 3rd Year of Phase I, Phase III Christlikeness, Ephesians Phase Hebrews Phase, Philemon Phase, James Phase, 1st & 2nd & 3rd John Phase
8. Year / Level / Book 4 Master Craftsman to Master Builder — A8
   Contents: Seeds of Phase IV Essential Elements of Discipleship (MEDS), Acts Phase 1 Corinthians Phase, Philippians Phase, Colossians Phase, 1 Thessalonians Phase 1 Timothy Phase, 1 Peter Phase
9. Year / Level / Book 5 Master Builder to Advanced Master Builder — A9
   Contents: Phase V. Healing, 2 Corinthians Phase, 2 Thessalonians Phase, 2 Timothy Phase
   Titus Phase, 2 Peter Phase, Jude/Revelation Phase, Genesis Phase, Proverbs Phase, Psalms Phase, Synoptic Gospels Phase
10. Consecration Plan / Worksheet — A10
11. MEDS / Things We Say — A11
12. Essential Elements / MEDS Phase IV — A12
13. Promotional Flyer — A13
14. Year One Practice Grid — A14
15. Galatians Practice Grid — A15

About the Author — 260

Most Effective Discipleship Seeds *(MEDS)*
DEFINITION OF SEEDS

SEEDS are units of spiritual revelation of Bible truth that progressively increases the Presence and Power of Jesus Christ in the experience of the believers, in direct proportion to their heart mastery of them.

PREFACE

As a student of God's Word and a lover of Christ's Church, I was perplexed and even somewhat grieved. It seemed obvious that much of the teaching taking place in the church environment among believers was being done in a random and haphazard manner often using methods that were not always consistent with or worthy of God's perfect plan. As a result, it was clear that significant spiritual growth was not common among believers. Some of the believers who were showing some spiritual growth were simply gaining "head knowledge", which is of little value when compared to the top benefit of permanently rooting, grounding and establishing scripture into the hearts of His people. Additionally, the substance of what they learned was too often laden with religious and traditional content not consistent with God's Word, and consequently was deficient in its measure of eternal value.

At the time I likened the situation to a math teacher who used unproven formulas and equations with no planned curriculum whose teachings lacked any significant order or congruency. The Word of God is the most important subject of every believer's learning. It emphasizes that everything in the church is to be done "decently and in order" and in the Person and Presence *(Name)* of Jesus Christ. Yet, too often it was being taught without the advantage of a clear and comprehensive *(Spirit led)* plan or curriculum.

Having sought the Lord diligently for nearly a decade at that time, I had become perplexed. I was thankful that the Lord had given me a strong measure of revelation and wisdom. Yet, admittedly my own effort to significantly help others grow in their relationship with Christ, through His Word, fell quite short of anything that I count as being successful with respect to getting the scripture truths permanently planted into their hearts.

One day while walking and praying *(perhaps more like complaining)* about the troublesome situation, suddenly the Lord, by His indescribable grace, instantaneously gave me a clear and detailed vision which lighted into my consciousness. I subsequently knew with much detail what the Lord would have me do to contribute to solving the "heart growth problem" that I had been communicating to Him about. The result of this vision and subsequent revelation is, in part, laid out in some detail in this book. This Christ centered Discipleship, while different from traditional approaches used by many Bible teachers, has proven itself to be highly effective for many believers who have successfully rooted, grounded, and established God's Word in their hearts in a practical and measurable manner.

Any accomplishment of this objective is simply one of the most, if not the most important thing a believer can accomplish in this life. It always results in greater success in every area of the believer's life, both now and eternally. Most Effective Discipleship Seeds *(MEDS)* is an organized, proven, and highly effective way to master God's Word in small part for the casual learner, or in large part for the serious and intentional seeker of God's heart. This learning primarily takes place through the enjoyment of MED'S structured fellowship, while enjoying the free and flowing lead of the Holy Spirit. Most Effective Discipleship Seeds *(MEDS)* is a CHRIST CENTERED WAY of learning through repetitively listening to and speaking the seed/scripture concepts in the enjoyment of godly fellowship.

MEDS avoids the idea of scripture memorization, which many find to be difficult or even intimidating. The Seeds focus instead on learning conceptually in an orderly manner specific biblical idea through fellowship, writing them on the heart of the believer as he speaks them with passion in his own words. By applying the approach and principles in this book each disciple will experience an uncommon and extraordinary growth in his Christian walk and will gain much greater intimacy with Christ as well as a much stronger confidence to minister God's Word to others.

Introduction

Dr. James Richards, Andrew Wommack, Randy Shankle, Bill Hybels and Witness Lee are just a few of many wonderful and skilled teachers who have greatly contributed to my growth through imparting truth to me through books and tapes. While I have never met any of these men personally, it has become clear to me even the most outstanding Bible teachers will sometimes disagree as to the proper understanding of a given scripture passage. It is important to stay mindful that on any given point, each believer may lack full knowledge, or might even have an inaccurate understanding of God's view.

Jesus made it clear if one thinks he sees completely, then he remains in his blindness *(John 9:39-41)*. In the writing and assembling of the Seeds and concepts in this Discipleship, every effort was made to back up each concept and teaching with specific scriptures. However, I trust that the Spirit also lives in you, and for this reason this Discipleship allows for, and even encourages, the user to modify or even change a seed concept where the user is convinced by the Word and the Spirit that he has received a more accurate or clearer understanding on a particular point or topic.

We always need to keep in mind that it is our common faith in Jesus Christ that makes us one, and we should allow no difference in our personal understanding *(outside genuine belief in Christ Jesus as Savior)* to separate us believers from each other in essence. So then, you can use the Seeds exactly as they are laid out in this book, or you can revise and adapt them according to your own spiritual revelation if you believe it improves the biblical accuracy of the teaching. However, I would ask that if you do make changes, that you do it only after careful study and serious consideration, and with sobriety, being led by the Holy Spirit.

In writing a book to explain Most Effective Discipleship Seeds *(MEDS)* I faced a particular and inherent problem. This Discipleship was not originally designed or intended to be learned by the means of reading a book, as its very unique dynamic involves learning primarily through listening to and then speaking back *(to that person)* the concepts *(in essence)* within a Seed. While the concepts can most assuredly be learned through reading this book, the Discipleship is divinely designed for the learning to take place primarily through the mutual fellowship between believers *(usually two, sometimes more)*. Only when practiced in the way of fellowship can you ever fully appreciate the power and effectiveness of MEDS. The combination of the divine biblical content of these Seeds, along with the inherent enjoyment of fellowship with the Spirit flowing freely, creates a synergy that is highly and uniquely conducive to extraordinary learning, all glory to God! It is likely that learning the Seeds through "book study" only, will not achieve the same level of outstanding results that this Discipleship has consistently produced when experienced through Spirit led personal mutual fellowship.

HISTORY AND TESTIMONIES OF MOST EFFECTIVE DISCIPLESHIP SEEDS (MEDS)

History

Most Effective Discipleship Seeds *(MEDS)* was initially inspired, developed, and informally tested by prison inmates late in 2005 through 2009 at Muskegon Correctional Facility located in Michigan. Over the course of a decade it spread to many other correctional facilities where thousands of inmates have experienced anywhere from moderate to extraordinary growth in their relationship with Jesus Christ by engrafting God's Word on their hearts through this discipling fellowship. Below are some of the comments taken from their own written and spoken testimonies, along with the approximate number of seeds and scriptures each one learned through MEDS.

Testimonies

- In quarantine facing a life sentence I fell on my knees and asked God to send me someone with whom I could be motivated to learn, share, and grow. God answered my prayer abundantly. The Seeds Ministry has changed my life. I now know how to understand life and how to love... just as God has asked me to do. Because of the seeds I now know who I am! The Seeds are the greatest thing I have done in my life!

    Troy Logan #497929 100 Seeds 140 scriptures

- Ever since I started doing the Seeds and teaching them to others I have so much more confidence when it comes to *(my knowledge of)* scripture. The Most Effective Discipleship Seeds *(MEDS)* is set up so systematically and is so well put together that there is no way possible, with some persistence, you will not internalize scripture truths and make the Word go to work in your life.

    Joseph Lee Davis #404884 180 Seeds 240 Scriptures

- Through the encouragement and love I received through the fellowship of doing the seeds, I have put a ton of God's Word in my heart and it has transformed me. Those who have offended me, I have forgiven. God is also using me to share His Word with others so their lives can likewise be transformed.

Tom LaForest #445337 252 Seeds 334 Scriptures

- I am 36 years old. I went to church twice on Sunday for most of my life. I went to a private Christian School K-12 and thought I knew almost everything about Christian living. In only one year, "The Seeds" have taught me more about Jesus Christ than I had learned in my previous 35 years. I used to be a hearer of the Word only, just sitting in Bible Study or Church. Now, all glory to God, I am a doer of the Word, leading Bible studies and being active in the Church. My prayer life and fellowship has abounded and I live for Christ daily.

Darrell Roseboom #737987 45 Seeds 80 Scriptures

- As a direct result of the Seeds Discipleship, I have greatly increased my understanding of the Word of God, and by God's grace have become more skilled at "rightly dividing the Word". In addition, through my growth in knowledge and personal relationship with Christ, I have developed many close friendships centered on Christ. In only a few months, I have been able to retain more Bible truths than I had in my previous 33 years of life. The Seeds have also given me confidence to share the Word of God with others.

Matthew Kaiser #648578 50 Seeds 60 Scriptures

- Not worldly knowledge, but "WORDLY" knowledge. MEDS has helped me immensely. I praise the Lord for this Spirit-empowered Discipleship.

Mark Woodbeck #358010 40 Seeds 70 Scriptures

- I was born again over 10 years ago and have been learning conceptually *(through MEDS)* for just over a year. I have learned, understood and grown more in my walk with Christ and in my personal relationship since last year than I did the whole ten years of being saved before that time.

Jeffrey Ellis 570382 35 Seeds 60 Scriptures

- "The Seeds" allowed me to abide in God like never before.

Michael Filipiak 598311 80 Seeds 200 Scriptures

- I have been doing MEDS for over two years, resulting in significant growth in my personal relationship with Jesus Christ through the Spirit. I've gained greater understanding of Scripture and now recognize God's purpose for my life with a desire to carry it out. I have witnessed magnificent growth in everyone who has participated in "The Seeds". I implore everyone to invest some time in this Discipleship. It has become a very effective way of redeeming my time here in prison.

George Bursler 639599 130 Seeds 400 Scriptures

- Before MEDS, when I would study God's WORD I usually ended up frustrated with myself or discouraged because I did not understand what I had read or could not retain what I had learned. Through MEDS not only have I learned Scripture, but I also understand what the Scriptures mean. What a great joy this has brought to my life.

    Larry Burns 390420 35 Seeds 60 Scriptures

- Through learning the Seeds, I realized God is not the least bit disappointed in me. I now understand that God wants to have a relationship with me "way more" than I want to have a relationship with Him...I, Doug Melven, years after I left prison, still have these truths burned in my heart. I wrote the above testimony 7 years prior to this typing, and I am still full of God and growing.

    Doug Melven 689036 200 Seeds 700 Scriptures *(At time of testimony, many more now)*

- I have been involved in MEDS for nearly two years. I would definitely recommend this Discipleship for anyone who is interested in gaining knowledge in the Bible, no matter where they are in their walk. I personally have benefited greatly.

    Neal Parker 301680 30 Seeds 50 Scriptures

- I've learned a lot from "The Seeds" and I am learning more about the LORD every day. I encourage others to learn "The Seeds". I am blessed each and every day because of what I have learned.

    Dave Rachar 470552 35 Seeds 58 Scriptures

- As I learned Scriptures via "The Seeds", I was able to combat the devil's daily attack of doubt, depression, and worry. "The Seeds" have become a new and rewarding way of getting God's WORD "etched" on my heart. For me learning Scriptures in this way has been a blessing.

    Wesley Vande Streck 756289 80 Seeds 200 Scriptures

- I had been praying for and believing for a solution to my spiritual impotence. After being introduced to this Discipleship, I was totally convinced that MEDS was for me. The past few months have marked an amazing growth in my understanding of truths in the Bible. Just last week, for the first time I taught the whole first pod *(4 seeds)* to my best friend. Spending my time in this Discipleship has been the wisest investment thus far in my life. I am ready to take the Gospel to the world!

  Justin John Morrison 598050 40 Seeds 70 Scriptures

- MEDS Discipleship is very powerful and effective. I have observed that many of the brothers when they first got here were shy about God's Word, not to vocal. But now they are bold, glowing, and growing up and starting to disciple others through "The Seeds". This Discipleship is advancing the Kingdom of God.

  Willie "Mac" McIntosh 135727

Five Christ-centered Philosophies of MEDS

Mutuality and Cooperation

Most Effective Discipleship Seeds *(MEDS)* is intended to always operate in Mutuality and Cooperation. Because the participating disciple's growth is usually so substantial, there is a danger of a person becoming competitive or of getting prideful when his progress exceeds that of those believers around him. Pride can be the most subtle of sins and consequently always needs to be carefully guarded against. The scripture tells us that we are not wise when we compare ourselves among ourselves *(2 Corinthians 10:12)*. Each believer who dispenses the Seeds for the learning of others should always approach this worthy endeavor not as a master, but as a servant. Indeed the one who brings the food to the table is not considered greater than the one being served. In this Discipleship, there is to be no fleshly judging, no manipulation, no guilt trips, nor any other kind of pressure to get the disciple to learn. Rather, generous doses of patient encouragement should always be offered. The things of God should never be forced on others. Even God Himself does not force or pressure us to do anything, but rather draws us and woos us to His Way through His great love for us. It is normal and proper for increased heart knowledge of God's Word to illicit greater confidence and thankfulness, but we need to keep on the lookout for the sneaky enemy called pride.

Inward Transformation

All "religion" focuses primarily on outward behavior modification. Genuine and true Discipleship of Christ Jesus always focuses primarily on Inward Transformation which is the result of an intimate relationship with Christ by His Spirit and Word. It is this kind of a developing ongoing bonding with Jesus Christ that will always, in time, produce its own fruit which will be ever increasing Christ like behavior. As will be emphasized throughout these Seeds, real transformation does not come by "trying harder", but rather by trusting Christ more and more through spending quality time in His presence, writing His Word on our hearts, and learning to yield to His Spirit.

Conceptual Learning

MEDS is not a Discipleship of memorization, but rather depend on a process we call Conceptual Learning. A child learns his own name by repetitive exposure to it. As adults we might come to know the words of a commercial or advertisement "jingle" simply because we heard it so many times, though we made no conscious decision or intentional effort to memorize it. Conceptual learning is not aimed at remembering the exact words of a scripture or idea, but rather is a "coming to know" the main ideas and concepts of a teaching *(Seed)* through a repetitive exposure of hearing it and SPEAKING it. One of the great benefits of this kind of learning is that typically the average person can learn 6 to 8 scripture passages or more, conceptually, in the same time that it take him to memorize one scripture passage word for word. Additionally will enjoy the added value of genuine fellowship, better comprehension, and greater practical application in the process. Many believers, who started out claiming a complete inability to learn scripture and its location, have through the MEDS approach conceptually learned dozens *(in some cases hundreds)* of scripture and their locations through enjoyable fellowship.

Enjoyment of Fellowship

The conceptual learning in this Discipleship is intended to be learned primarily through the enjoyment of fellowship. While personal study of these Seeds can and will complement and increase the growth rate of the individual, many have enjoyed a great measure of success learning and developing a closer relationship with Jesus Christ simply through fellowshipping in the Seeds, with little or no personal study. Consequently, even one that does not enjoy reading or is illiterate can enjoy tremendous spiritual growth through Most Effective Discipleship Seeds *(MEDS)*.

All Become Equipped to Teach

In MEDS there is no practice of the giving or taking of any rank, status, or titles. Rather, every disciple/learner is considered to be a servant minister qualified to teach each Seed he has learned just as soon as he masters its concepts. In this way, God's Kingdom can expand rapidly as it did in the early days of the Church through a "pay forward" mindset which progressively does away with the faulty clergy/laity mentality. The clergy/laity mindset promotes the false belief that only very few among us are qualified to operate in the anointing and teach God's Word to others *(2 Timothy 2:24)*. Such unbiblical thinking is inconsistent with and cripples individual and corporate spiritual growth. The Lord desires for all believers to be progressively equipped to teach others.

STRUCTURE OF MEDS

Book 1 of Most Effective Discipleship Seeds *(MEDS) (this publication)* covers the first year of Phase One and the Galatians Phase. This first year content includes 12 Pods *(a group of 4 or 5 Seeds)*, 50 Seeds, 88 scripture passages, *(including 17 specials)* and over 400 concepts. MEDS is not a finite Discipleship program to be completed, but rather is designed as a Discipleship lifestyle of continuously and habitually engraving godly truth on the heart of each participant. At the time of this writing more than 2200 Seeds have been developed which represents 5 years/levels of solid, organized, prioritized, and measurable growth in spiritual knowledge and maturity. *(See Appendixes #3 thru #9 for five year overview and Seed content for Years/Levels 1-5)*.

Each succeeding level increases substantially in the number of Seeds, Scriptures, and Concepts to be mastered. Many Disciples easily master the first 50 Seeds *(88 scriptures)* in the first year or in some cases much less time, while some may master only 10 to 20 seeds over the same period of time. In either case these results will significantly benefit each believer in their walk and in their ability and confidence to minister to others. Indeed, any amount of growth accomplished by engrafting God's Word in the heart of the believer, even if it is only a few Seeds, will richly benefit that disciple in a observable and transformative measure, as well as those taught by him.

This first book contains what a serious disciple of Christ should know after one year of effective Discipleship. Few Christians have reached this basic measure of mastery even after many years of being a being believers. This may be due to the lack of an organized, comprehensive and specific curriculum or of not having an effective and enjoyable method of imparting truth to permanently engrafting it on each believer's heart. Most Effective Discipleship Seeds *(MEDS)* has proven to be an outstanding solution to both of these problems.

PROCESS OF MEDS

Each Seed is set in priority order so that each learner increases in knowledge in a logical and practical way according the planned curriculum. Each Seed is learned with the intent and purpose of its scripture and concepts being permanently written on the heart of the disciple for his own benefit, but also to enable him to skillfully and spiritually minister to others out of his own established heart knowledge, and equip those he teaches to do the same. In the proper practice of MEDS the second Seed is not learned until the first Seed is mastered. The third Seed is not learned until after the first Seed is reviewed and the second Seed is mastered, and so on until all the Seeds of each year *(level)* are mastered.

Regular review through fellowship will insure that each Seed will continue to be established in the heart and not "here today and gone tomorrow" which happens too often in many current traditional approaches and personal practices. Ultimately, the goal is that each Seed is progressively and deeply rooted, grounded, and established in each believer's heart. Rooted as the disciple continues to hear and speak it, grounded as the disciple consistently explains it to others in his own words, and established in his identity as the disciple comes to discern, own, and love its truth.

This learning takes place through Balanced Conversational Fellowship in which the servant minister speaks the concept to his peer and his peer speaks it back to him. This is done repeatedly until the one being ministered to can easily recall and speak the Seed name, concepts, and associated scriptures without any help. Keep in mind "to speak the concept" does not necessarily mean "word for word" but rather to speak the main thought or idea of the teaching in one's own words. Through this repetitive and persistent fellowship, each truth will be progressively rooted more deeply in the hearts of both the disciple dispensing the Word, as well as in the disciple hearing and speaking it **back**. This ***enjoyable fellowship results in an ongoing building up of both parties in each Seed topic and its concepts.***

RESULTS OF MEDS

Those who have used this approach over a period of time, have found it to be by far, the most effective and efficient Christ centered Way to grow and mature as a sincere disciple of Jesus Christ. Dozens to hundreds of scriptures, addresses and concepts have been mastered by many believers who had previously struggled with learning even just a few scriptures and addresses. The results of Most Effective Discipleship *(MEDS)* includes each participant having much greater understanding of scriptures and how to rightly divide them. In addition, each disciple testifies to a wonderful increase in intimacy in their personal relationship with the Lord Jesus and find themselves spending more and more time with Him than ever before as the Lord continues to transform them from the inside out. They also discover a much greater confidence to minister to and disciple others as the power of the Spirit enables them.

Finally, they report gaining increased spiritual insight enabling them to understand thousands of other scripture passages that they had previously little or no success in understanding and applying to their lives. Amazingly many also report their ability to retain and recall other important information is significantly improved regardless of the subject matter. It is our belief that those who set their heart to learn God's Word through the spiritual enjoyment and fellowship of Most Effective Discipleship Seeds *(MEDS)* will experience greater success than through any other method. We strongly encourage every ministry, minister, and believer to give MEDS an honest try. We are convinced you will be pleased, impressed, and wonderfully transformed by the Holy Spirit as the result of practicing this outstanding fellowship.

HOW TO USE THIS BOOK

A Grid of Truth

Most people who live in big cities understand the main north and south streets and the main east and west streets form a grid like pattern. Consequently such a person who know the main streets of a city well, can be placed anywhere in that city and by traveling a few blocks in any direction he will soon come to one of those main streets and will be able to quickly figure out his exact location. MOST EFFECTIVE DISCIPLESHIP SEEDS *(MEDS)* is designed to work in a similar fashion. Each seed consists of one or more concepts and represents and expresses an important Bible topical truth *(A main street)*. When the disciple masters all 100 Seeds of PHASE 1 *(the first 3 years)*, he will possess an excellent practical overview of the essential teachings of the entire scriptures.

First things First

A Seed is a unit of spiritual revelation and bible truth that increases the Presence and Power of Jesus Christ in the experience of the believer who masters it. The seeds are formatted generally in the order of their relative importance so that the disciple, relative to his relationship with Jesus Christ develops and matures from the most foundational matters *(milk)* to the more advanced Truths *(meat)*. The believer who permanently learns even a limited amount of seeds will be rooted, grounded and established in the Word in a way that will consistently benefit both himself and others with whom he is led into fellowship. Indeed, the potential for individual and corporate growth through the use of this discipling fellowship has proven to bring an exponential growth that is likely well beyond what most Christians would even dare to imagine.

Special Aids

A Pod is a set grouping of 4 or 5 seeds. The Pods and Seeds are ordered and their learning is simplified by the use of simple acronyms. In this Discipleship an acronym is a series of letters used to recall something formerly learned. For example, the first Pod contains the first 4 seeds which are Faith-righteousness, Assurance, Clearance and Consecration. After being learned, these seeds can be easily recalled by the acronym FACC. Additionally, more acronyms are used as you move into some of the longer and more complex concepts. Feel free to adapt the acronyms in whatever way makes the writing of God's Truth on your heart easiest.

Humility is Key

MEDS also makes use of various "associations" and "learning devices". For example, similarly numbered Scriptures are called "cousins". You can use these "helps" as outlined in this book, or you can come up with your own. A few believers have attempted to learn the seeds without the use of acronyms and other such helps; however, not with much success. You will have the best results if you are open to what is perhaps a new way of learning for you. Humility is an important key in all matters pertaining to growth in Christ.

Your Unique Expression

Always keep in mind, the main thrust of the Seeds is not memorization, but rather conceptual learning. This means the goal is NOT to remember specific words or phrases but to put these important Bible truths in your heart in a way that will allow you to speak them with whatever words come to your mind as you start to express the concepts in your own mind or to others. When a truth is learned conceptually, the exact words will often vary significantly depending on with whom you are fellowshipping *(or serving)* and on how the Holy Spirit may be leading you.

God's Word Prevailing in You

As you learn each seed be sure to continue to review it periodically by fellowshipping and meditating in it until you own it; that is to where you will never lose it. It is better to learn a smaller number of Seeds thoroughly than to learn a large number of seeds superficially or incompletely. As you minister God's important truth to others, you equip and encourage them to do the same. In that way, God's Word can prevail in you and in those with whom you fellowship in a genuine and permanent manner, *(both now and throughout eternity)*. May God's Grace and Peace abound in you throughout your life and ministry.

Outline Formats – Simple Outline and Sample Fellowship

Every Seed is presented first in a Simple Format *(a basic outline)*. The initial Seeds in the First Year, as well as other selected Seeds throughout the First Year, are given additionally in a Sample Fellowship Format. In the Sample Fellowship Format a fundamental example of how MEDS spoken fellowship might normally take place is given. Keep in mind that in these rudimentary written examples, the servant minister gives the concept and receives it back only once. In actual fellowship, a concept normally needs to be given and spoken back a couple of times or more as needed for the disciple learner to be able to give it back by his own recall and without any help from his peer.

Further Explanations

Each of the 30 Seeds in the first year of Phase I is followed by a Further Explanation. These explanations are designed to further explain each Seed and answer the most commonly asked questions about it. All the Seeds in the Galatians Phase *(Chapters 8 to 13)* are given in the Simple Format and do not include a Further Explanation, but are of course designed to be learned through the enjoyment of fellowship.

Seed Numbering System

For the purpose of the written seeds, each seed is identified by a three-digit number.

The "First Digit" is the placement of the seed within the pod.
The "Second Digit is the placement of the Pod within the Year or Phase.
The "Third Digit" designates the Year of Phase 1.

For example, Faith-Righteousness is Seed 111 meaning it is the First Seed in the First Pod of the First Year. *(Of Phase I)*.

Seed 432, which is called "Grace, Glory, Hope and Life is the Fourth Seed in the Third Pod of the Second Year.

The Fifth Seed in the Eighth Pod of the Third Year is "Spiritual Liberty which is designated 583. *(The final seed of Phase 1)*.

IMPORTANT NOTE: During fellowship the Seeds are normally referred to in the way they are written in the bold type above.

Gender Designation

Whenever the pronoun "Him" or "He" is capitalized *(except at the beginning of a sentence)* it refers to deity *(Father, Son or Holy Spirit)*.

Otherwise, all other references in this book to "him" or "his" are intended to mean all people without respect to gender.

BOOK 1

Year One of Phase I and Galatians Phase

Little Child to Young Man Level

88 Seeds – 108 Scripture Passages

FACC

Chapter One

The First Pod - Acronym: FACC

Pod Clue: calendar flip

Seed 111 – Faith Righteousness

(In fellowship Seed 111 is referred to as the 1st Seed of the 1st Pod of the 1st Year)

Simple Format

I. The name of the 1st Seed in the First Pod is **FAITH RIGHTEOUSNESS**.
   1. The concept of the 1st Seed is **I AM RIGHTEOUS BECAUSE OF MY FAITH IN JESUS CHRIST**.

   A. The first scripture for faith righteousness is **ROMANS 9:30-32** *(hint: 30 days has September on the Romans calendar)*
      1. The concept of this scripture is **THE GENTILES RECEIVED RIGHTEOUSNESS BY FAITH, BUT THE JEWS DID NOT ATTAIN TO RIGHTEOUSNESS BECAUSE THEY TRIED TO GET IT BY THE LAW** *(trusting their own ability)*.

   B. The second scripture for faith righteousness is **PHILIPPIANS 3:9** *(hint: flip/ph-lip the Romans 9:30/drop the zero to remember Philippians 3:9)*
      1. The concept of this scripture is that **PAUL OBTAINED HIS RIGHTEOUSNESS BY FAITH, NOT BY WORKS**.

Note 1
The word "righteousness" as used in the New Testament refers primarily to a "right standing with God". "Right behavior" is the fruit of the gift of righteousness, not the cause of it.

Note 2
The word "concept" means the "main thought" or "idea" of a seed or scripture (freely expressed in one's own words).

Note 3

FACC

All Seeds and concepts should be spoken in a way that makes them:
Personal *- applied to myself*
Positive *- with strong expectancy of fruit (in the natural realm)*
Present tense *– reckoned as already done (in spiritual realm)*
Poetic *– spoken passionately with conviction*
Prophetic *- in humility led by the Holy Spirit to engrave it on the speaker's heart to establish him in true identity (Proverbs 23:7).*

Note 4
When one partner in fellowship asks or prompts the other for a seed concept or scripture concept the intent is NEVER to test the other person but rather to give him an opportunity to speak it until it is engrafted in his heart. If he does not have the concept mastered it simply means he has not heard it and said it enough yet. Solution: Encourage and help him hear and speak it until the concept is mastered. The intent of this fellowship is to always be an enjoyment as in eating a good meal together with a friend, the food being God's Word. For this reason if the learning disciple cannot express the concept within 6 to 10 seconds after asked for, it is usually best just to speak to him again. When he hears it and says it enough times he will be able to easily recall it at will.

FACC

Sample Fellowship Format

Disciple's reply is in **bold type**

"The name of the first seed is...faith righteousness. The concept of faith righteousness is...I am righteous through my faith in Christ - What is the name of the 1st Seed?"
"Faith righteousness"...

"That is correct. What is the concept *(main idea)* of faith righteousness"...
"I am righteous by my faith in Jesus."

"Very good. The first scripture is... Romans 9:30-32. You can recall that by remembering...September has 30
days on our Romans Calendar. The concept of Romans 9:30 is...The Gentiles received righteousness by faith, the Jews stumbled trying to get right with God by works. What is the first scripture for faith righteousness?"

"Romans 9:30-32"

"Yes. What is the concept?"
"The Gentiles received righteousness by faith, the Jews stumbled trying to get right with God by works."

"Very Good. The second scripture is Philippians 3:9...you can recall this scripture by flipping *(to remember ph-lip/pians)* the position of the numbers 9 and the 3 of the Romans 9:30 *(dropping the zero)*. The concept of Philippians 3:9 is...Paul received his righteousness by faith, not by works of the law. What is the second scripture"?

Philippians 3:9.

"That's correct - what is the concept of Philippians 3:9."
"Paul attained to his right standing with God by believing, not by his own works."

Excellent!

FACC

Note

In this Sample Fellowship examples each seed, scripture, and concept is immediately learned without the need of repetition. While there are a few that can learn that quickly, with most believers it will take hearing and speaking a concept 2-5 times (or more) for the believer to master the concepts of a seed. Normally a seed can be learned with by most individuals in less than ten minutes. However, the speed of the learner does not matter. What matters is getting these important truths engraved into his heart.

END OF SEED 111 FAITH RIGHTEOUSNESS

REVIEW SEED UNTIL MASTERED

FACC

Seed 111   Faith Righteousness – Further Information

The 1st Seed in the 1st Pod of the 1st Year

Under the Old Testament Law and Covenant, righteousness was based on outward behavior. If a righteous man was ever to sin, he at once became unrighteous. If an unrighteous man did the right thing, he became righteous *(Ezekiel 18:25-28)*. Such is the unstable situation when attempting to live under The Law. The Law of God, given primarily through Moses, demands a supply of perfection that is way beyond what mortal man can consistently deliver. But praise be to God, under the New Covenant grace provides all The Law demands and even more *(Romans 5:21)*. It meets God's desire and righteous requirement in and through faith in Jesus Christ.

The Law demands perfection. If you break The Law, even at only one point, you are considered guilty of breaking all of it *(James 2:10)*. The Law demands perfection, yet supplies none of the Life of God which is necessary to meet that need *(Galatians 3:21)*. But that no man is justified by The Law is evident *(Galatians 3:11)*. The righteousness which is a gift to the believer through faith in the Work of Christ supplies and exceeds what is needed to please God *(Romans 3:24, 25)*.

In general, the Bible portrays two kinds of righteousness. The first is self-righteousness, which is based on human effort and human ability to keep God's Law. God Himself refers to this kind of righteousness as filthy rags *(Isaiah 64:6)*. Paul explains his righteousness as not being his own achieved by keeping The Law, but rather it was the righteousness which was a gift of God by faith *(Philippians 3:9)*. Jesus confirmed this position by explaining to His Disciples that, of themselves, they could do nothing to satisfy Him *(John 15:5)*.

Some Christians today still believe that righteousness is the result of outward behavior. That is, if you continue to do right, then you become righteous in God's sight. But that is spiritual dyslexia *(backwards thinking)*. In truth, our Lord God imputes *(credits our account)* righteousness to us freely at the time of regeneration *(new birth)*, apart from any work on our part *(Romans 4:6)*. Now, to the degree that we believe and possess that righteousness and yield to it, to that degree we will experience, enjoy, and express the fruit of the Spirit. So then, we do not "get holy" to go to God, but rather we go to God to be transformed and sanctified to be holy. The Holy Spirit is always the only true source of genuine righteousness operating in man. This is the Bible's Way of Christ Jesus as The Way of our righteousness *(2 Corinthians 5:21)*.

In this age of grace, it is never behavior that brings righteousness, but rather it is the righteousness freely given to each believer that brings him to a positional and objective right standing with God. In this standing, God sees us continually as sinless and perfected in the Spirit based on the finished work of The Cross. When we speak of "The Cross", we are not referring to a piece of wood *(not obvious to everyone)*, but rather to the entire redemptive results accomplished by the death, burial, and resurrection of Jesus Christ. Each believer has been reconciled to God and no longer has sin imputed to him *(2 Corinthians 5:18, 19; Romans 4:8)*. This is experienced by and according to the believer's faith.

This righteousness standing, when trusted, then produces the good works, for as a man thinks in his heart, so he is *(Proverbs 23:7)*. We need to fully understand that the only righteous behavior that is acceptable to God comes from this imputed righteousness and never of man's own ability or effort. Only then will we recognize we have no place to boast, but rather ALL glory and praise rightfully belong to God alone. As a result, our attitude becomes one of great gratitude and high worship for the God of the Bible who is so generous, merciful, and loving toward us apart from any human work. When the truth of righteousness *(that is freely given through faith)* is rooted, grounded and established in the heart of the believer, only then is man empowered to experience and express the very holiness of God in Christ Jesus for whom he was created and to whom he was called. All glory to God!

As with every important Bible truth, we need to, by the Spirit of God, passionately and repeatedly confess our righteous standing with God in His sight. Our confession of God's Word and Truth should also be personal *(spoken in the first person)*, Positive *(recognizing our current oneness with Christ in the Spiritual Realm)* and in the Present Tense *(as a current Spiritual Truth)*. Additionally, these Bible truths should be spoken by the power of the Spirit *(Prophetically)*, and with true passion *(Poetically)*.

fAcc

Seed 211 - Assurance

(In fellowship Seed 211 is referred to as the 2nd Seed in the 1st Pod of the First Year)

Simple Format

II. The name of the second seed is **ASSURANCE**.
   1. The concept of Assurance **is I KNOW FOR SURE THAT CHRIST LOVES ME AND LIVES IN ME** *(clue L-L)*.

      A. The Scripture for Assurance is **1 JOHN 5:13** *(clue: Little Johnny first went to school when he was 5 years old and to middle school when he was 13 years old)*.
      2. The concept is **I KNOW FOR SURE I HAVE ETERNAL LIFE BECAUSE IT IS WRITTEN** *(clue: E-L)*.

Note: Eternal Life includes the fullness of the Christ Life that is dwelling currently in the spirit of every believer. This Eternal Life is characterized by perfect love, perfect peace, perfect joy, and perfect wisdom. These blessings and many more are experienced by the believer to the degree he believes they are in him and to the extent he learns to progressively access them.

fAcc

Sample Fellowship Format

Disciple's reply is in **bold type**

"The name of the 2nd seed in the first pod is… Assurance. What is the name of the second seed?"
"Assurance. Yes, that is correct".

"The concept is… I know for sure that Christ loves me and lives in me. What is the concept of Assurance?"
"I know for sure that Christ loves me and lives in me."

"Very good. The Scripture for Assurance is… 1 John 5:13. The concept of 1 John 5:13 is… I know for sure I have eternal life because it is written *(hint: EL)*.
What is the Scripture for Assurance"?
"1 John 5:13"

"That is correct. What is the concept for 1 John 5:13?
I know for sure I have eternal life because it is written. Excellent."

End of Seed 211 Assurance

REVIEW SEED UNTIL MASTERED

fAcc

Seed 211   Assurance - Further Information

The Second Seed in the First Pod of the First Year

If our eternal destination depended on our good behavior, no believer could ever know with certainty if his "good behavior" was "good enough". Such uncertainty in man tends to breed an ungodly fear which will ultimately result in discouragement and backsliding. But God, in His loving wisdom, wants each one of His children to have an assurance of the Eternal Life which is by grace through faith, so that it might be sure to all who believe in Him *(Romans 4:16)*.

Eternal Life is not only a future reward, but is also a present redemptive reality, for this Eternal Life is the very life of Jesus Christ that currently lives within each believer. This Eternal Life, both NOW and always, provides each believer access to the love, wisdom, peace, and joy of Jesus Himself. Indeed, all that Jesus Christ is and has is made available to each believer through faith. With maturity of faith and experience, each believer learns to experience and express Christ in a greater way through growth in knowing Him *(John 17:3)*. Confession of Eternal Life as a present and future reality is needed and is always of great benefit to each believer *(Hebrews 4:14)*

F A C C

Seed 311 - Clearance

(In fellowship Seed 311 is referred to as the
3rd Seed in the 1st Pod of the First Year)

Simple Format

III. The Name of the 3rd seed is **CLEARANCE** *(clue: A good way to remember: Have you ever known personally or known of anyone by the name of Clarence? For example, the Supreme Court Justice Clarence Thomas. That person's name will help you remember the name of this seed).*

  1. The concept of Clearance is **I CAN GO TO GOD ANYTIME I WANT BECAUSE I KNOW HE IS NOT ANGRY WITH ME** *(This concept expresses when I can go and why I can go to God).*

Note 1
All of God's wrath against sin was put on Jesus at the Cross of Calvary which brought in the blessing of this present Age of Grace. God hates sin and never just overlooks it, but has dealt with it already. Therefore, He is never upset with the believer who sins. God is just and cannot be unjust to punish again that which He already dealt with at the Cross.

  A. The scripture is **HEBREWS 4:16** *(1st clue: In the Bible women never make coffee because He brews it. 2nd clue: 4 cups of coffee made for 4 tables of 4 people... 4x4=16 cups of coffee).*

    1. The concept is **I GO BOLDLY TO GOD'S THRONE OF GRACE** *(This concept expresses with what attitude I can go to God – e.g. confidently, without any fear, boldly).*

F A **C** C

Sample Fellowship Format

Disciple's reply is in **bold type**

"The name of the third seed is... Clearance.
The concept of Clearance is... I can go to God anytime I want because I know He is not mad at me".
What is the third seed in the first pod?"
"Clearance."

"That is correct! What is the concept of Clearance?
(Clue: The concept of this seed explains WHEN and WHY I can go to God)".
"I can go to God anytime I want because I know He is not mad at me!"

"Very good! The Scripture for Clearance is... Hebrews 4:16. HE-brews 4:16 can be recalled by...
The man made 4 cups of coffee for 4 tables of 4 people" - 4 x 4 = 16 for Hebrews 4:16.
Just think...A clearance sale on coffee... to recall the name and scripture for this seed.
The concept of Hebrews 4:16 is... Let us go BOLDLY to the throne of grace.
Speak all these truths with a strong emphasis/enthusiasm/emotion. The concept of this Scripture tells me HOW I can go to God.

The word "boldly" here means "with complete confidence, having no fear.
What is the Scripture for Clearance?"
"Hebrews 4:16."
"That is right!
What Is the concept?
"I go BOLDLY to the throne of God."
Very good!

END OF SEED 311   CLEARANCE

REVIEW SEED UNTIL MASTERED

F A C C

Seed 311   Clearance - Further Information

The 3rd Seed in the 1st Pod of the 1st Year

The parable of the forgiving and loving Father in Luke Chapter 15 *(commonly named after the prodigal son)* is a beautiful illustration of what God requires of each of us to return to Him when we have sinned or made ungodly choices. The answer is simple... just return to Him in earnest. This is the meaning of repentance in its simplest form. Indeed, even before the prodigal son ever spoke a word to the Father or even reached Him, the Father ran to His son and emphatically kissed him and embraced him. This perfectly and beautifully illustrates God's consistent love for and faithfulness to His own children in Christ Jesus, even when they fall short of His glory. This is because our gracious Lord always freely forgives and restores. This is fully experienced simply by believing in Him and returning to Him.

The older brother in this parable represents the ugly attitude of a religious person who insists that forgiveness and restoration must be triggered, earned, or deserved by a specific ritual or action of some kind by the believer. The older brother greatly resented and was angered that the Father would dare *(have the audacity)* to so freely forgive and restore the formerly wayward younger brother. After all, wasn't it the older brother who had lived a more "holy" life through his loyalty to the Father? Was it not the older brother who actually deserved to have a party thrown for him based on his clearly more favorable behavior? This is the foolishness and folly of religion. Belief that God's goodness toward a true believer is based on the believer's good behavior is serious error. The idea that each believer can forever and always go to God with a bold confidence is a fundamental principal of true Christianity that every believer needs to have firmly rooted and grounded in his heart *(Romans 5:2)*. This is because it is only in the presence of the Father that real transformation and sanctification can take place. We do not become holy in order to go to the Father, rather we go to the Father to become holy.

Many believers fail to go consistently and boldly to God in fellowship. This is because they wrongly believe that they can go to our Lord only when they are "living right" in their own eyes. They make the fleshly error spoken of in Colossians 1:21 of being separated from God "in their own mind" due to their wicked works. It is important for each believer to become rooted and grounded in the truth of our eternal reconciliation to Him which was accomplished by the finished work of The Cross. Only then will we go to Him often with boldness, not only when we are walking strong after Him, but especially when we fall short of his glory. He is always faithful to extend His grace and mercy which we always need but especially need in times of trials and tribulation *(Hebrews 4:16)*.

Sin is always abhorrent and we are to hate it. It can certainly take us where we do not want to go and cost us more than we want to pay. But as a believer, finished sin will never block your fellowship with God unless you are deceived into believing that it does. Each sincere believer needs to understand that it is our faith in "Christ crucified" *(1 Corinthians 2:2)* that is the one truth that *(in God's eyes)* completely deals with and removes our sin eternally.

F A C **C**

Seed 411 – Consecration

(In fellowship Seed 411 is referred to as the 4th Seed in the 1st Pod of the First Year)

Simple Format

IV. The name of the fourth seed in the first pod is **CONSECRATION** *(clue: A way to remember... Think hard and your "concentration" (sounds like) can help recall "Consecration".*

Note 1
Consecration means "to give, set aside, dedicate or recommit".

1. The concept for consecration is **I GIVE MYSELF TO GOD AT LEAST ONCE PER DAY** *(seed clue: give-seek-give. 1st give is in the above concept, seek is concept of first scripture (Matthew 6:33), and the 2nd give is the concept of 2nd scripture (Romans 12:1)*

Note 2
The more a believer gives himself to the Lord the better. It is impossible to be over-consecrated. A person can be too religious, but he can never be too spiritual.

A. The first scripture for consecration is **MATTHEW 6:33** *(A way to remember. The math equation 6=3+3 to remember Matthew 6:33.*
   1. The concept for Matthew 6:33 is **I SEEK FIRST THE KINGDOM OF GOD.**

B. The second scripture is **ROMANS 12:1** *(double the 6 from the previous scripture Matthew 6:33).*
   1. The concept is **I GIVE MYSELF TO THE LORD AS A LIVING SACRIFICE.**

Note 3
The Kingdom of God is the realm in which God rules and reigns or wherever King Jesus has rule. In other words, the Kingdom of God is the influence of God. To seek His kingdom is to seek His influence. Some of the ways to do this is by praying, studying the Word, abiding in Him, Yielding to Him, praising Him, and fellowshipping with other believers).

F A C **C**

Sample Fellowship Format

Disciple's reply is in **bold type**

"What is the name of the 4th Seed in the 1st Pod?"
"Consecration"

"That is correct. What is the concept of consecration?"
"I give myself to God at least once per day".

"Very good! What is the Scripture for Consecration?"
Matthew 6:33

"That is correct. What is the concept of Matthew 6:33?"
"Seek first the Kingdom of God".

"Excellent! The second Scripture for consecration is Romans 12:1
A way to remember. Double the 6 from the previous verse.
The concept of Romans 12:1 is "I give myself as a living sacrifice to God".
What is the second Scripture for consecration?"
"Romans 12:1"

"Yes. What is the concept for Romans 12:1?"
"I give myself as a living sacrifice to God. That is correct."

END OF SEED 411   CONSECRATION
REVIEW SEED UNTIL MASTERED

FAc**C**

Seed 411 Consecration – Further Information

The 4th Seed of the 1st Pod of the First Year

Consecration is to give or dedicate or re-commit our lives to God at least once per day. As believers, we need to be progressively and consistently fixing our hearts on the Lord. This important habit needs to be developed and practiced by every sincere believer as an important aspect of assuring a continuous growth in our spiritual lives. Such an ongoing re-dedication and recommitment cannot be overemphasized or overdone. For each time we sincerely give ourselves to the Lord we our further marked by the Holy Spirit for God's purpose in our lives.

After consecrating ourselves, we need to continually seek the Kingdom of God, which simply means to seek the influence of the King, Jesus Christ. Prayer, Bible study, praise, and fellowship are just a few of a multitude of ways to seek and enter God's Kingdom while still on earth. Each of these activities are profitable and proper ways to redeem our time in "The Way" that God has ordained for us. Daily consecration and seeking are excellent habits that need to be rooted, grounded, and established in every believer's heart

FACC

Overview of the First Pod

I. Faith Righteousness

    1. I am righteous because of my faith in Jesus.

        A. Romans 9:30-32
           1. The Gentiles received righteousness by faith. The Jews did not, as they stumbled by trying to earn it.

        B. Philippians 3:9
           1. Paul received his righteousness by faith not by the Law.

II. Assurance

    1. I know for sure that Christ loves me and lives in me.

        A. 1 John 5:13
           1. Because it is written, I know for sure that I have eternal life.

III. Clearance

    1. I can go to God anytime because I know He is not angry with me.

        A. Hebrews 4:16
           1. I go boldly to the Throne of Grace.

IV. Consecration

    1. I give myself to the Lord at least once per day.

        A. Matthew 6:33
           1. I seek first the Kingdom of God.

        B. Romans 12:1
           1. I give myself to God as a living sacrifice.

F A C C

Epilogue for Chapter One

The model conversation of MEDS that is illustrated throughout the first seven chapters reflects the general pattern of the interaction between the participants. While there is no exact way this fellowship has to be done, the general idea is to build and establish each seed with its concepts from the ground up. This is done by first giving the concept, second hearing back that concept, third giving the next concept and last hearing back both concepts, and so on. The idea is to make sure each concept is alternately vocalized by both Disciples until it is fully conceptualized and established in both of their hearts as they move along. This normally requires reliance on the patient persistence that exists within the believers through Christ. But the results are well worth whatever effort is needed.

The first four seeds make up a critical foundation that needs to be established deep in the heart of every believer, particularly those who are young in the Lord. To be skilled in righteousness *(Hebrews 5:13)* is to understand how it works and how to use it. First, you have to receive righteousness as a gift and know you possess it. Then, as you mature and learn to abide and walk in it, it produces the "fruit of righteousness" *(Philippians 1:11)*; and as a result, all glory goes to God. Next, the believer needs to know that the matter of his eternal destiny is a settled issue in God's eyes and that the life of the risen Christ dwells in him. This will give the believer the freedom and confidence to pursue God without constantly trying to measure himself against the law or anything else that is not Christ in him. If he can learn to keep his focus stayed *(kept)* on Christ, and not on self, his growth will be consistent and proper.

The third seed, Clearance, gives the believer the confidence to keep going to God, even when his behavior falls short of his own desire and God's standard. Getting consistently in our Lord's presence is the most important key to increased practical holiness.

However, what if a believer understands he is righteous by faith, and knows he possesses the eternal life and nature of God? What if he realizes the veil that separated man from God has been torn from top to bottom; yet he rarely spends time with God? Certainly, he will not experience substantial growth in his covenant benefits including holiness. So it is important for each believer, particularly the young ones in the Lord, to be encouraged to consecrate themselves to the Lord at least once per day.

SISL

Floating Seed - Implorer/Beseecher Seed

Seed 000 Shared Initiative and Shared Leadership (SISL)

The SISL Seed is designed for the discipler *(servant-leader)* to use as he feels led by the Spirit. Normally it is taught right after the disciple masters the first pod. However it may be learned at any point after the first pod is completed. The discipler may feel that the encouragement and understanding this seed brings is not yet needed. On rare occasions the SISL seed may be taught as an introductory seed prior to the first seed of the first pod. This may be optimal when the disciple is already very strong in God's Word and is learning the seeds primarily to use as a teaching tool for others.

The SISL Seed is designed to help root and establish each disciple in a proper attitude, clear motive, and biblical philosophy that will serve to keep the fellowship Christ-centered so that the disciples experience stays both highly effective and enjoyable.

Simple Format

I. The name of the Implorer/Beseecher Seed is **SHARED INITIATIVE AND SHARED LEADERSHIP *(SISL)*.**

   1. The First Concept **is I TAKE THE INITIATIVE TO REVIEW THE SEEDS I'VE LEARNED AND TO LEARN THE NEXT ONE WHEN I AM READY**
   (acronym for these 3 concepts: IQI).

   2. The Second Concept is **I AM QUALIFIED TO TEACH THE SEEDS THAT I HAVE LEARNED.**

   3. The Third Concept **is I TAKE THE INITIATIVE TO TEACH *(PAY FORWARD)* AS A SERVANT-LEADER THE SEEDS I HAVE LEARNED.**

      A. The scripture for SISL is **1 CORINTHIANS 7:35**
   (clue: 7 X 5=35) (acronym for concept PLuM)
   1. **I TEACH YOU FOR YOUR PROFIT, NOT TO PUT YOU ON A LEASH, BUT THAT YOU MAY STAY MINDFUL OF THE THNGS OF GOD.**

SISL

Floating Seed - Implorer/Beseecher Seed

Sample Fellowship Format

This special seed is to beseech and implore each disciple
To continue to grow and to teach others in The Way
of this Discipleship.
The name of this seed is Shared Initiative and Shared Leadership.

Use the acronym IQI to recall these three concepts.
First, I take the Initiative to review the seeds I've learned
And I learn a new one when I am ready.
Second, I am Qualified to teach others the seeds I have learned.
And last, I take the Initiative to "pay forward" to others the seeds I have learned,
And I always do this with the attitude of a servant

What is the name of the Implorer Seed?
"Shared Initiative and Shared Leadership."

"What are the three concepts for this seed?"
**"I take the Initiative to review the seeds I've learned and to learn the next one when I am ready.
I'm Qualified to teach to others the seeds I have learned.
I take the Initiative to teach others with a servant attitude and as led by the Spirit** *(acronym IQI)."*

"That's right. Very good. The Scripture for SISL is 1 Corinthians 7:35 *(7 X 5 = 35)*.
The concept of the Scripture is...I teach you for your Profit, not to put you on a Leash, so that you may stay Mindful of the things of God *(Acronym: PLuM)*.
What is the Scripture for Shared Initiative and Shared Leadership?
1 Corinthians 7:35

That is correct.
What is the concept of the Scripture?
I teach you for your Profit, not to put you on a Leash, so that you may stay Mindful of the things of God.

That's right. You got it

SISL

Floating Seed - Implorer/Beseecher Seed

END OF SEED 000   SHARED INITIATIVE AND SHARED LEADER-
SHIP

REVIEW SEED UNTIL MASTERED

B DSR

Chapter Two

The Second Pod - Acronym: BDSR

Pod Clue: The Two 2ⁿᵈ's

Seed 121 – Bible Reliability

(In fellowship Seed 121 is referred to as the 1ˢᵗ Seed in the 2ⁿᵈ Pod of the First Year)

Simple Format

I. The name of the 1st Seed in the in the second pod is **BIBLE RELIABILITY**

1. The concept has three parts:
    a) The first part is **TODAY'S BIBLE** *(without respect to translations)* **IS RELIABLE.**
    b) The second part is **AND IT CAN BE PROVEN BOTH LEGALLY** *(in a courtroom)* **AND HISTORICALLY** *(in a classroom).*
    c) The third part is recalled by the acronym **MAPS.CC** which stands for..."

MANUSCRIPTS - *handwritten copy of original autograph writings.*
ARCHAEOLOGY – *dug up artifacts prove the veracity of the Bible.*
PROPHECY – *Specific events foretold hundreds of years earlier came to fruition in perfect detail, many about Jesus Christ Himself.*
SCRIPTURE ITSELF – *The Bible professes to be God's Word.*
CONGRUENCY – *40 Inspired writers in perfect agreement when the Word is rightly divided.*
CHANGED LIVES – *Billions of lives and whole societies dramatically changed throughout the course of history by God's Word.*

   A. The first Scripture is **2 TIMOTHY 3:16** *(Can be recalled by "The most famous number in the Bible -316 – as many already know John 3:16).*
      1. The concept is **ALL SCRIPTURE IS INSPIRED BY GOD AND IS PROFITABLE".**

   B. The second Scripture is **2 PETER 1:21** *(This can be recalled by thinking twice of the legal age to drink in most states...2 Peter 1:21).*

B D S R

2. The concept is **ALL SCRIPTURE IS INSPIRED BY GOD BUT GIVEN THROUGH MEN"**.

Note 1

The clues and hints given in parenthesis are used initially and throughout fellowship as needed. They are an important part of triggering recall for most MEDS Disciples.

Note 2

Reading all these clues/hints may seem to the reader to be overdone or cumbersome. However, in fellowship they are very effective for most add to the enjoyment of learning.

B DSR

Sample Fellowship Format

Disciple's reply is in **bold type**

"What is the name of the first seed in the second pod?"
"Bible Reliability."

"Correct. What is the concept of Bible reliability?"
**"Today's Bible is reliable and can be proven both legally and historically by
Manuscripts, Archaeology, Prophecy, Scripture itself, Congruency and Changed lives."**

"Very Good. What is the first Scripture?"
"2 Timothy 3:16."

"That is right. What is the concept?"
"All Scripture is inspired by God and is profitable."

"Correct. What is the second Scripture?"
2 Peter 1:21

"Very good. What is the concept of the second Scripture?"
"All Scripture is inspired by God but given through men"

"That is very good."

END OF SEED 121   Bible Reliability
REVIEW SEED UNTIL MASTERED

B D S R

Seed 121   Bible Reliability – Further Information

The 1ˢᵗ Seed in the 2nd Pod of the 1st Year

God's Word calls for every believer to be an ambassador for Jesus Christ. Since Jesus is the living Word, we are to be those who present and defend God's Word. Very few current believers would ever have any need to be persuaded of the inerrancy and reliability of the Bible. However, each saint *(believer)* should be equipped to instruct those with a lack of confidence so that they would not be fooled by the most common worldly attacks against God's Word.

There are two very common attacks against the truth that the Bible is reliable. The first attack incorrectly claims that the Bible finds its inspiration from the mind of men; simply expressing the wisdom, reasoning, and philosophy of man. Consequently, they would argue, it carries no divine authority. Any serious student of God's Word to whom the Spirit has revealed some of the Bible's deeper and higher truths knows with great surety the folly of attributing the Excellency and power of the scriptures to mere man.

The second most common attack against the Bible is the claim that over the centuries the Word has been changed and degraded by man so as to make it untrustworthy. Serious and proper study reveals at least six kinds of strong proofs that today's Bible is completely reliable. Through these truths, we can know well beyond any doubt that the Bible we have today is completely reliable.

The six proofs are as follows:

1. **M**anuscripts - These are the ancient handwritten copies of the originals that exist still today in various locations around the world. These copies date back in relatively close proximity to the original autograph writings. The number of these manuscripts that are In existence today are over 24,000; this unusually high number along with their age, prove the Bible we have today is wholly consistent with the original writings in every major Bible teaching.

2. **A**rchaeology - This is the practice of digging up artifacts *(ancient objects)* that have, by their very existence, proven the Bible to be true and accurate. For example, at one time some historians and scientists

claimed that the Bible, at least in part, must be fiction because there was no historical proof of the existence of Babylon *(a city in the Bible)*. Consequently, they claimed that because there was no historical proof of Babylon's existence, the Bible could not be trusted. Just a few years later, archaeologists dug up nearly the whole city. This kind of event has occurred many times over the centuries.

3. **Prophecy** - Hundreds of scriptures foretelling events regarding Israel and the Church have been fulfilled in perfect detail. Professional statisticians have determined that the odds against all these prophecies coming true by chance or by human manipulation are astronomically high. The numbers do not lie, the Bible we have today is inspired by God and entirely reliable. In addition, there are nearly three hundred references that refer to the coming of the Messiah *(Jesus)* written in the Old Testament. All of them were fulfilled in the New Testament. They solidly establish and confirm Jesus' credentials as the one true Christ and God, as well as the reliability of God's Word. Below are some of the most well-known prophecies concerning the Messiah:

   a. Born of the seed of Woman predicted in Genesis 3:15 and fulfilled in Galatians 4:4 and Matthew 1:20
   b. Born of a virgin predicted in Isaiah 7:14 and fulfilled in Matthew 1:18, 23, 25
   c. Would be of the Tribe of Judah predicted in Genesis 49:10 and fulfilled in Luke 3:23, 33
   d. Born in Bethlehem predicted in Micah 5:2 and fulfilled in Matthew 2:4-7
   e. Shall be called Lord predicted in Psalm 110:1 and fulfilled in Luke 2:11 and Matthew 22:43-45
   f. Would have a ministry of miracles predicted in Isaiah 35:5, 6 and fulfilled in Matthew 9:32-35 and John 9:6-11
   g. Concerning His resurrection, predicted in Psalms 16:10 and fulfilled in Acts 2:31, 32
   h. Would be betrayed by a friend predicted in Psalm 41:9 and fulfilled in Matthew 10:4
   i. His life sold for thirty pieces of silver predicted in Zechariah 11:12 and fulfilled in Matthew 26:14-16.
   j. Would be forsaken by His Disciples predicted in Zechariah 13:7 and fulfilled in Mark 14:49, 50
   k. Smitten and spit upon predicted in Isaiah 50:6 and fulfilled in Matthew 26:67

B DSR

    l. Hands and feet would be pierced predicted in Psalms 22:16 and Zechariah 12:10 and fulfilled in Luke 23:33 and John 20:25
    m. Would be hated without cause predicted in Psalms 69:4 and fulfilled in John 15:25

4. **S**cripture Itself - The Bible clearly claims itself to be the perfect Word of God. While there are some other books that make the same claim, none of them have the manuscript, archaeological, or prophetic evidence the Bible has.

5. **C**ongruency - The Bible was written through the inspiration of God by approximately forty different authors, from great kings to lowly fishermen. Yet, when the Word of God is rightly divided and properly interpreted, all of its teachings fit together perfectly. This perfect agreement is known as congruency. Every other book that claims divinity is written by one man who claimed an angelic visitation. The Bible has at least forty solid witnesses inspired by God.

6. **C**hanged Lives - The Bible, the annual and all-time best seller, has positively touched billions of lives over the centuries. No other book in existence of mankind had ever carried the universal notoriety and respect that the Bible has been accorded worldwide. Today's Bible continues to change millions of lives day after day and year after year.

B **D** S R

Seed 221 – Deity of Christ

(In fellowship Seed 221 is referred to as the 2nd Seed in the 2nd Pod of the First Year)

Simple format

II. The name of the second seed in the second pod <u>**DEITY**</u> **OF CHRIST.**

   1. The concept is **JESUS IS GOD.**

      A. The first Scripture for this seed is **JOHN 1:1, 14.**
      (The first words of verse 1 "In the beginning" can remind you that this Scripture address is in the very beginning of John).
        1. The concept is **IN THE BEGINNING WAS THE WORD, AND THE WORD WAS WITH GOD, AND THE WORD WAS GOD, AND THE WORD BECAME FLESH.**

      B. The second Scripture for Deity of Christ is **ROMANS 9:5.**
      (This can be recalled by "banker's hours" or "Dolly's song").
      The concept is **JESUS IS GOD OVERALL, ETERNALLY BLESSED.**
      (Some use the acronym JOE to remember... <u>J</u>esus is God <u>o</u>verall, <u>e</u>ternally blessed).

B D S R

Sample Fellowship Format

Disciple's reply is in **bold type**

"What is the name of the second seed in the second pod?"
"Deity of Christ."

"Yes. What is the first Scripture?"
JOHN 1:1, 14

"Right. The concept of this Scripture is, "In the beginning was the Word and the Word
was with God and the Word was God and the Word became flesh.
What is the first Scripture for Deity of Christ?"
JOHN1:1, 14.

"Very good. What is the concept?"
**"In the beginning was the Word and the Word was with God
and the Word was God and the Word became flesh."**

"That is correct. The second scripture is Romans 9:5 which says Jesus is God.
. What is the second Scripture for Deity of Christ?"
"Romans 9:5"

"Very good. What is the concept of Romans 9:5?"
"Jesus is God overall, eternally blessed
That's right."

END OF SEED 221   Deity of Christ

REVIEW SEED UNTIL MASTERED

B D S R

Seed 221 Deity of Christ – Further Information

The 2nd Seed in the 2nd Pod of the 1st Year

The scriptural evidence that Jesus is God who manifested Himself in the flesh is overwhelming. It is a clear teaching of scripture and yet is still strongly resisted or misunderstood by many sincere seekers of truth. As is true in many doctrinal matters, a person needs to put aside all personal bias, preconceived notions, and human logic, all of which are of little or no value when desiring to understand and receive the great truths of God and His Word.

That God is one in essence is a fundamental truth of scripture. Yet God, unlike man, is not limited by time or space. Consequently, it is not at all too difficult for Him to manifest Himself in many different ways in many different places simultaneously. In truth, a man in Chicago can be experiencing God as "Daddy Father" while a woman in New York City is experiencing God the Son as a Brother and a Friend. Simultaneously, a teenager can be experiencing God as the Spirit of Truth, the Comforter, the Teacher and Helper while in Detroit. This is not greater and lesser gods, or forces of God, but rather the One True God revealing Himself in three different ways to three different people in three different places at the same time. Wonderfully, God can easily do this unlimited thousand and endless millions of times over simultaneously.

In the New Testament Age, God can and does manifest Himself as the Father, the Son, and the Holy Spirit. Some are confused by the clear distinction between the Father and Son because of times such as when Jesus prayed to the Father. There is a simple and important reason for this which is explained fully in Seed 431 "Kenosis". Kenosis is a Greek word whose meaning is critical to the proper understanding of the duality of Jesus being both God and Man. That the "Kenosis" is not commonly understood or even taught among many believers contributes greatly to the lack of a full revelation and acceptance of Christ as God by many people.

Nonetheless, the scripture is clear, the only way to really know the Father is to know the Son *(John 8:19, 14:7-9)*. To know One of Them is to know the Other, because They are One. But while God is One, He certainly is not limited to one way of expressing and manifesting Himself. Following is a list of just a very small percentage of scriptures that prove that Jesus is God:

B D S R

Isaiah 9:6,7; John 14:7-9; John 20:27-29; 1 John 5:20; Titus 2:13; Isaiah 45:18 and 44:24 compared to Colossians 1:15-17 and Hebrews 1:10; Isaiah 44:6 and 43:10 compared with Revelation 1:8-17; and Isaiah 42:8 and 48:11 compared with Matthew 24:30 and John 17:5.

Keep in mind that whenever you see the word LORD *(all caps)*, such as in the above Old Testament scriptures, it is always referring to the Divine Name of the Father which is represented in the original Hebrew text as YHWH *(usually spelled out "Yah-weh" and pronounced "Yah-way")*. After examining these scriptures carefully *(as well as many others)*, the Deity of Jesus Christ should be as clear as the sun at noontime on a clear day.

B D S R

Seed 321 – Spirit, Soul, and Body

*(In fellowship Seed 321 is referred to as the
3rd Seed in the 2nd Pod of the First Year)*

Simple format

III. The name of the third seed in the second pod is **SPIRIT, SOUL AND BODY.**

    1. The first concept is **MY SPIRIT IS ONE WITH GOD AND IT IS PERFECT.**
    2. The second concept is **MY SOUL IS MY SELF-CONSCIOUSNESS AND CONSISTS OF MY MIND, MY WILL AND MY EMOTIONS.**
    3. The third concept is **"MY BODY IS MY WORLD CONSCIOUSNESS AND IS HOW I COMMUNICATE WITH THE WORLD.**

        A. The Scripture for this seed is **1THESSALONIANS 5:23**
            1. The concept if **MY SPIRIT, SOUL AND BODY EACH NEED TO BE TOUCHED *(SANCTIFIED)* BY GOD.**

B D **S** R

Sample Fellowship Format

Disciple's reply is in **bold type**

"The name of the third seed in the second pod is
Spirit, Soul, and Body.
What is the name of the third seed in the second pod?"
"Spirit, Soul and Body"

"Correct. What are the three concepts for Spirit, Soul and Body?"
**"My spirit is my God-consciousness and my oneness with God.
My soul is self-consciousness.
My body is how I communicate with the world."**

"That is correct. What is the Scripture for Spirit, Soul and Body?"
"1 Thessalonians 5:23"

"Correct. What is the concept or the Scripture?"
"Each part of my being spirit, soul and body needs to be touched by God."

"Very good."

End of Seed 321 Spirit, Soul, and Body
REVIEW SEED UNTIL MASTERED

B D S R

Seed 321   Further Information – Spirit, Soul, and Body

The 3rd Seed in the 2nd Pod of the 1st Year

God forming the spirit of man *("Inmost Man" or "Hidden Man")* the highest, deepest, and most profound part of man is given equal importance with God laying the very foundation of the earth *(Zechariah 12:1)*. Indeed, that which is born of the Spirit is the spirit *(John 3:6)*. So when a person is born again, it is his spirit that is suddenly made new *(2 Corinthians 5:17)* and miraculously changed and made perfect forever *(Hebrews 10:14 and 12:23)* in oneness with Christ Jesus *(1 Corinthians 6:17)*. Therefore, our experiences with God and our ability to express His life and nature always works primarily from the inside-out *(Philippians 2:12)*.

The spirit of man serves three major functions. The first function is discernment which is an inward knowing *(intuition)* of various revelations of God apart from any outward teaching *(Hebrews 8:11)*. The second function is the conscience which determines by the Holy Spirit if an activity or information is of God or not. The third function of the spirit of man is to experience direct fellowship with God, which is always received initially through the spirit of man *(John 4:23, 24)*. It is only through the spirit of man that his soul can directly experience the things of God.

The soul of man *(Inward man)* is made up of our mind *(thoughts)*, our will *(choices)*, and our emotions *(feelings)*. This is the part of the active believer that is being sanctified and transformed from faith to faith, and from glory to glory. The soul of man *(the natural self)* is instructed to yield to the spirit *(Galatians 5:16)*, which is one with God's Spirit in life and nature. In this way, the Fruit of the Spirit is expressed out of man's spirit through his soul.

The body *(temple or vessel)* is the outward physical part of man which is the vessel that contains the spirit and soul. It is through our body that our soul experiences the world outside of us. This is done through the five senses: seeing, hearing, smelling, tasting, and touching. Interestingly, each of those functions is spoken of in God's Word as having operational counterparts in the spiritual realm as well. So it appears that all the outward physical functions are simply types and shadows of the higher spiritual and eternal senses of the eternal spirit of man.

Understanding the tripartite nature of man is critical to the right dividing of the Word of God. It is only the Word of God that can pierce to the dividing of the spirit of man from the soul of man *(Hebrews 4:12)*. Many "seeming contradictions" of God's Word can be quickly resolved by rightly dividing the scriptures that are speaking of man's spirit from the scriptures that are speaking of man's soul or flesh *(2 Timothy 2:15)*. The distinction and division the Word makes of the spirit and the soul is never a literal separation, but rather is a distinguishing of the spirit from the soul for proper cooperation between the two parts. The ultimate goal is that the soul of man *(the natural man)* be totally yielded to the spirit of man which is one with God's Spirit. More will be explained about recognizing proper scripture division in the next Seed, Rightly Dividing the Word *(421)*.

BDSR

Seed 421 – Rightly Dividing The Word

(In fellowship Seed 321 is referred to as the
4th Seed in the 2nd Pod of the First Year)

Simple format

IV. The name of the fourth seed in the second pod is **RIGHTLY DIVIDING THE WORD**
(Associate this seed name with your right hand),
1. The concept is **COMPARING SCRIPTURE WITH SCRIPTURE TO UNCOVER TRUTH.**
(Put your hands together, then open them up like a book to remember this).

   A. The first Scripture is **2 TIMOTHY 2:15**. In fellowship we call this the bottom cousin *(at the bottom of this pod)* because it is closely related to the first scripture *(at the top of the pod...2 Timothy 3:16...the top cousin).*
   1. The concept of the Scripture is **"STUDY TO SHOW YOURSELF APPROVED TO GOD BY RIGHTLY DIVIDING THE WORD OF TRUTH".**

   B. The second Scripture for this seed is **ACTS 17:11**
   (This Scripture can be recalled by an ice-cold Slurpee. You get them at 7-11 to trigger 17:11).
   1. The concept is **"I SEARCH THE SCRIPTURES DAILY".** Good.

B D S **R**

Sample Fellowship Format

Disciple's reply is in **bold type**

"The fourth seed in the second pod is called rightly dividing the Word.
The concept is I study to show myself approved by rightly dividing the Word.
What is the name of the fourth seed in the second pod?"
"Rightly dividing the Word."

"Yes, that is right. What is the concept?"
"Comparing Scripture with Scripture to uncover truth."

"The first scripture for this seed is 2 Timothy 2:15. The concept is I study to show myself approved by rightly dividing the Word. What is the first Scripture for rightly dividing the Word?"

"2 Timothy 2:15"

"Good. What is the concept?"

"I study to show yourself approved by Rightly dividing the Word of truth."

"Very good. The second scripture is Acts 17:11. The concept is I search scriptures daily.
What is the second Scripture for rightly dividing the Word?"
"Acts 17:11."

"Very good. What is the concept of the Scripture?"
"I search the Scriptures daily."

"Great."

END OF SEED 421   Rightly Dividing the Word

REVIEW SEED UNTIL MASTERED

B D S R

Seed 421   Further Information – Rightly Dividing the Word

The 4th Seed in the 2nd Pod of the 1st Year

To the carnal man and perhaps even to the immature spiritual man, the Bible says many things that are hard to understand. Indeed, there are even certain scriptures that seem to clearly contradict each other. Of course in truth, when the Word is rightly divided and correctly understood, there is perfect harmony in all its thoughts and teachings. But to be able to consistently rightly divide and explain the Word of God accurately requires much humility, revelation, and experience in yielding to the Holy Spirit. There is a multitude of matters that need to be considered in correctly handling God's Word. In learning more about this Seed, we will touch on three *(of eight)* important kinds of rightly dividing the Word.

The first kind of division is the discerning of what passages in the Bible are simply a God inspired record of what man said or thought *(a natural or fleshly man's word or opinion)* but not God's wisdom or instruction to us. For example, God told Adam not to eat of the Tree of Knowledge of Good and Evil "lest you die." *(Genesis 3:3)*. This is clearly God's instruction to Adam. However, the Bible also records the serpent telling Eve 'Ye shall not surely die" *(Genesis 3:4)*. In this particular passage it is very obvious that the words spoken to Eve were not of God and were a lie. However, sometimes making this kind of division is NOT so obvious.

For example, many people, believing they are quoting God's wisdom will say, "The Lord gives, and the Lord takes away *(Job 1:21)*. While there is no doubt that the author of Job *(probably Moses)* was divinely inspired to include that statement of Job's, it is nonetheless clear after careful study that Job was speaking according to his carnal and natural understanding *(Job 42:3)*. Indeed, in truth it is always our God who blesses and the enemy who takes away. John 10:10 tells us, "The thief does not come except to steal, and to kill, and to destroy." Job was mistaken, God did not bring the trouble into Job's life, Satan did. Most of Job's speaking throughout this book was not inspired by God, even though the accurate recording of what he said certainly was inspired. While most scripture is a record of God's view and opinion, we must be careful to recognize when it is simply a record of the opinion or sentiments of man.

The second kind of division is that of recognizing the dispensational difference in scripture, particularly between the Old Covenant and the New Covenant; that is, between the Dispensation of the Law *(pre-cross)* and the Dispensation of Grace *(post-cross)*. While it is true that God is the same yesterday, today, and forever *(all glory to His Name!)*, the way He deals with man after the Cross has greatly changed *(all glory to God!)*. A simple example of this is Jesus explaining to His Disciples during the Sermon on the Mount, "But if you forgive not men their trespasses, neither will your Father forgive your trespasses" *(Matthew 7:15)*. This statement was true under the Dispensation of the Law *(pre-cross)*. But after the resurrection of Christ, the Apostle Paul, inspired by the Holy Spirit, explained the New Covenant reality of forgiveness saying, "...forgiving one another...even as Christ forgave you, so also you do" *(Colossians 3:13)*.

Under the Dispensation of Grace, we are not told to forgive to get forgiveness. Rather, we are instructed to freely extend to others the same kind of forgiveness that has been freely been given to us. For a believer to be unforgiving is a serious matter. Such unforgiveness is foolish and costly. However, such foolishness is not greater than, nor does it cancel the effectiveness and atoning power of the shedding of the blood of Christ on the Cross and what that bought for us. There are a multitude of scriptures written after the resurrection of Christ that teach without controversy that man's forgiveness is a "done deal". Such forgiveness depends totally upon faith in Jesus, not any act of man *(Ephesians 1:7; Colossians 1:14; Romans 4:6-8; Hebrews 10:9, 10, 16-18 and many others)*. The well-known Christian song, "What can wash away my sins? NOTHING but the blood of Jesus" is actually true.

The Old Covenant Law is not made for a righteous man, but for the unregenerate man *(1 Timothy 1:8-9)*. Once we have received Christ, the Law serves no purpose for us in regards to righteousness *(Romans 10:4)*. Indeed, if we turn back to the Law after coming to Christ, we separate ourselves from Christ and fall from grace *(Galatians 5:1-5, Romans 3:19-21)*.

The third kind of division *(which is very important)* is using the Word of God to divide the born-again spirit of a man from his soul *(natural)* man *(Hebrews 4:12)*. These separations and divisions are essential in order to properly understand and explain the plain and clear meaning of certain scriptures. Here are some examples of proper division of spirit of man from the soul of man:

B D S R

1. 2 Peter 1:3, 4 states that as believers we have already been given "all things" that pertain to life and godliness as compared TO verses 5-7 of the same passage lists seven attributes that we need to add to our faith. But if we have already been given all things then why would there be any need to add anything? Proper understanding of this passage becomes easy when we simply divide it properly, understanding that in our born-again spirit man we have Christ Jesus, and in Him we have all things needed for life and godliness. However, in our soul *(natural man)*, there is always a need to add to our faith these attributes of God in an ever-increasing measure.

2. Now compare 1 John 3:2 which says, "...when He *(Jesus)* shall appear, we shall be like Him, for we shall see Him as He is" compared to 1 John 4:17 which says "...because as He *(Jesus)* is so are we in this world." Again we need to rightly divide. In our soul man we are being transformed into His likeness progressively as He is revealed to us, with the ultimate fulfillment being at His return. But in our born again spirit man, which is one with God, we are already like Jesus *(in life and nature, not in deity)*, even right now in this world.

3. Also study 1 John 2:20, "But you have an unction from God, and you know all things" compared to 1 Corinthians 8:2 which says, "And if any man thinks he knows anything, he knows nothing yet as he ought to know." Again without proper division *(assignment)* of spirit and soul to each scripture there appears to be a plain contradiction. But once again, the teaching is simple if you understand that in your *(born again)* spirit man you have the Mind of Christ *(1 Corinthians 2:16)* and consequently in your spirit man you truly do know all things. But in your soul *(natural man)* if you think you know anything, you know nothing yet as you ought to.

These divisions of spirit and soul are common throughout God's Word and should establish us in two important truths. The first truth is that in our natural man *(soul)*, apart from Christ, we have nothing, we can do nothing, and we are nothing. This truth should keep us ever humble. However, the greater Second Truth is that in Christ we have every positive thing, we know all things, and we can do all things even as the Spirit leads us and enables us. Indeed, we can do all the works Christ Jesus did and even greater works *(John 14:12)*. This Second Truth should create in us a great confidence and an eternal gratitude. These two truths *(the first and second)* working together, when fully understood and applied, will result in the mature Christian living in a very balanced way, as a son of God with a stronghold of humility and meekness, but also with a rock solid and unshakable confidence in his position and identity in Jesus.

B D S R

Overview of the Second Pod

I. Bible Reliability
   1. The Bible as we have it today is reliable and it can be proven both legally and historically by Manuscripts, Archaeology, Prophesy, Scripture itself, Congruency, and Changed Lives.

     A. 2 Timothy 3:16
       1. All scripture is inspired by God and profitable.

     B. 2 Peter 1:21
       1. All scripture is inspired by God and given through men.

II. Deity of Christ
   1. Jesus is God

     A. John 1:1,14
       1. In the beginning was the Word, and the Word was with God, and the Word was God. The Word became flesh.

     B. Romans 9:5
       1. Jesus is God overall eternally blessed!

III. Spirit, Soul, and Body
   1. My spirit is one with God and it is perfect.
   2. My soul *(mind, will, and emotions)* is my consciousness of self.
   3. My body is how I interact with the world *(through the five senses)*.

     A. 1 Thessalonians 5:23
       1. My spirit, soul, and body each need to be touched *(sanctified)* by God.

IV. Rightly Dividing the Word
   1. I compare scripture with scripture to uncover the truth.

     A. 2. Timothy 2:15
       1. I study to show myself approved, a workman that needs not be ashamed, rightly dividing the Word of Truth.

     B. Acts 17:11
       1. I search the Scripture daily!

Epilogue for Chapter Two

Keep in mind that the "typical" conversations in these written sections do not reflect the fact that most people need to hear something and speak it many times before it gets deeply engraved onto their hearts. An important part of this Discipleship is the persistent repetitive feeding and speaking that occurs until the concept is mastered by the disciple. Research shows we remember 10% of what we read, 20% of what we hear, 30% of what we see, 70% of what we discuss with others, and 95% of what we teach others. Some people have an unrealistic expectation that they can "preach" various truths once and that the listener will automatically always know those truths. In actual practice, that is rarely ever the case.

Most of the time a seed in Most Effective Discipleship Seeds *(MEDS)* can be learned in five to ten minutes and will become eternal knowledge when it is reviewed regularly for 30-60 days. However, it may take some believers 20-30 minutes or more to learn a single seed. This is okay. For the important thing is that the seed is learned by the disciple that it would become instrumental in bringing the believer into a stronger and closer relationship with the Lord to have a greater maturity in Christ. Additionally, as the believer matures, he will be equipped to be able to help others grow through the same process.

3 B 2 K

Chapter Three

The Third Pod - Acronym: 3B2K

Pod Clue: Next 3 out of 4

(Scriptures are in Corinthians)

Seed 131 – 3 Aspects of Salvation

(In fellowship Seed 131 is referred to as the 1st Seed in the 3rd Pod of the First Year)

Simple format

I. The name of the first seed in the third pod is 3 ASPECTS OF SALVATION.
   1. The first concept is **MY SPIRIT SALVATION TOOK PLACE WHEN I WAS BORN AGAIN** *(regenerated)* **THIS HAPPENED IN THE <u>PAST</u> WHEN IS FIRST BELIEVED.**

   2. The second concept is **MY SOUL SALVATION IS MY PRACTICAL TRANSFORMATION** *(sanctification)* **WHICH IS TAKING PLACE IN THE <u>PRESENT</u>.**

   3. The third concept is **"MY BODY SALVATION IS THE RECEIVING OF A GLORIFIED** *(transfigured/ redeemed)* **BODY WHICH WILL OCCUR IN THE <u>FUTURE</u>".**

      A. The Scripture is **1 CORINTHIANS 1:30**. *(Recall by associating what are you normally doing at 1:30 p.m.).*
         1. The concept is **CHRIST IS MY WISDOM, WHICH IS MY RIGHTEOUSNESS** *(Spirit salvation)*, **MY SANCTIFICATION** *(soul salvation)* **AND MY REDEMPTION** *(body salvation)*.

3 B 2 K

Sample Fellowship Format

Disciple's reply is in **bold type**

"What is the name of the first seed in the third pod?"
"3 Aspects of Salvation"

"Good. What are the three concepts?"
"My spirit has been born again (regenerated) **in the <u>past</u>."**

"My soul is being transformed (sanctified) **in the <u>present</u>."**

"My body will be redeemed (transfigured glorified) **in the <u>future</u>."**

"Excellent. What is the Scripture for 3 Aspects of Salvation?"
"1 Corinthians 1:30"

"Good. What is the concept of that Scripture?"
"Christ is my Wisdom which is my righteousness *(Spirit salvation)*, **Sanctification** *(soul salvation)* **and Redemption** *(body salvation.)***"**

"Great."

END OF SEED 131   3 Aspects of Salvation
REVIEW SEED UNTIL MASTERED

3 B 2 K

Seed 131   Further Information – 3 Aspects of Salvation

The 1st Seed in the 3rd Pod of the 1st Year

Further Information for Seed 131
The 1st Seed in the 3rd Pod of the 1st Year
3 Aspects of Salvation

By the finished work of the Cross, our salvation, relative to "eternity", can be thought of as a single act; however, "in time" and in our experience, salvation is a progressive event that has three aspects. The first aspect of salvation is when a person initially believes in his heart that Christ is truly the Messiah Savior, in God's sight that man becomes eternally righteous in his human spirit *(John 3:6, Hebrews 10:14)*. He is automatically baptized into the death of Christ and is immediately part of the Church of Christ: one of the "firstborn whose names are registered in the Book of Life and whose spirits have been made perfect" *(Hebrews 12:23)*.

However, the scripture teaches that after being born again, another process begins. While the spirit of man has been perfected, the soul still needs to be saved through sanctification *(James 1:20, Hebrews 10:39)*. This process is also known as transformation *(2 Corinthians 3:17, 18; Romans 12:1, 2)*. In this second aspect of salvation, each believer progressively takes on the nature and life of Christ in his experience and expression.

After two decades in Christian ministry, Paul stated that he had not yet attained to, nor arrived at, his ultimate spiritual maturity *(Philippians 3:12)*. In our natural life *(soul life)*, there is always a higher level of love and spiritual maturity into which to grow The purpose is to become more like Christ each and every day of our lives. As we mature in holiness, we will sin less, but will probably never be completely sinless. While it may theoretically possible to be sinless, that should not be our focus; rather, our focus should always be on Jesus Christ.

As we spend time seeking Him and abiding in Him, and in learning to yield to Him, our sanctification and holiness will increase spontaneously, effortlessly, and automatically. This process will transform us from

3 B 2 K

the inside-out. The way of man and religion focuses on behavior modification *(outside-in)*. Such an approach is not Christ as The Way, The Truth, and The Life.

The third and final aspect of salvation is reserved for the future. This is when Christ Jesus returns and each believer receives an incorruptible, glorified body *(Philippians 3:20, 21; 1 Corinthians 15:35-55)*. So then, while it is proper for the believer to say, "I have been saved," it is at the same time also correct to understand salvation as an ongoing process in the soulish life of the child of God, whereby he is consistently able to receive an even greater measure of his inheritance from God in Christ Jesus.

3 **B** 2 K

Seed 231 – Books of the New Testament

*(In fellowship Seed 231 is referred to as the
2nd Seed in the 3rd Pod of the First Year)*

Simple format

II. The name of the second seed in the third pod is **"BOOKS OF THE NEW TESTAMENT."**
(acronyms: MM's ARCC, General Electric Power Company, the 5 T's, Peanut butter Ham and Jelly, the Home stretch)

1. The first concept is MM's which is **MATTHEW, MARK, LUKE AND JOHN.**
2. The second concept is ARCC which is **ACTS ROMANS, 1 CORINTHIANS AND 2 CORINTHIANS.**
3. The third concept GEPC which is **GALATIANS, EPHESIANS, PHILIPPIANS, AND COLOSSIANS.**
   (find some phrase to recall GEPC like General Electric Power Company)
4. The fourth concept is 5T's which is **1 & 2 THESSALONIANS, 1 & 2 TIMOTHY AND TITUS.**
5. The fifth concept is PHJ which is **PHILEMON, HEBREWS AND JAMES.**
6. The sixth concept is the Home stretch which is **1 & 2 PETER, 1, 2 & 3 JOHN, JUDE AND REVELATION** *(Sometimes shortened to "2 Peters, 3 Johns, Jude and Revelation).*

3 B 2 K

Sample Fellowship Format

Disciple's reply is in **bold type**

"What is the name of this seed?"
"Books of the New Testament."

"Yes. What are the 27 books of the New Testament?"
"Matthew, Mark Luke and John
Acts, Romans, 1 & 2 Corinthians
Galatians, Ephesians, Philippians and Colossians
1 & 2 Thessalonians, 1 & 2 Timothy, and Titus
Philemon, Hebrews and James
1 & 2 Peter, 1, 2, and 3 John, Jude and Revelation"

"Excellent."

END OF SEED 231   Books of the New Testament

REVIEW SEED UNTIL MASTERED

3 B 2 K

Seed 231   Further Information – Books of New Testament

The 2nd Seed in the 3rd Pod of the 1st Year

The Seeds are a most excellent way to develop a good and strong topical overview of the Bible. At this point in the process, it is beneficial to learn the order of the books of the Bible, particularly those in the New Testament. Not only will mastering the books in order contribute to the believer's confidence when studying the Word, but it will engender confidence in others as the believer ministers to them. The New Covenant *(New Testament)* books should be mastered first since it is the covenant we are currently living under. That is the goal of this seed.

The learning of the names of Old Testament books will remain optional for now. However, acronyms to aid in the learning of Old Testament books are included in this seed explanation. Many believers *(through fellowship)* have mastered the books of the New Testament in 10-30 minutes at the most using the breakdown and acronyms provided on the next page. Old Testament aids are on the page after that for those who desire to master the Old Testament as well.

3 B 2 K

OLD TESTAMENT BOOKS (optional)

1. GEL ND	<u>G</u>enesis, <u>E</u>xodus, <u>L</u>eviticus, <u>N</u>umbers, <u>D</u>euteronomy
2. Josh is Judgmental of Ruth	<u>J</u>oshua, <u>J</u>udges, <u>R</u>uth
3. 2 <u>SKC</u>'s	1 Samuel, 2 Samuel, 1 Kings, 2 Kings, 1 Chronicles, 2 Chronicles
4. East North East	Ezra, Nehemiah, Esther
5. Poetic Books JPPES	Job, Psalms, Proverbs, Ecclesiastes, Song of Solomon
6. Major Prophets IJ LED	Isaiah, Jeremiah, Lamentations, Ezekiel, Daniel
7. Minor Prophets - 4 Groups of 3 - 1st group of 3 is HJA for	Hosea, Joel, Amos
2nd group of 3 is Orange Juice and Milk for	Obadiah, Jonah, Micah
3rd group of 3 is N*(HZ)* for	Nahum, Habakkuk, Zephaniah
4th group is 3 is *(HZ)* M for	Haggai, Zechariah, Malachi
39 Old Testament Books	
66 Books in the Bible	

3 B **2** K

Seed 331 – 2 or 3 Witnesses

(In fellowship Seed 331 is referred to as the 3rd Seed in the 3rd Pod of the First Year)

Simple format

III. The name of the third seed in the third pod is **2 OR 3 WITNESSES.**

    1. The concept is **EVERY <u>MATTER</u> IS ESTABLISHED** *(PROVEN)* **BY 2 OR 3 WITNESSES.**

        A. The Scripture for 2 or 3 witnesses is **2 CORINTHIANS 13:1.** *(This is a cousin to 1 Corinthians 1:30.)*
           1. The concept for the Scripture is **EVERY WORD** *(scripture)* **IS ESTABLISHED** *(proven)* **BY 2 OR 3 WITNESSES".**

3 B 2 K

Sample Fellowship Format

Disciple's reply is in **bold type**

"What is the name of the third seed in the third pod?"
"2 or 3 witnesses."

"Great.
What is the concept of 2 or 3 Witnesses?"
"Every matter is established *(proven)* by 2 or 3 witnesses."

"That's correct."

"The scripture for 2 or 3 witnesses is 2 Corinthians 1:30.
The concept is… Every word is established by 2 or 3 witnesses.
What is the Scripture for 2 or 3 witnesses?"
"2 Corinthians 13:1"

"Good. What is the concept?"
**"Every Word *(Scripture)* is established *(proven)* by
2 or 3 witnesses."**

"That's right."

END OF SEED 331   2 or 3 Witnesses

REVIEW SEED UNTIL MASTERED

3B **2** K

Seed 231   Further Information – 2 or 3 Witnesses

The 2nd Seed in the 3rd Pod of the 1st Year

A basic principle of hermeneutics *(the rules for proper interpretation of the Bible)* is that each truth in scripture needs to be established by two or three scripture witnesses. This is to help assure that an individual scripture is not misunderstood or used out of proper context, or used improperly in any way. Failure to follow the 2 or 3 Witnesses principle can easily result in Disciples trusting ideas and concepts that are not consistent with the teaching of the whole scripture. As scripture witness is multiplied, the truth is confirmed and the result is greater confidence in Christ and Him as The Way, The Truth, and The Life.

The 2 or 3 Witnesses principle can also be applied in regards to agreement in prayer *(Matthew 18:19)* which can bring a greater confidence in the expectation of answered prayer. The principle was also used in the Old Testament to establish the reliability of testimony against a person who was accused of a violation of The Law *(Deuteronomy 17:6)*. Finally, in the New Testament, the scripture requires 2 or 3 Witnesses to bring any accusation against an elder in the Church *(1 Timothy 5:19)*.

3 B 2 K

Seed 431 – Kenosis

(In fellowship Seed 431 is referred to as the 4th Seed in the 3rd Pod of the First Year)

Simple format

IV. The name of the fourth seed in the third pod is **KENOSIS**.

   1. This concept has 4 parts *(Acronym: JCTS)*.
   JESUS IS GOD WHO
   CAME TO EARTH AND LIVED AS A MAN...
   TOTALLY DEPENDENT ON GOD TO...
   SET AN EXAMPLE FOR US".

     A. The Scripture for Kenosis is **PHILIPPIANS 2:6-8.**
     (Associates: "2 4 6 8 who do we appreciate?" But drop the 4).
       1. The concept is... **JESUS DID NOT CONSIDER IT ROBBERY TO BE EQUAL WITH GOD.**
       HE EMPTIED HIMSELF or "made Himself nothing", or "of no reputation" and **HE HUMBLED HIMSELF EVEN TO DEATH ON THE CROSS"**.

3B2 K

Sample Fellowship Format

Disciple's reply is in **bold type**

What is the name of the fourth seed in the third pod?
Kenosis

Yes. What is the concept of Kenosis?
Jesus is God, He came to earth to live as a man,
Totally dependent on God to set an example for us.

Excellent. What is the Scripture for Kenosis?
Philippians 2:6-8.

Very Good. What is the concept?
Jesus did not consider it robbery to be equal with God.
He emptied Himself and He humbled Himself even to death on the cross.

Good.

END OF SEED 431   Kenois

REVIEW SEED UNTIL MASTERED

Seed 431   Further Information – Kenosis

The 4th Seed in the 3rd Pod of the 1st Year

"Kenosis" is a Greek word that is used in Philippians 2:7 in the original text which is variously translated into English as to empty self, to make oneself of no reputation, to strip oneself, or to make oneself nothing. In context, it is referring to Jesus, who realized He was God in the flesh, choosing not to grasp to or focus on that truth, but instead to live as a man, fully and completely trusting God by the Spirit. This fundamental teaching of the New Testament *(2 Corinthians 8:9)* helps us to understand the relationship and oneness of the Father, Son, and Holy Spirit.

Jesus our God took on flesh and walked this earth living as a man. Even though Jesus was both fully man and fully God, equal to God in every way *(because He is God)*, He laid aside His right to live as God. He never ceased to be God, but only by His own choice gave up the prerogative *(right)* to live according to the power of His own deity. Instead, Jesus operated only in His humanity, totally trusting God the Father by the Spirit, allowing the power of God to be experienced by and expressed through His humanity as Jesus the Son of Man.

Because of the "kenosis", our Lord fully took part in humanity and experienced every weakness and temptation of natural man. So while Jesus was God in the flesh and the Son of God, all He did while in human flesh He did as a man yielding to the Holy Spirit. Because he lived as the Son of Man, He is our perfect example of how to live trusting fully in the Spirit. If Jesus had lived as God, He could not have been our perfect example *(the first of many brethren)*. But He was the perfect man, even though in essence He never ceased to be God.

The fundamental teaching of "kenosis" fully answers the often asked question, "Why did Jesus pray to God, if He were God?" The simple answer is, "Although He truly was God in the flesh, He was living as a man fully trusting God in the Spirit; therefore, He prayed to the Father in order to set an example of what we as believers should do in all situations *(John 11:41,42)*. During His time on earth, Jesus spoke repeatedly of the fact that He did nothing or judged nothing by Himself, but did all according to what the Father showed Him *(John 5:19,30)* and told Him. Yet when Jesus was asked to show the Disciples the Father, He did not hesitate to explain that when they saw Himself *(the Son)*, they saw the Father *(John 14:8-11)*.

3 B 2 K

Overview of Third Pod

I. 3 Aspects of Salvation
   1. Spirit Salvation means the believer has been "BORN AGAIN" *(regenerated)* which took place a the time he first accepted Christ Jesus as the Messiah through heart belief.

   2. Soul Salvation is the believer being transformed *(sanctified)* as he abides in and yields to Christ day by day.

   3. Body Salvation is when the believer receives a glorified *(redeemed, incorruptible)* body at the Return of Christ.

   A. 1 Corinthians 1:30
   1. Christ is our wisdom; which is our righteousness, sanctification, and redemption.

II. Books of the New Testament
   1. Matthew, Mark, Luke, John...
   Acts, Romans, 1 Corinthians, 2 Corinthians...
   Galatians, Ephesians, Philippians, Colossians...
   1 Thessalonians, 2 Thessalonians, 1 Timothy, 2 Timothy, Titus...
   Philemon, Hebrews, James...
   1 Peter, 2 Peter, 1 John, 2 John, 3 John, Jude, Revelation

III. 2 or 3 Witnesses
   1. Every matter is established by 2 or 3 witnesses.

   A. 2 Corinthians 13:1
   1. Every Word is established by 2 or 3 witnesses.

IV. Kenosis
   1. Even though Jesus is God, when He came to earth He LIVED as a man, totally dependent on God to set a proper example for us.

   A. Philippians 2:6-8.
   1. Jesus did not consider it robbery to be equal with God.
   2. Instead, He emptied Himself *(made Himself nothing)*.
   3. Jesus humbled Himself, even to death on the Cross.

3 B 2 K

Epilogue for Chapter Three

Remember that as you speak these scriptures and concepts, it is important to speak them with vision and passion: seeing them as being done. Information plus emotion is what causes these truths to be written on the heart permanently. There are many scriptures that make it clear that you need to be diligent in guarding your heart and writing God's truth on it. Your speaking can be done according to God's wonderful redemptive truths to write victory into your heart, or in a negative worldly fashion that will bring defeat. By the leading of the Lord, you need to take care of your heart: the Word says "...out of the heart springs the issues of life" *(Proverbs 4:23)*.

The input programming of your heart can originate from many diverse sources. Indeed, one of the enemy's main schemes is to provide you with many deceptions and lies. You alone are the gatekeeper of your heart. You decide what to let in and what to keep out by the sincere confession of the words of your mouth. By consistently abiding in Christ and speaking God's Word you will be well able to guard your heart from the enemy, and fill it with the abundance and power of God's Word.

4 PK3K

Chapter Four

The Fourth Pod - Acronym: 4PK3K

Pod Clue: Big and long

Seed 141 – 4 Laws, 4 Lifes, SOS

*(In fellowship Seed 141 is referred to as the
1st Seed in the 4th Pod of the First Year)*

Simple format

V. The name of the first seed in the fourth pod is 4 LAWS, 4 LIVES, SOSL.

1. The concept is **SOSL, "THE STRENGTH OF SIN IS THE LAW"** *(which means if a believer "tries" to achieve holiness by human effort through law keeping, he may have some temporary success but ultimately his self-effort will only serve to strengthen his flesh's desire to sin).*

   A. The first Scripture is **1 CORINTHIANS 15:56**.
   *(Associate: "The Big" because of the high chapter number and the high verse number...
   Note: There will be an associated clue with the second scripture).*
   1. The concept of this Scripture is **THE STRENGTH OF SIN IS THE LAW"** *(See 1 above).*

   B. The second Scripture is **ROMANS 7:1-8:2**. *(We refer to this as The Long because of its length. So with the 2 Scriptures of this seed we have "The Big and Long"). (Read this entire passage of Romans 7:1-8:2 carefully. Be sure to note the many Scriptures (vs. 5-11) that speak of the effect of the law and commandments activating and strengthening sin. Additionally, notice the many Scriptures that refer to the Apostle's "desire to do good" (Law of the Mind), yet not being able to successfully carry out his desire (because of the Law of Sin).*
   1. The concept is **"THE 4 LAWS AND 4 LIVES"**.
      (The first 3 laws below are referring to a principle or power which "exerts a constant force" within each believer. The 4th law is God's written Law outside the believer).

(1) The first Law *(weakest)* and Life is the **LAW OF THE MIND** which is in the **SOUL LIFE**. This law always desires to do good by keeping Moses' Law *(commandments)*. However, the harder the self tries to keep the written Law of God, the stronger the Law of Sin gets.

(2) The second Law, *(stronger than first)* and Life is the **LAW OF SIN** in the **FLESH LIFE.** The Law of Sin cares neither about God or Man and wants to do what feels good to itself at the moment with little regard of whatever the long-term consequences might be. It is aroused and strengthened by the First Law *(The Law of the Mind)*.

(3) The Third Law *(strongest and undefeatable)* and Life is the **LAW OF THE SPIRIT OF LIFE** *(Romans 8:2)* that dwells permanently in every believer which is in the man's SPIRIT LIFE. This is the presence of the Godhead in the believer working as a law that God has placed in your heart. To the extent that the disciple yields to this law only, to that extent he will experience the fullness of deliverance and victory.

(4) The Fourth Law is the written O.T. LAW OF GOD *(or Moses' Law)* which the Law of the Mind tries to keep. The Fourth Life is the BODY LIFE which always follows the decision of the soul to either walk after the Spirit or the Flesh.

4 PK3K

Sample Fellowship Format

Disciple's reply is in **bold type**

What is the name of the first seed in the fourth pod?
4 Laws, 4 Lives SOSL

Good. What does SOSL stand for?
The strength of sin is the law; which means, if I try to keep the law, I will inadvertently strengthen the desire of the flesh to sin.

Excellent. What is the first Scripture for 4 Laws 4 Lives SOSL?
1 Corinthians 15:56

What is the concept of 1 Corinthians 15:56?
The strength of sin is the law.

What is the 2nd scripture of this seed?
Romans 7:1-8:2.

That's right. What is the concept?
The 4 laws and the 4 lifes.

Right! What is the First law and Life?
The Law of the Mind in the Soul life which desires to do good by keeping God's Law

Yes, but what does it end up doing?
It strengthens the law of sin in the flesh.

Great. What is the Second Law and what does it do?
The Law of Sin in the flesh life and it does whatever it wants to do with no regard for God or man. Great.
What is the Third Law and where is it located?
The Law of the Spirit of Life in my spirit. It is the Life and Person of Christ living in me *(as a Law)* that empowers me to be able to live holy and blameless as I progressively learn to rely on it.

That's right.

4 PK3K

Tell me about the Fourth Law and the Fourth Life?
The Fourth Law is the Law of Moses, a written law outside of man *(in the Bible)*. The Fourth life is the Body life which always follows the leading of the soul of each man.

Very good. Great job

END OF SEED 141   4 Laws, 4 Lifes SOSL
REVIEW SEED UNTIL MASTERED

4 PK3K

Seed 141 Further Information – 4 Laws, 4 Lifes, SOS

The 1st Seed in the 4th Pod of the 1st Year

SOSL stands for the "Strength of Sin is the Law" *(1 Corinthians 15:56)*. While the Law of God is good and holy, it contains none of the Life of God and consequently possesses no power to defeat sin. The Law simply demands human will power, of itself, to supply what ultimately human will power simply cannot supply which is perfect submission to the Law of God *(James 2:10)*. This is why every person needs Jesus Christ as Savior. He is the Life and Power that has defeated and defeats sin. What then is the purpose of the Law? It was added through Moses long after the promise through faith *(Galatians 4:17)* was given to Abraham *(Genesis chapters 12 and 15)*.

The main purpose the Law was given was to direct and regulate the flesh of man in part until Christ *(the Promise fulfilled)*, had come into the believer at the time of regeneration *(being born again)*. Once the believer has Christ in his life, the Law no longer has any role in regards to holy living or righteous standing *(Romans 10:1-4)*. Holy living is always accomplished through trust and faith in the finished work of Jesus operating in, on, and through the believer by the power of the Holy Spirit. Only Christ through the Holy Spirit possesses the consistent effective power which has and does overcome all sin and death.

When a believer seeks, or tries strive for holiness through keeping the Law by his own human will and strength, he unwittingly empowers the sin in his flesh. Hence, the Strength of Sin is the Law *(SOSL)*. while "self will" and "human ability" can defeat sin for a relatively short period of time, eventually, the Law of Sin will defeat a man's own best effort *(Romans 7:15-23)*. But when the disciple turns to Christ Jesus he is empowered for consistent victory in Christ. Consequently, Christ Jesus, not the believer, is worthy of and receives all glory and praise for the victory. The believer's appropriate response is never pride or self-righteous smugness, but rather humility and thankfulness.

The word "law" as used in Romans 7:23 *(and certain other times throughout this seed)* refers to "a spiritual principal, power, or person that exerts a consistent and constant force." An example from the natural realm would be the law of gravity, which is a consistent and constant force that causes physical objects to fall to the ground when released in mid-air. The law of aerodynamics when properly applied will defeat the law of gravity which explains how birds and airplanes fly.

Therefore, some laws are more dominant than others. A greater law will defeat or overcome a lesser law. The same principal applies in the spiritual realm. The believer needs to understand the various laws that that operate in the spiritual realm in order to experience consistent victory over sin. In this Seed, the disciple learns about 4 laws and 4 lifes that are important to understand in order to live a consistent victorious life and help others to do the same.

The word "life" as we use it in this Seed means "a person or force which can bring movement, activity, and growth." Each of the first 3 laws and all 4 lives are inherent in every born-again believer. The First Law, the weakest of the three, is the Law of the Mind *(Romans 7:23)* which is in the Soul Life. The Law of the Mind in the Soul Life delights in God's Law *(Romans 7:22)* and tries to do good by keeping God's Law. However, in the self-effort to do good, the Law of the Mind inadvertently enlivens and strengthens the Second Law, the Law of Sin *(Romans 7:23)* in the Flesh Life, which is stronger than the Law of the Mind in the Soul life.

This is the wretched situation of each born again believer that Paul is explaining in Romans 7:14-20, which is the struggle of a believer trying to overcome sin apart from Christ by self-effort and self-will. Although he may experience a measure of temporary success, ultimately self-dependent "doing" is a fruitless endeavor doomed for failure.

Jesus Christ, as the only Way to genuine victory over sin, is the essential meaning of the Third Law called the Law of the Spirit of Life *(Romans 8:2)* which is in our Spirit Life. This law is the strongest of all; indeed, it is undefeatable. The Law of the Spirit of Life is the fullness of the Godhead operating in us and through us by faith *(Colossians 2:9, 10)*. This wonderful law is the "My Law" which God foretold through His prophets that He would put in our mind and write on our hearts *(Hebrews 8:10)*.

The fourth and final law is the Law of God, also commonly known as the Law of Moses. Remember it is the application of The Law of God that serves to strengthen the power of sin *(Law of Sin)* in the believer when the keeping of the Law of God is trusted for achieving righteousness. The

Law of God is the written law which is outside of us, which once held us captive. When we received Jesus Christ as our Savior, we were set free from the bondage that had come as a result of the Law of God *(Romans 7:1-6; Galatians 4:1-7).*

The Law of God, which was prevalent before Christ came, is referred to in 2 Corinthians 3:9 as now being a ministry of condemnation and in 3:7 as a ministry of death. Verse 7 confirms that this passage is speaking of the Moral Law of God saying it was "written and engraved on stones". This Law will always kill us if it is not used lawfully; that is, for its intended purpose, which was to restrain men, expose men, and keep men ONLY until they received Christ as their Lord and Savior *(1 Timothy 1:7-9).* Any attempt to use the Law in an unlawful way will always ultimately result in condemnation and death.

So the Law today is not to be the regulator of our flesh, as it was given only as a shadow to operate as a temporary "guardian" or "tutor" of the flesh until Christ should come *(Galatians 3:24,25; Hebrews 10:1).* Indeed, the Bible contrasts Moses' Law, calling it "weak and unprofitable", with the Melchizedek priesthood of Christ, calling the latter "the Power of an Endless Life" *(Hebrews 7:15-19)* which is synonymous with the Law of the Spirit of Life. To attempt to fight the flesh with the written Law *(once you have Christ)* is a foolish and futile endeavor.

The flesh *(Law of Sin)* may be temporarily restrained by human effort and will power, but the flesh can never be consistently defeated by human ability. So our victory comes NOT by beating down the flesh, it rather by annulling and ignoring it *(Hebrews 7:18),* and then turning to the Law of the Spirit of Life, which is where victory is already won by Christ in the spiritual realm *(Romans 8:2).*

In summary, SOSL signifies the Strength of Sin is the Law. The weakest law is the Law of the Mind in the Soul Life. Stronger than the Law of the Mind is the Law of Sin in the Flesh Life. But the strongest and greatest law of all, the law that has already defeated sin and death, is the Law of the Spirit of Life which God has freely given us, which is Christ in us. The Law of God *(of Moses)* is the law outside of us on which we no longer focus, as it is only a shadow of Christ Jesus *(Hebrews 10:2; Colossians 2:16, 17).* The life of the believer's body always follows the ultimate decision of the soul to follow the Spirit or the flesh. Only in Christ do we have genuine victory. To Jesus Christ be all the glory!

4 P K 3 K

Seed 241 – Pride vs. Godly Humility

*(In fellowship Seed 241 is referred to as the
2nd Seed in the 4th Pod of the First Year)*

Simple format

VI. The name of the Second Seed in the Fourth Pod is **PRIDE & GODLY HUMILITY"**.

1. The concept of Pride & Godly Humility is **PRIDE IS DEPENDENCE ON SELF. HUMILITY IS DEPENDENCE ON GOD.**

   A. The first Scripture is **PROVERBS 16:18.**
   (Associate: Legal age to drive 16, Legal age to vote 18.)
   1. The concept is **PRIDE COMES BEFORE A FALL.**

   B. The Second Scripture is **MATTHEW 23:12.**
   (Associate: Easy as 1 2 3 1 2 and the first 1 is the first Book of the NT.
   1. The concept is **IF YOU EXALT YOURSELF YOU WILL BE HUMBLED, IF YOU HUMBLE YOURSELF YOU WILL BE EXALTED.**

   C. *The third Scripture for this seed is **1 PETER 5:5-7** (Associate: Rabbit driving the speed limit - 55).*

   1. The first concept is **GOD RESISTS THE PROUD, BUT GIVES GRACE TO THE HUMBLE.**

   2. The second concept is **I HUMBLE MYSELF BEFORE GOD KNOWING HE WILL EXALT ME IN DUE TIME."**

   3. The third concept is **I CAST ALL MY CARE UPON HIM BECAUSE HE CARES FOR ME.**
   (v. 5 = What God does.
   v. 6 = What we should do because of what God does.
   v. 7 = How God wants us to do it.)

Sample Fellowship Format

Disciple's reply is in **bold type**

What is the name of the Second Seed in the Fourth Pod?
Pride & Godly Humility.

Very good. What is the concept for Pride & Godly Humility?
Pride is dependence on self.
Humility is dependence on God

That is correct.

What is the 1st scripture for Pride and Godly Humility?
Proverbs 16:18

Good. What is the concept for Proverbs 16:18?
Pride comes before a fall.

Great. What is the second Scripture for this seed?
Matthew 23:12

Excellent. What is the concept of the Scripture?
If you exalt yourself you will be humbled,
if you humble yourself you will be exalted

What is the 2nd scripture for Pride vs. Godly Humility?
Matthew 23:12.

Correct. And what is the concept?
If a man exalts himself he will He will be brought down, but I humble
myself and God exalts me!

Very Good. The 3rd scripture is 1 Peter 5:5-7.
What is the concept for verse 5?
God resists the proud, but gives grace to the humble.

Good. What is the concept for verse 6?
I humble myself before God knowing He will exalt
me in due time

4  K 3 K

That is correct. What is the concept for verse 7?
I cast all my care upon Him because He cares for me

Correct. Great Job!

END OF SEED 241   Pride vs Godly Humility
REVIEW SEED UNTIL MASTERED

Seed 241 Further Information – Pride vs. Godly Humility

The 2nd Seed in the 4th Pod of the 1st Year

Our confidence to experience the best God has for us and to live a victorious life should never spring out of self-confidence, self-reliance, or self-esteem, but rather should emanate out of our confidence in God, our reliance on Him, and our understanding of the esteem He has for us that evolves entirely out of our oneness with our Lord Jesus Christ. All dependence on self, apart from Christ, is pride. The Bible teaches: Cursed is the man who puts his trust in man *(including our own self)* but blessed is the man who puts his trust in God *(Jeremiah 17:5, 7)*. To the extent that the believer relies on his own ability, to that degree he is operating in sinful pride, and that pride will always cause him to stumble.

The simplest definition of Godly humility is "total dependence on God". The more we seek Him and continue to gain a greater revelation and understanding of His nature and His love relative to us, the more we will develop a perfect confidence in Him. The result will be true Godly humility.

Contrary to what many believe, to be humble does not mean to judge ourselves harshly, but rather to be sober, not thinking higher of ourselves than we ought *(Romans 12:3)*, but rather abiding in Him and submitting ourselves to Him which will result in His exalting us in His own time and way *(James 5:5-7)*. The word "pride" is never used in scripture with a positive connotation. Therefore, it is probably wise to always think of pride as being something completely of the flesh, the world, and the devil, that results in destruction *(Proverbs 16:18)*.

As we progressively see ourselves the way our Father sees us, we will develop a healthy balance between confidence and humility. Our confidence comes not from any personal attributes of self, but rather is based on our experience of the reality of who we are and what we have in Jesus. This confidence should continue to increase as we spiritually mature.

However, balancing that confidence in Him should be an ever increasing sobriety that reminds is how utterly useless we are apart from our Lord and how meaningless is our life apart from our oneness with

Him. As we *(through Christ)* maintain a proper balance *(temperance)* between confidence and humility *(constantly increasing in both)*, our Lord will surely do great things through us for the building up of ourselves, others, and His kingdom. We should not be "proud" of ourselves or others, but rather should give God all the thanks and praise with joy; He is the only source of all that is pleasing in His sight.

Confidence and boldness are often needed in our daily lives, but our sureness should rely completely on who He is and who we are in Him. Then as we experience success and blessings, we will know to give God all the glory.

4 P **K** 3 K

Seed 341 – Kingdom of God

*(In fellowship Seed 341 is referred to as the
3rd Seed in the 4th Pod of the First Year)*

Simple format

VII.   The Third seed in the Fourth Pod is **KINGDOM OF GOD.**

    1. The concept is **"THE KINGDOM OF GOD IS THE REALM WHERE GOD RULES AND REIGNS"** (*or wherever King Jesus has influence*).

       A. The first Scripture is **LUKE 17:20-21**
          (*Associate: 17 is the common number in this Scripture and the next.
          For this Scripture think 17+3=20, for the next 3+14=17 for 14:17*)
          1. The concept here is **THE KINGDOM OF GOD DOES NOT COME BY OBSERVATION BUT IS WITHIN ME.**

       B. The second Scripture is **ROMANS 14:17.**
          1. The concept is **THE KINGDOM OF OF GOD IS RIGHTEOUSNESS, PEACE AND JOY IN THE HOLY GHOST.**

Sample Fellowship Format

Disciple's reply is in **bold type**

What is the name of the seed in the fourth pod?
Kingdom of God

Great. What is the concept of Kingdom of God?
**The Kingdom of God is where God
rules and reigns** *(or wherever King Jesus has influence)*.

Very Good. What is the first Scripture?
Luke 17:20-21.

Excellent. What is the context of the Scripture?
The kingdom of God does not come by observation but is within you

That is correct. What is the second Scripture for this seed?
Romans 14:17

Excellent. What is the concept of that Scripture?
**The Kingdom of of God is
Righteousness, Peace and Joy in the Holy Ghost**

Very good.

END OF SEED 341   Kingdom of God

REVIEW SEED UNTIL MASTERED

Seed 341 Further Information – Kingdom of God

The 3rd Seed in the 4th Pod of the 1st Year

The Kingdom of God includes all that God is and all that God has. But more specifically, it is the realm in which God rules and reigns; that is, where His influence is dominant. Consequently, to seek or enter God's kingdom is accomplished when a disciple diligently seeks or enters the realm of God's influence. Jesus taught that no one can see or enter God's realm and influence *(kingdom)* unless they are born again *(John 3:5-7)*.

Jesus went on to explain how this can be; it is the person who looks to and believes in Jesus Christ and the work of the Cross that has eternal life *(John 3:14-17)*. When a person truly believes in his heart that Jesus is the Savior, at that moment that believer becomes born again and is baptized into the death of Jesus Christ and into the body of Christ *(the church)* and becomes a child of God's kingdom *(Mark 16:16, Romans 6:3)*.

The kingdom of God is God's overall general reign from eternity past to eternity future. The kingdom of Heaven is a term used exclusively in the book of Matthew. It is likely referring to the part of the kingdom of God that is on earth which would be composed of the church today and the heavenly part of the coming Millennial Kingdom. So then, the kingdom of God always existed wherever God's influence was present, but the kingdom of Heaven drew near when John the Baptist came preaching his message. The power and glory of the kingdom of Heaven exists today through the Church and will be fully manifested during the Millennial Reign.

4PK**3**K

Seed 441 – 3 Aspects of Love

*(In fellowship Seed 441 is referred to as the
4th Seed in the 4th Pod of the First Year)*

Simple format

VIII. The Fourth Seed in the Fourth pod is **3 ASPECTS OF LOVE**.

1. The first aspect of love is **AGAPE LOVE** which is **GOD'S UNCONDITIONAL LOVE** for us.
2. The Second aspect of love is **PHILIA LOVE** which is the **HIGHEST HUMAN LOVE**.
   This love is **CONDITIONAL**.
3. The Third aspect of love is "**EROS LOVE**" which is **PHYSICAL** attraction and/or Interaction.

   A. The Scripture for 3 Aspects of Love is **1 CORINTHIANS 13**.
   1. The concept is there are **THE 16 CHARACTERISTICS OF LOVE** *(divided into 4 groups.*
      (Acronym: PinK/PuRSE/EBKiD/RiP THe PuN)

      The first group characteristics *(PinK)* are **LOVE IS PATIENT, LOVE IS KIND**.

      The second group characteristics *(PuRSE)* are **LOVE IS NOT PROUD, RUDE, SELF-SEEKING OR EASILY ANGERED**.

      The third group characteristics *(EBKiD)* are **LOVE DOES NOT ENVY, BOAST, KEEP A RECORD OF WRONGS OR DELIGHT IN EVIL**.

      The fourth group *(RiP THe PuN)* **LOVE DOES REJOICE IN THE TRUTH, PROTECT, TRUST, HOPE, PERSEVERE AND NEVER FAIL**.

4 P K **3** K

Sample Fellowship Format

Disciple's reply is in **bold type**

What is the fourth seed in the fourth pod?
3 Aspects of Love.

Great. What is the first aspect of love?
Agape Love, which is God's unconditional love for me.

That is correct. What is the second aspect of love?
Philia Love which is the highest human love. This love is conditional

What is the 3rd aspect of love?
Eros Love which is physical attraction and/or interaction.

Excellent. What is the Scripture for 3 Aspects of Love?
1 Corinthians 13.

Good. What are the 16 characteristics of Love?
Love *is* Patient, Love is Kind.
Love *is not* Proud, Rude, Self-Seeking, or Easily angered.
Love *does not* Envy, Boast, Keep a record of wrongs, or Delight in Evil.
Love does Rejoice in the Truth, Protect, Trust, Hope, Persevere, and Never fail.

That is right. Excellent.

END OF SEED 441   3 Kinds of Love

REVIEW SEED UNTIL MASTERED

4 P K **3** K

Seed 441 Further Information – 3 Kinds of Love

The 4th Seed in the 4th Pod of the 1st Year

Biblical love can be better understood through contrasting 3 Greek words that refer to the different aspects of love that can be experienced by mankind. The first aspect is "Eros Love". This Greek word speaks of physical touching and romantic or sexual love. This love is a creation of God and is extremely beautiful, enjoyable, and useful when carried out according to God's standards and ways.

The second aspect of love expressed by the original Greek language is "Philia Love". Philia love is the highest human love possible, apart from the work of the Holy Spirit working in, on, and through a person. Unfortunately, philia love is always conditional and is sometimes motivated primarily by self-gain. Philia love can become stronger and more consistent if it is touched and uplifted by the highest kind of love, which in the Greek language is called Agape Love.

Agape Love is the third and highest love taught in this seed. This love is exemplified by the unconditional love of the heavenly Father for His children. The expression of agape love never depends on the goodness or behavior of the one being loved, but rather on the character of the one doing the loving. This high and deep love is described in some detail by the 16 characteristics of love in 1 Corinthians 13:4-8. Agape Love toward God and others is an important part the greatest command and becomes a major operation and expression of our lives as we mature in our trust in the Father, our abiding in the Son, and yielding to the Holy Spirit.

The characteristics of love are learned in this seed through the use of four acronyms. They are PinK, PuRSE, EBKiD, and RiP THe PuN. The PinK acronym stands for love IS Patient and Kind. PuRSE stands for love IS NOT Proud, Rude, Self-seeking, or Easily angered. EB KiD stands for love DOES NOT Envy, Boast, Keep a record of wrongs, or Delight in evil. Finally, the acronym RiP THe PuN stands for love DOES Rejoice in truth, Protect, Trust, Hope, Persevere, and Never fails.

As we better understand and experience God's agape love, we will learn that agape is not primarily about a feeling, but rather it is an attitude that always wants the best for others and consistently expresses such in our actions. The more we experience the reality of God's love for us in our own lives, the more we will consistently and freely pour out this kind of wonderful love for others.

Here are a couple of good questions to ask ourselves. Is our love becoming warmer? Or is it inconsistent and growing cold? These questions are important; the answers to which will be a good measure of how we are doing in our Christian growth. Only to the extent that God's agape love is flowing through us are we genuinely expressing Christ Jesus in us. We will learn much more about the height, depth, and width of this kind of love in Seed 323 "Comparing Two Loves" which will, in greater detail, give practical examples of the difference between man's philia love and God's Agape Love.

Seed 541 – Kingdom Qualified

(In fellowship Seed 541 is referred to as the 5th Seed in the 4th Pod of the First Year)

Simple format

IX. The Fifth seed in the Fourth Pod is **KINGDOM QUALIFIED"**.

1. The concept is **"The Father has qualified me for His Kingdom"**.

    A. The Scripture for this seed is **COLOSSIANS 1:12, 13.**
       1. The concept is **"I HAVE BEEN DELIVERED OUT OF THE KINGDOM OF DARKNESS INTO THE KINGDOM OF HIS BELOVED SON"**.

4 P K 3 **K**

Sample Fellowship Format

Disciple's reply is in **bold type**

What is the Fifth Seed in the Fourth Pod?
Kingdom Qualified

Yes. What is the concept of the seed?
The Father has qualified me for His Kingdom

Excellent. What is the scripture for Kingdom Qualified?
Colossians 1:12, 13.

Yes. What is the concept?
I have been delivered out of the kingdom of darkness into the Kingdom of His Beloved Son.

Very Good.

END OF SEED 431   Kingdom Qualified
REVIEW SEED UNTIL MASTERED

4 P K 3 **K**

Seed 541 Further Information – Kingdom Qualified

The 5th Seed in the 4th Pod of the 1st Year

When a believer is born again through heart belief in Jesus the Messiah, that believer is spiritually delivered by the Lord from the kingdom of darkness *(Satan's rule and influence)* into the Kingdom of God's beloved Son. At that point, the believer's objective identity in God's sight is perfectly one with Jesus in the spiritual realm. All this takes place by grace through the genuine faith of the believer, irrespective of any work or effort on his part. This qualification is wholly the operation of the Father through the Holy Spirit in Christ Jesus. This perfect, objective identity of the spirit of man in God's sight may be at various levels in contrast to his soulish subjective experience of his identity in his own sight. The distance of this difference will depend on the level of the believer's revelation of Bible Truth and his maturity relative to his dying to self and walking after the Holy Spirit.

While it is certainly true that each believer is made for and called to faith works, it is important to understand that it is never the works or efforts of the believer that establish who he is. But rather, the believer is qualified by the Father's Work accomplished by the blood at the cross at Calvary. For that reason, our attitude as born again children of God should always be one of gratitude and worship for our Lord. As we learn and mature through consistent abiding in Christ, the result will always be good spiritual fruit. All glory to God!

4 P K 3 K

Overview of the Fourth Pod

I. 4 Laws, 4 Lives, S.O.S.L.
  1. S.O.S.L. stands for the Strength of Sin is the Law.

    A. 1 Corinthians 15:56
      1. The Strength of sin is the Law.

    B. Romans 7:1-8:2
      1. The Four Laws and Four Lifes *(as outlined below)*.

    The "Weakest Law" *(in the Soul Life)* is the Law of the Mind. This law wants to do good by keeping God's Law, but instead it inadvertently strengthens the Law of Sin.

    The "Stronger Law" *(in the Flesh Life)* is the Law of Sin. It desires to do whatever it feels like doing with no regard for others or God. It is aroused by the Law of the Mind.

    The "Strongest Law" *(in the Spirit Life)* is the Law of the Spirit of Life which is synonymous with the Godhead living inside the believer. When we yield to this Law, we never sin or fall short of God's glory. The Body Life always follows the lead of the Soul Life *(the Soul Life chooses which life it will follow, Spirit or flesh)*.

    Law of Moses *(God's Law)*, a written law outside of man *(in the Bible)*. The Fourth life is the Body life which always follows the leading of the soul of each man.

II. Pride and Godly Humility
  1. Pride is dependence on self. Godly Humility is total dependence on God.

    A. Proverbs 16:18
      1. Pride goes before the fall.

    B. Matthew 23:12
      1. If I exalt myself, I will be brought down, if I humble myself, I will be exalted.

4 P K 3 K

    C. 1 Peter 5:5-7
        1. God resists the proud, but gives grace to the humble.
        2. I humble myself before God and He exalts me in due time.
        3. I cast my cares on the Lord because He cares for me.

III. Kingdom of God
    1. The realm where God rules and reigns *(or wherever God has influence)*.

    A. Luke 17:20,21
        1. The Kingdom of God does not come by observation but it is within me.

    B. Romans 14:17.
        2. The Kingdom of God is not food or drink, but is righteousness, peace, and joy in the Holy Spirit.

IV. 3 Aspects of Love
    1. Eros- physical touching and romantic love.
    2. Philia- the highest human love. It is conditional.
    3. Agape- God's unconditional love for His children.

    A. 1 Corinthians 13
        1. Love IS Patient and Kind
        2. Love IS NOT Proud, Rude, Self seeking, or Easily angered
        3. Love DOES NOT Envy, Boast, Keep a record of wrongs, or Delight in evil.
        4. Love DOES Rejoice in truth, Protect, Trust, Hope, Persevere, and Never fail.

V. Kingdom Qualified
    3. I am qualified for the Kingdom of God because the Father qualified me.

    A. Colossians 1:12,13
        1. I have been delivered out of the Kingdom of Darkness into the Kingdom of Light.

Epilogue for Chapter Four

The Apostle Paul explained to those in the city of Philippi that it was not tedious for Him to keep saying the same things to them over and over again. He added that it made them safe *(Philippians 3:1)*. The repetitive attentive hearing and passionate speaking of God's Word by the Spirit of God causes it to be engrafted on the heart. This engrafting of God's Word on the heart of the believer is the highest meaning of "being a doer of the Word".

Hearing and speaking God's important truths over and over again with passion, moves them from being only "head knowledge" and "writes them on the heart" of the believer. Only as this occurs is the saint transformed from the inside-out and truly becomes a sanctified vessel who experiences Christ in order to express Christ. This is God's ultimate plan for each believer and is each believer's destiny.

5 PPT

CHAPTER FIVE

THE FIFTH POD - ACRONYM: 5PPT

POD CLUE: LUKE SANDWICH WITH ROMANS BREAD

Seed 151 – 5 Aspects of Obedience

(In fellowship Seed 151 is referred to as the 1st Seed in the 5th Pod of the First Year)

Simple format

I. The First seed in the Fifth Pod is **5 ASPECTS OF OBEDIENCE.**

   1. The First concept is "There are **2 ASPECTS OF UNGODLY OBEDIENCE** *(Dead Works).*
   (Associate: Physical Education)

   The first aspect is **PERFORMING** which is when a believer does a work or deed to impress others".
   (All work should be done by the Spirit through the believer to express the Life and Nature of Jesus).

   The second aspect is **EARNING**. Earning is when a believer does a work or deed for his own profit or reward.

   2. The second concept is "There are **3 ASPECTS OF GODLY OBEDIENCE".**
   (Associate: Dock of the BAY)

   The first aspect is **BELIEVING** which is the **ONE THING REQUIRED".**

   The second aspect is **ABIDING** which is the **ONE THING NEEDED.**

   The third aspect is **YIELDING** which is **BENEFICIAL** (or profitable to us and others)".

5 P P T

A. The first Scripture is **ROMANS 1:5**
   1. The concept is **BELIEVING IS OBEDIENCE**.

B. The second Scripture for 5 Aspects of Obedience is **LUKE 10:42.**
   1. The concept is **MARY WAS ABIDING AT THE FEET OF JESUS WHICH HE SAID WAS THE ONE THING NEEDED.**

C. The third Scripture for 5 Aspects of Obedience is **ROMANS 6:19.**
   1. The concept is **I YIELD TO THE WORD AND THE SPIRIT IN ALL MATTERS.**

5 PPT

Sample Fellowship Format

Disciple's reply is in **bold type**

What is the first seed in the fifth pod?
5 Aspects of Obedience

That's right.
What are the 2 ungodly aspects of obedience? Explain each one.
Performance is when a believer does a work or deed to impress others *(a dead work).*
Earning is when a believer does a work or deed for his own profit or reward *(a dead work).*

Excellent. What is the 2nd Scripture for 5 Aspects of Obedience?
Luke 10:42.

Yes. What is the concept?
Mary was abiding at the feet of Jesus, which He said was the one thing needed.

What are the 3 aspects of Godly obedience and how important are they?
Believing which is the one thing absolutely required.
Abiding which is the one thing needed.
Yielding which is beneficial *(to us and others).*

Very good. What is the 1st Scripture for 5 Aspects of Obedience?
Romans 1:5

Good. What is the concept?
Believing is Obedience.

Great. What is the 3rd Scripture for this seed?
Romans 6:19.

Excellent. What is the concept?
I yield to the Word and the Holy Spirit in all things.

That is correct.

5PPT

END OF SEED 151 5 Aspects of Obedience
REVIEW SEED UNTIL MASTERED

5 PPT

Seed 151 Further Information – 5 Aspects of Obedience

The 1st Seed in the 5th Pod of the 1st Year

To walk successfully in God's kingdom, it is important not only to spiritually distinguish good from evil, but also to distinguish the difference between religious ungodly obedience and spiritual godly obedience. We are not called just to "do good", but rather to be vessels that contain Christ in order to express Christ. Christless religion can do good, but it cannot express the life of Jesus Christ Himself. Being a yielded vessel, enjoying Christ Jesus, and allowing Him to have His way and His expression through us is God's way.

God's way of "entering the rest" *(Hebrews 4:10, 11)* is much higher, more beautiful, and much more effective than man's way of "try your best". As we trust and rely on our Lord, we truly learn to walk in His abundant life *(John 10:10)*. In this seed, we learn how to identify religious, ungodly obedience from spiritual godly obedience in order that we may properly fulfill God's purpose for us, which is to be conformed to the image of His Son by grace through faith.

There are two aspects of ungodly obedience *(acronym PE)*. The first ungodly aspect is "Performance". Performance is when the believer does good works out of self-righteousness with the motive of impressing others or God *(Isaiah 64:6; Philippians 3:9)*. To attempt to impress God demonstrates a misunderstanding of God's complete satisfaction with every believer, which is not based on what a believer does, but rather on his inherited righteousness and oneness with Christ Jesus through faith *(Hebrews 11:6)*. The proper godly motive for spiritual good works is to always radiate and express Christ, out His righteousness and love in us, for us, and through us; not with a motive to IMPRESS, but rather with the aim to express Christ's love and nature.

The second aspect of ungodly obedience is "Earning". Earning is the believer doing a good work motivated primarily by a desire for reward or payment *(Romans 4:4)*. In other words, instead of operating out of God's other centered love, the believer acts based on a carnal motive of self-gain. This kind of self-centered doing misses the mark of true godly obedience. Both performing and earning are "dead works" in the sight of God

(Matthew 6:1-6; Hebrews 6:1, 2; 9:14).

The first aspect of Godly Obedience is "Believing". Heart belief in Jesus Christ as our Savior is the one thing required to be born again of the Spirit, to have our sins blotted out and to have our names remain written in the Book of Life *(John 3:36; Romans 10:10)*. After this initial salvation it is important and profitable to continue to believe each Word of God, according to the Doctrine of Christ, as it is revealed to us, that we would a continual growth in sanctification *(soul salvation)* which will bear the fruit of holiness.

The Second Aspect of Godly Obedience is "Abiding". Jesus explained to Martha, who was worried and distracted by much serving, that her sister Mary *(who was abiding at Jesus' feet)* was doing the one thing needed *(Luke 10:38-42)*. Only through abiding in the Vine do we produce much fruit. Of ourselves, we can do nothing *(John 15:5)*. Abiding simply means to continue to turn to, focus on, and trust in the Jesus Christ that is in us. Abiding can be accomplished through prayer, praise, thanksgiving, godly fellowship, Bible study, or by many other means or methods that genuinely acknowledge and practice the presence of God. It is inevitable, as we abide, we will progressively be sanctified and transformed into His likeness from grace to grace, faith to faith, and glory to glory. Our labor is not a yoke that binds us, but rather a yoke that is easy and a enjoyment of fellowship that brings us into true liberty *(Matthew 11:28-30; John 8:30-32)*.

The third aspect of obedience is "Yielding" *(Romans 6:13)*. To yield to the Holy Spirit is beneficial to the kingdom of God, for ourselves, and for others. To yield in this context means "to give in to, surrender to, or submit to" the Lord Jesus. So in the highest sense, we do not "do what Jesus would do", but rather, "Jesus expresses Himself and executes His life through us as we continue to die to self-reliance and self-glory". Because He is the source of not only the direction, but He is also Himself the very Power to carry it out, to Him goes all the glory and praise.

If the believer will keep his focus on believing, abiding, and yielding instead of on performing and earning, he will have a stronger walk and a more perfect holiness "by accident" than he could ever accomplish "on purpose" through dependence on self-effort and human ability.

5 **P** P T

Seed 251 – Power of the Tongue

(In fellowship Seed 251 is referred to as the
2nd Seed in the 5th Pod of the First Year)

Simple format

II. The Second Seed in the Fifth Pod **THE POWER OF THE TONGUE.**

This Seed has Five Concepts
(Acronyms: LB NN HH HH PP)

1. The First concept is **I SPEAK LIFE AND BLESSINGS** *(LB)*.
2. The Second concept is **I SPEAK NO NEGATIVES** *(NN)*.
3. The Third concept is **I SPEAK HEALTH AND HEALING** *(HH.)*
4. The Fourth concept is **I SPEAK HOPE AND HIGHER TRUTHS** *(HH)*.
5. The Fifth concept is **I SPEAK GOD'S WORD PROPHETICALLY AND POETICALLY BECAUSE I AM A DOER OF THE WORD** *(PP)*.

   A. The first Scripture is **Proverbs 18:21.**
      (Associate: Voting age and drinking age)
      1. The concept is **MY TONGUE HAS THE POWER OF LIFE AND DEATH".**

   B. The second Scripture is **JAMES 1:21-25**
      (Hint: Drop the 8 from the first Scripture to get 1;21).
      1. The concept is **"I AM NOT A HEARER ONLY, BUT BE A DOER OF THE WORD".**
      (That means to be a Prophetic Poetic speaker of God's Word)

   C. The third Scripture for Power of the Tongue is **JAMES 3:2.**
      1. The concept is **IF ONE DOES NOT STUMBLE IN WHAT HE SAYS, HE IS A PERFECT MAN ABLE TO BRIDLE HIS WHOLE BODY.**

5 **P** PT

Sample Fellowship Format

Disciple's reply is in **bold type**

What is the second seed in the fifth pod?
Power of the Tongue.

Great. What are the 5 concepts of this seed?
**I Speak Life and Blessings
I Speak No Negatives
I Speak Health and Healing
I Speak Hope and Higher Truths
I Speak God's Word Prophetically and Poetically
because I am a doer of the Word**
That is excellent.

What is the first Scripture for Power of the Tongue?
Proverbs 18:21.

Correct. What is the concept?
The tongue has the power of life and deat

Great. What is the second Scripture for Power of the Tongue?
James 1:21-25.

Good. What is the concept?
**I am not a hearer only, but be a doer of the Word".
*(That is a Prophetic Poetic speaker of God's Word)***

Excellent. What is the third Scripture for Power of the Tongue?
James 3:2.

Very good. What is the concept?
If a man does not stumble in what he says, he is a perfect man able to bridle his whole body.

Great job!.

5 **P** PT

END OF SEED 251   Power of the Tongue
REVIEW SEED UNTIL MASTERED

5 P P T

Seed 251 Further Information – Power of the Tongue

The 2nd Seed in the 5th Pod of the 1st Year

The word "confession" in scripture is translated from the Greek word "homologia" which literally means "to say the same". To yield our tongue to the Holy Spirit, to consistently and passionately "say the same" as God's Word, reveals the truest and highest meaning of God's instruction: "Don't be a hearer only but a doer *(poetic speaker)* of the Word)" *(James 1:22)*. Indeed, whatever we say in faith, we receive either the things of Life or the things of death *(Proverbs 18:22)*.

In this seed, the disciple learns 5 aspects regarding the power of the tongue. The first aspect of the Power of the Tongue is "speak blessing". To speak blessing is to speak forth both to self and to others the multifaceted wisdom of God. This includes the abundance of His grace *(Colossians 4:6)*, His promises regarding the blessing, and all that we need for life and godliness has already been bequeathed to us *(2 Peter 1:3,4)*. We need to consistently and passionately speak these truths.

The second aspect is "speak no negatives" either to self or to others. An example of this would be Joshua, knowing the Israelites' tendency toward murmuring and complaining, instructed the people to "not say a word" for six days *(Joshua 6:10)*. Most certainly, Joshua understood that negative speaking can hinder, delay, or even cut off the inheritance of God's promise to God's people. Scripture teaches us to speak only that which is useful for building up others *(Ephesians 4:29)*. While in this world, we will have some trouble, our focus in speaking should be about the spiritual and unseen things of God *(2 Corinthians 4:13-18)*.

The third aspect is to "speak health and healing" to both ourselves and others. Each believer needs to understand that in the spiritual realm we are never the sick trying to get healed, but rather we are healed, learning to grasp and hold on to our health.

The fourth aspect is to "speak hope and higher truths". To speak hope is to continually confess a positive expectation of our sure inheritance, knowing it is according to God's Word, and that God cannot lie. To speak a higher truth is to confess and claim each of God's promises, particularly in the face of opposing circumstances or forces. We should always speak the higher truth repeatedly over any anti-Word *(anti-Christ)* whether it is spoken to us or by us. By consistently speaking God's Word by the Spirit, we keep ourselves in an ideal place to progressively inherit all that God has promised us.

The fifth aspect of the Power of the Tongue is "speak God's Word prophetically *(by the Spirit)* and poetically *(with fervent passion)* because I am a doer of the Word and not a hearer only" *(James 1:21-25)*. The word translated "doer" in James is the Greek word "poetis" *(from which the English word "poet" is derived)*. The first definition in both the Strong's Concordance and the Young's Concordance for "poetis" is "to speak poetically".

To speak prophetically in the Old Testament was often referring to "fore-telling". However, in the New Covenant age prophetic speaking usually refers to "forth-telling". To speak God's Word poetically means to say it with a godly passion influenced by the clear vision of the fulfillment of God's promises with the love, peace, and joy they bring. As much as possible, always strive to believe and to see with the eyes of your heart, using your God-given imagination to experience the high joy of the fulfillment of the numerous redemptive truths of God.

Seed 351 – Praise and Worship

(In fellowship Seed 351 is referred to as the 3rd Seed in the 5th Pod of the First Year)

Simple format

III. The Third Seed in the Fifth Pod is **PRAISE & WORSHIP**.
  (Acronym: SpaCe CAT)

Note
This Seed has Six concepts. Three for Praise, Three for Worship.

The Three Concepts for Praise:
1. The first type of praise is **SACRIFICIAL PRAISE, WHICH IS DYING TO SELF.**
2. The second type of praise is **PROPHETIC PRAISE, WHICH IS YIELDING TO CHRIST IN ME PRAISING THROUGH ME.**
3. The third type of praise is **CELEBRATION PRAISE WHICH IS CELEBRATING FOR STRENGTH AND THANKING GOD FOR ALL HE HAS DONE.**

The 3 Concepts for Worship:
1. The first type of worship is **COMMUNICATION WORSHIP, LISTENING TO GOD AND SPEAKING TO HIM FOR INTIMACY.**
2. The second type of worship **is ADORATION WORSHIP, WHICH IS BEING TRANSFORMED BY HIS PRESENCE.**
3. The third type of worship is **THANKSGIVING WORSHIP, WHICH IS THANKING GOD FOR WHO HE IS.**

   A. The first Scripture for Praise & Worship is **HEBREWS 2:12.**
      1. The concept is "Jesus foretold that He would praise the Father's name in midst of the congregation.

   B. The second Scripture is **JOHN 4:23-24.**
      1. The concept is **"GOD IS SPIRIT. THOSE WHO WORSHIP HIM MUST DO IT IN SPIRIT AND IN TRUTH".**

5P **P** T
Sample Fellowship Format

Disciple's reply is in **bold type**

What is the name of the 3rd seed in the fifth pod?
Praise and Worship.

That's right. What are the three kinds of praise?
Sacrificial praise is dying to myself during praise.
Prophetic Praise is allowing Christ to praise through me.
Celebration Praise is praising for strength and thanking God for all He has done.
Very good.

What are the three kinds of worship?
Communion worship is listening first and then speaking to gain intimacy with God.
Adoration is me being transformed by His Presence as I adore Him.
Thanksgiving Worship is thanking God foe Who He is Excellent.

What are the two scriptures for Praise and Worship?
Hebrews 2:12 and John 4:24.

Very Good. What is the concept for Hebrews 2:12?
Jesus said He would stand in the midst of the congregation and praise the Lord.

That's right. What is the John 4:24?
God is Spirit and those who worship Him must worship Him in spirit and in truth.

Perfect.

END OF SEED 351   PRAISE AND WORSHIP
REVIEW SEED UNTIL MASTERED

5P **P** T

Seed 351 Further Information – Praise and Worship

The 3rd Seed in the 5th Pod of the 1st Year

God's desire for us to praise and worship Him is not born out of any need He has for our approval or admiration, but rather is commanded out of God's wisdom and knowledge of how praise and worship greatly benefits us, His children. For indeed, as we praise and worship our Lord in sincerity, we are always gradually being transformed and conformed more and more into His image and character.

Praise is a celebration of what God has done, is doing, and will do for us. In praise, we express our joy and gratitude through various Bible instructed means including singing, shouting, clapping, dancing, and raising hands to the Lord.

Worship is a centering of our focus on the beauty of the very nature and character of God. This form of abiding normally includes such activities as singing, reflecting, holy meditation, lifting hands, and adoration.

While there may be some exceptions, praise is usually more physically active, louder, and more excited than worship. Worship tends toward less physical movement and normally is softer in volume and gentler in tone. In this seed, the disciple learns about the 3 main aspects of praise and 3 main aspects of worship.

3 Aspects of Praise

The first aspect of praise is "sacrificial praise". The idea in sacrificial praise is to be so totally absorbed in celebrating God's accomplishments for mankind, that we lose all consciousness of self, putting away all worries and problems. This kind of praise is a "dying to self" and a celebrating of everything Christ is in and through us and all that He has done for us.

The second aspect of praise is "prophetic praise". The idea of prophetic praise is to be so completely yielded to the Spirit of Christ that we are able to sense and release a higher level of praise in which the Son of God praises the Father's Name through us *(Hebrews 2:12)*.

The third aspect of praise is "celebration praise". In this aspect of praise there is an impartation of godly strength to our natural man activated through our praise. King David wrote in Psalms 8:2, "Out of the mouth of babes and nursing infants You have ordained strength...that you may silence the enemy". Jesus later revealed the fulfillment of David's prophecy in Matthew 21:16 saying, "Out of the mouth of babes you have ordained praise..." In proclaiming the fulfillment of the Psalms 8:2 prophecy, Jesus replaced "perfected strength" with "perfected praise", teaching us that as He perfects our praise His strength is perfected in us.

3 Aspects of Worship

The first aspect of worship is "communication worship". This worship involves a sensitive and reflective inner listening to the Lord alternated with speaking back to Him as led by the Holy Spirit. The focus here is on a loving interaction with the Lord, which magnifies Him and His relationship with us through our adoration of Him and our personal realization of our oneness with Him in spirit and in purpose.

The second aspect of worship is "adoration worship". This aspect of worship means to be completely absorbed and lost in active reflection regarding the Lord and the beauty of His holiness. In this worship, there is always at least a gradual transformation, from glory to glory, into His likeness by fully experiencing His presence as we continue to adore Him.

The third aspect of worship is "thanksgiving worship". This aspect of worship allows us to focus on who God is as well as on thanking Him for the beauty of His holiness and the generosity of His character. There is likely no worry or problem that strong doses of thanksgiving praise will not decrease or eliminate altogether.

5PP **T**

Seed 451 – Totally Equipped

(In fellowship Seed 451 is referred to as the 4th Seed in the 5th Pod of the First Year)

Simple format

VI. The Fourth seed in the Fifth Pod is **TOTALLY EQUIPPED**.
  1. The concept is **I LACK NOTHING BECAUSE CHRIST LIVES IN ME.**

    A. The first Scripture is **2 PETER 1:3-4.**
      1. The concept **is I HAVE BEEN GIVEN EVERYTHING I NEED FOR LIFE AND GODLINESS.**

    B. The second Scripture is **COLOSSIANS 2:9-10.**
      1. The concept is **THE FULLNESS OF THE GODHEAD DWELLS IN CHRIST AND I AM COMPLETE IN HIM.**

5PP T

Sample Fellowship Format

Disciple's reply is in **bold type**

What is the Fourth Seed in the Fifth Pod?
Totally Equipped

Great. What is the first Scripture for Totally Equipped?
2 Peter 1:3-4

That is right. What is the concept?
We have been given everything we need for life and godliness.

Excellent. What is the second Scripture?
Colossians 2:9-10

Excellent. What is the concept?
We are complete in Christ

Very good.

END OF SEED 451   Totally Equipped

REVIEW SEED UNTIL MASTERED

5PP T

Seed 451 Further Information – Totally Equipped

The 4th Seed in the 5th Pod of the 1st Year

"Totally Equipped" is the higher truth that the fullness of Jesus Christ our Lord dwells in our born again spirit man. Therefore, we already legally possess every gift, blessing, and promise bequeathed to us as a result of His death; for Christ is the Testator of the New Covenant. Not only do we have all that He has *(except for deity)*, but because we *(the body of Christ)* possess spiritual oneness in Him *(the Head of the Body)*, our true identity is no longer reckoned to be according to the flesh or the world, but rather our identity is one with Him.

When the Father looks at us, He sees us, loves us, and receives us exactly as He looks at Jesus, sees Jesus, loves Jesus, and receives Jesus; for in Him we are already perfect spiritual beings. So then, we are inherently fully prepared *(by Him)* in our spirit man *(the deepest and most profound part of our being)* which assures us of the availability of complete victory because we have been totally equipped for every good work. To be established in our high and true identity is a very important matter, for as a man thinks in his heart, that is the way he really is *(Proverbs 23:7)*.

5 P P T

Overview of the Fifth Pod

I. **5 Aspects of Obedience**

   (The first 2 Aspects are Ungodly)
   1. Performing *(which is doing it to **IMPRESS**. In proper Christianity our actions should never be with the motive to impress others but rather with the motive to **EXPRESS** Christ)*
   2. Earning *(which is good works primarily motivated by profit or reward to self)*

   (The last 3 Aspects are Godly)
   3. Believing *(which is the one thing required)*
   4. Abiding *(which is the one thing needed)*
   5. Yielding *(which is beneficial)*

   A. Romans 1:5
      1. Believing is obedience.

   B. Luke 10:42
      1. Jesus said that Mary was doing "the one thing needed" *(she was abiding at the feet of Jesus, learning of Him)*.

   C. Romans 6:19
      1. I yield myself to the Holy Spirit.

II. **Power of the Tongue**
   1. I speak life and blessings.
   2. I speak no negatives.
   3. I speak health and healing.
   4. I speak hope and higher truths.
   5. I speak God's Word prophetically *(by the Spirit)* and poetically *(with passion)* because that is the primary meaning of being a "Doer of the Word".

   A. Proverbs 18:21
      1. My tongue has the power of life and death.

   B. James 1:21-25
      1. I am **NOT** be a hearer **ONLY** of the Word, but be a Doer of the Word *(engraft the Word on your heart by speaking it with emotion)*.

 C. James 3:2
  1. If a man can be perfect in what he says, he will be able to bridle his whole body.

III. Praise and Worship *(SPC CAT)*
 (3 Kinds of Praise)
 1. Sacrificial Praise *(dying to self)*
 2. Prophetic Praise *(Christ, or the Spirit, praising through me)*
 3. Celebration Praise *(celebrating for strength and praising God for what He has done)*

 (3 Kinds of Worship)
 1. Communion Worship *(listening to God and speaking with God resulting in increased intimacy with Him)*
 2. Adoration Worship *(being transformed by God's presence)*
 3. Thanksgiving Worship *(thanking God for Who He is)*

  A. Hebrews 2:12
   1. Jesus stands in the congregation and praises the Father's Name through me.

  B. John 4:23, 24
   1. God is Spirit. I worship God in Spirit and in Truth.

IV. Totally Equipped
 1. I lack nothing because Christ lives in me.

  A. 2 Peter 1:3,4
   1. I have been given everything I need for life and godliness.

  B. Colossians 2:9,10
   1. I am complete in Christ.

Epilogue for Chapter Five

"Religion" normally focuses on doing what is right in order to please God. This is misguided. The proper focus of the believer is simply on Christ, believing in Him, abiding in Him, and yielding to Him. It is being in His presence as much as possible that allows the Holy Spirit to transform us from the inside out. Human philosophy and psychology looks to our natural thinking and doing as the way to wholeness. The Bible looks to what Christ has done, trusting what He has done, and learning to tap into His accomplishments which always results in genuine transformation and sanctification.

The world system looks toward and focuses on "outward behavior modification". But, the Holy Spirit is looking for "inward transformation" that will always produce the Fruit of Righteousness and results in all glory going to God alone. A person's doing *(apart from Christ)* can never make himself even a bit more holy in God's eyes. In as much as the believer is spending time in the presence of Jesus Christ, receiving His free love and acceptance; Christ will always bring that person toward the holiness desired, planned, and accomplished through the working of the Holy Spirit. We need to constantly look to Him, not to ourselves.

6DSP

CHAPTER SIX

THE SIXTH POD - ACRONYM: 6DSP

POD CLUE: A TALL HEBREW

Seed 161 – 6 Elementary Principles of Christ

*(In fellowship Seed 161 is referred to as the
1st Seed in the 6th Pod of the First Year)*

Simple format

I. The First Seed in the Sixth Pod is **6 ELEMENTARY PRINCIPLES OF CHRIST**. *(Acronym: RooFeD-LoRE)*.

1. The First Elementary Principle is **REPENTANCE FROM DEAD WORKS**.
   **The concept is I AM TOTALLY PERSUADED THERE IS NO DEED OR WORK OF ANY KIND A
   I CAN DO TO ACHIEVE, RIGHTEOUSNESS IN GOD'S SIGHT**
   (Righteousness is a gift that is given only through faith).

2. The Second Elementary Principle is **FAITH TOWARD GOD**.
   The concept is **GOD IS WHO HE SAYS HE IS, I AM WHO GOD SAYS I AM AND HE ALWAYS KEEPS HIS PROMISES**.

3. The Third Elementary Principle is **DOCTRINE OF BAPTISMS**
   The concept is Every baptism is either a type or reality of **PUTTING OFF THE OLD MAN** *(Adam)* **AND PUTTING ON THE NEW MAN** *(Jesus)*.

4. The Fourth Elementary Principle is **LAYING ON OF HANDS**.
   The concept is **AN OUTWARD RITUAL THAT SYMBOLIZES AN INWARD REALITY**

5. The Fifth Elementary Principle is **RESURRECTION OF THE DEAD**.
   The concept is **RESURRECTION POWER IS THE FUEL FOR ALL SALVATION** *(Spirit, soul and body)*.

6. The Sixth Elementary Principle is **ETERNAL JUDGMENT**.
   This principle has 4 important aspects:
   1) The 1st judgment is… In the past **ALL MY SIN WAS JUDGED AT THE CROSS**.

2) The 2nd judgment is... **I JUDGE MYSELF AS INNOCENT** *(not guilty of sin)* due to the finished work of the cross.

3) The 3rd judgment is... **THE JUDGMENT OF ALL BELIEVERS WORKS AT THE JUDGMENT SEAT OF CHRIST** *(after natural death)*.

4) The 4th judgment is... **THE JUDGMENT OF UNBELIEVERS AT THE GREAT WHITE THRONE** *(the Second Death)*.

   A. The Scripture for Six Elementary Principles is **HEBREWS 5:11-6:3**.
   1. The first concept is **BY NOW YOU OUGHT TO BE TEACHERS BUT YOU NEED TO BE TAUGHT THE BASIC ORACLES OF GOD**.
   2. The second concept is **THE 6 ELEMENTARY PRICIPLES** *(as outlined in the seed concepts above.*

6 D S P

Sample Fellowship Format

Disciple's reply is in **bold type**

What is the name of the First Seed in the Sixth Pod?
6 Elementary principles of Christ.

Good. What is the first elementary principle and its concept?
Repentance from Dead Works.
I have become totally persuaded there is nothing I can do to earn Righteousness

That is right. What is the second elementary principle and its concept?
Faith Toward God.
God is who He says He is, I am who God says I am and He always keeps His promises.

Very good. What is the third elementary principle and its concept?
Doctrine of Baptisms.
I put off the Old man and put on the New Man

Great. What is the fourth elementary principle and its concept?
Laying on of Hands.
An outward ritual that symbolizes an inward reality

Excellent. What is the fifth elementary principle and its concept?
Resurrection of the Dead.
The same power that raised Jesus from the dead is the same power that accomplishes every aspect of my salvation in my life.

Very good. What is the sixth elementary principle?
Eternal Judgment.

Good. What are the four eternal judgments?
All my sin was judged at the cross

I judge myself as innocent (*not guilty of any sin*) due to the finished work of the cross.
The Judgment of the believers works at the Judgment seat of Christ.
The Judgment of unbelievers at the Great White Throne (*the Second

6 D S P

Death)

Excellent.

What is the Scripture for 6 Elementary Principles of Christ?
Hebrews 5:11-6:3.

Great. What is the first concept?
By now you ought to be teachers yet you still need to be taught the Basic Oracles of God.

Very good. What is the second concept?

The 6 Elementary Principles and their concepts are outlined in the seed above

Excellent.

END OF SEED 161   6 Elementary Principles of Christ
REVIEW SEED UNTIL MASTERED

6 D S P

Seed 161 Further Information – 6 Elementary Principles of Christ

The 1st Seed in the 6th Pod of the 1st Year

In Chapter 5 of the book of Hebrews, the author *(probably Paul or one of his associates)* is starting to teach the importance of the Priesthood of Melchizedek. But in the midst of the author's explanation, he takes a turn away from the subject of Melchizedek, stating that he has much to say regarding Melchizedek, but that it was hard to explain because his readers were "dull of hearing". The author writes that the inability of the readers to understand was due to the fact that they were not learned in the "milk of the Word", that is, in the basic oracles of God *(Hebrews 5:5-12)*. Early in the 6th chapter, the God-inspired author goes on to list 6 oracles which he calls "the elementary principles of Christ". He gives the first two principles as being foundational and the last four as being doctrinal.

If ever a passage in scripture had a flashing blue light saying, "Pay attention, this is important", this passage does. In Hebrews 5:11 the writer says, "... by now you ought to be teachers but you need someone to teach you..." It is amazing that yet today, a high percentage of believers know little or nothing regarding the existence and/or the importance of this Bible passage. Consequently, through this passage we can see that there may be many who believe they are mature Christians, yet according to scripture, are still in need of the milk of the Word and regarding some of the fundamentals are still babes in Christ. In this seed, the believer will master the 6 elementary principles of Christ and their important basic meanings.

The First Two Principles are Foundational

The first elementary principle is "repentance from dead works". This principle, being listed first, is undoubtedly of special importance. Repentance from dead works can be clearly understood through carefully studying Matthew chapters 3 through 6. In Matthew 3, John the Baptist appears on the scene as a forerunner of Jesus Christ to "Prepare the way..." Not surprisingly, his very first proclamation is in perfect agreement with the first elementary principle. John says, "Repent, for the kingdom is near." John's baptism, also referred to in scripture as John's baptism of repentance *(Mark 1:4; Luke 3:8; Acts 19:4)*, is not related to common sin, but rather symbolizes a dying to any remaining self-righteousness and living according to the righteousness *(right standing with God)* that the believer receives by faith.

The teaching of John's baptism of repentance *(from dead works)* is succinctly and clearly explained in Acts 19:4 "...That they should believe on Him who should come after him *(John)*, that is, in Christ Jesus." In John's baptism, when the person being baptized went under the water, it signified dying to the self-reliance of law-keeping; the coming up out of the water signified putting total trust and reliance on the Spirit *(the Law of the Spirit of Life; Romans 8:2)*, the One *(Jesus)* who came after John. Because it involved water, it is too often mistakenly associated with Christian water baptism.

The water baptism that Jesus commanded, without a doubt, is different and separate from John's baptism of repentance. The water baptism that Jesus commanded symbolizes the believer dying with Christ and being resurrected with Him, and was never commanded or practiced in scriptures until after the resurrection of Christ *(Matthew 28:18-20)*.

Today, the correct application of John's baptism of repentance *(from dead works)* can be simply explained as a believer coming to be fully persuaded that there is nothing the believer can do, apart from heart belief in the Messiah, to attain righteousness *(right standing with God)*. The actual nature of John's baptism is further proven by the fact that Jesus proclaimed John's baptism to be fitting for Himself in order to fulfill all righteousness. If John's baptism had anything to do with sin, then it would, of course, not be fitting for Jesus to undergo, as He knew no sin. *(2 Corinthians 5:21)*. However, Jesus from His youth was raised as a Jew and would have been taught from a young age the necessity of law-keeping.

By willingly submitting to John's baptism, Jesus acknowledged that irrespective of the fact that He was fully God, since He was living as a man in His human living, He would no longer trust His own human ability; but rather would totally rely on the Spirit of the Father as the only source of everything He did and everything He said. *(John 5:19, 30; 14:10)*. After John's baptism, the Holy Spirit *(as a dove)* lighted on Jesus and the Father proclaimed, "This is My beloved Son, with Whom I am well pleased." Jesus had not yet begun His ministry, nor had He performed a single miracle, yet the Father was extremely pleased with Him. This was likely, at least in part, because of His understanding of the Father's will and His own willingness to be submitted to it as His Source for everything which is the main idea of John's Baptism. In Matthew chapter 4, the devil challenged Jesus' identity by chiding Him with these words: "IF thou be the Son of God, command these stones to be made bread." Jesus having undergone being baptized by John, refused to fall into the trap of trying to prove who He was by what He did. Instead, He simply proclaimed that it was God's Word alone in which he was trusting. He clearly understood that He did not have to "do to be". Once a believer repents from dead works, he too no longer does work in order to prove who he is, but rather the works of the believer are simply the fruit of yielding to the Spirit of Christ in him *(Philippians 2:13)*.

Matthew 5 portrays believers as "the salt of the earth" and "the light of the world" *(vs. 13-16)*. Our God, not ourselves, is always the source of all genuine saltiness and all true shining. Matthew 6 warns us not to do our own righteous works with the motive of being seen by men. He further explains that we should operate in such a way that our left hand does not know what our right hand is doing. This indicates a doing that is not motivated by self-gain or outward show, but rather is the natural outflow of abiding in the True Vine *(Jesus)*. The fruit of the Spirit proceeds forth in a spiritual and unforced way as we keep our mind focused properly on Him while yielding to Him.

The second elementary principle is "faith toward God". This principle includes three main concepts:

1. God is who He says He is.
2. I am who God says I am.
3. God always keeps His Word *(promise)*, as he cannot lie.

The Next Four Principles are Doctrinal

The third elementary principle is the "doctrine of baptisms". The concept of this principle is "dying to the old and living to the new" or "putting off of the old and putting on the new". Each baptism taught in the New Testament is a kind of putting off and putting on, the old man *(Adam)* dying, and the New Man *(Christ)* rising up in his place. Some teachings errantly claim, based on Ephesians 4, that there is only one baptism. But by carefully comparing scripture to scripture we can uncover the truth that the "one baptism" in Ephesians 4 is teaching that there is only one baptism that brings us into the One Body, which is the "baptism into the Body" *(1 Corinthians 12:13; Galatians 3:27)*. But without question, there are additional baptisms into repentance, death, Spirit, water, fire, and Moses, all mentioned specifically and separately in the New Testament *(Seed 171 thoroughly covers each of these baptisms)*. As sons of God, we should never divide what God has made one, nor should we make one what God has clearly divided.

The fourth elementary principle is the "doctrine of laying on of hands". The laying on of hands is an outward act *(ritual)* that symbolizes, identifies, imparts, or confirms an inward spiritual reality. It may also serve to activate the faith for a particular purpose in the person who is having hands laid on him. Here are some scriptures that teach the various purposes for the laying on of hands:

1. Healing *(Mark 16:16; Acts 9:12)*
2. Baptism of the Holy Spirit *(Acts 8:17, 18; 19:6)*
3. Impartation or activation of gifts of the Spirit *(1 Timothy 4:14; 2 Timothy 1:6)*
4. Ordination or appointment to specific office or function in the Church *(Acts 1:22; 6:6; 13:1-3)*
5. Blessing others *(Genesis 48:13, 14; Matthew 19:15)*

The fifth elementary principle is the "doctrine of resurrection of the dead". The concept of this principle is that the resurrection Power that raised Jesus from the dead is the "Fuel of all salvation". Every aspect of salvation including regeneration and justification of the believer's spirit, sanctification of his soul, and even redemption of the believer's body are all accomplished by the one and same resurrection Power. This explains why Paul in Philippians 3:10 *(compare to Ephesians 1:18-23)* longed to know "the Power of the resurrection" and the "fellowship of His suffering". Paul understood that as the "suffering of dying to self" increased, so did the experience and influence of the resurrection power in his life. The more we die to self and submit completely to the Holy Spirit, the more the resurrection power will operate in, on, and through us.

The sixth and final elementary principle is the "doctrine of eternal judgments". The four most important aspects of eternal judgment with which every believer should be familiar are:

Judgment of Sin at the Cross - This occurred at the Cross of Cavalry approximately 2000 years ago. For the saint, there should be absolutely no fear of God's judgment of his personal sin, as he should fully understand that God's wrath against all the believer's sin was satisfied by the blood at the time of the crucifixion of Jesus *(once and for all those who trust in Jesus)*. Sin was completely judged and punished at the Cross; from God's perspective it does not need to be judged or punished ever again. Indeed, if God was to re-judge or re-punish a believer's sin, which would be an application of double jeopardy, and it would cause God to become unjust. That, of course, is not possible *(Hebrews 10:16-18; 9:12)*.

The Believer's Judgment of Self as Innocent - Because God's wrath against sin is complete, the believer now needs to make a proper and perpetual judgment of self. He judges in his own conscience to line up his view of himself with God's view of him, that he has been cleansed by his faith in the FINISHED WORK OF THE CROSS from all his sin: past, present, and future. This positive self-judgment is that which needs to be seen by the believer and fully appreciated that he never takes the elements of communion in an unworthy manner.

The Judgment Seat of Christ. This is where all believers will be judged. Good works done in faith will be rewarded, but all dead works *(performing and earning)* will burn up and the believer will suffer loss of reward. However, the believer himself will surely be saved through this final baptism of the Refiner's fire *(2 Corinthians 5:10; 1 Corinthians 3:8-15; Malachi 3:2)*.

The Great White Throne Judgment - This is the judgment when and where all the unbelievers *(described as the cowardly, unbelieving, abominable, murderers, sexually immoral, sorcerers, idolaters, and all liars)* will be judged and cast into the lake of fire as their final judgment. This is the second death *(Revelation 20:11-15; 21:8)*.

Undoubtedly, Satan delights in the great ignorance *(not knowing)* among many believers regarding the important teaching of these elementary principles of Christ. We are told in scripture not to be ignorant of Satan's devices. Believers too often suffer a lack of full blessings simply due to ignorance of the truth *(Hosea 4:6)*. Only after believers understand, are rooted, and are established in these truths in their hearts are they ready to move on to the "meat of the Word". To the extent that they do not

6 DSP

know, understand, or apply these truths to their lives, they are unskilled in the Word of Righteousness. They are still babes.

6 D S P

Seed 261 – Doctrine of Christ

(In fellowship Seed 261 is referred to as the
2nd Seed in the 6th Pod of the First Year)

Simple format

II. The Second Seed in the Sixth Pod is **DOCTRINE OF CHRIST.**
  1. The concept is **BUILDING UP OTHERS BY DISPENSING GOD'S WORD (CHRIST).**

    A. The Scripture is **1 TIMOTHY 1:3-4.**
      1. The concept is **TEACH NO OTHER DOCTRINE EXCEPT FOR GODLY EDIFICATION** *(Dispensation of Grace)* **WHICH IS IN FAITH".**

6 D S P

Sample Fellowship Format

Disciple's reply is in **bold type**

What is the Second Seed in the Sixth Pod?
Doctrine of Christ

Great. What is the concept?
Building up others by dispensing God's Word

Excellent. What is the scripture for Doctrine of Christ?
1 Timothy 1:3, 4.

Teach no other doctrine except godly edification which is in faith.

That is right. Good Job.

END OF SEED 261   Doctrine of Christ
REVIEW SEED UNTIL MASTERED

6 D S P

Seed 261 Further Information – Doctrine of Christ

The 2nd Seed in the 6th Pod of the 1st Year

The concept of the "doctrine of Christ" is to "build up others by dispensing Christ *(the Word)*". The word "doctrine" simply means "a teaching". If a teaching does not rise to the "build up others" standard, it is not part of the Doctrine of Christ and should not be taught in the church *(among believers)*. The minimum standard is simply "the teaching must build by adding truth". This, of course, does not mean adding to the Word of God, but rather adding more of the Word of God to the believer in a way which edifies. If we abide in this teaching, it is evidences that we have the Father and the Son *(2 John 9)*. You cannot have One without having the Other *(1 John 2:22)*.

So then, the doctrine of Christ is not referring primarily to the teachings of Jesus, but rather to the truths about Jesus Himself, His ministry, His way, and Him as God. Indeed, the doctrine of Christ is the same as the apostle's doctrine referred to in Acts 2:42. Scripture instructs us not to give heed to myths *(rumors and fables)* and unending genealogies *(commonly accepted traditional teaching not supported by scripture)*, but rather to teach nothing other than "godly edification which is in faith" *(1 Timothy 1:3, 4)*.

Paul's epistles contribute greatly to the completion of the divine Revelation concerning God's eternal purposes accomplished through the dispensation of grace. God's grace is dispensed primarily through the speaking of God's Word. The word "dispensation" is translated also as administration, stewardship, and economy *(Ephesians 1:10; 3:9; Colossians 1:25; 1 Corinthians 9:17)*. It is translated in these ways from the Greek word "okionomia" which literally means "the Law of the House".

This dispensation or stewardship is for God *(through His many sons)* to dispense Himself through Christ into His chosen people so that He may have a house to express Himself; this house is the church. This economy and practice is the very essence of the doctrine of Christ. Any teaching that is not done in God's love according to God's Word, with the motive of building up others for God's purposes, is not the doctrine of Christ and has no rightful place in true New Testament ministry.

6 D S P

Seed 361 – Sense of Worthiness

*(In fellowship Seed 361 is referred to as the
3rd Seed in the 6th Pod of the First Year)*

Simple format

III. The Third Seed in the Sixth Pod is **SENSE OF WORTHINESS *(361)*.**

  1. The first concept is **EVERY PERSON HAS TWO CRITICAL NEEDS.**

     The First Need is **TO BE LOVED AND ACCEPTED WITH A PERFECT LOVE AND ACCEPTANCE.**

     The Second Need is **TO HAVE A STRONG SENSE OF PURPOSE.**

  2. The second concept is **THE ONLY WAY TO GET THESE TWO NEEDS PERFECTLY MET IS THROUGH AN INTIMATE RELATIONSHIP WITH JESUS CHRIST.**

     A. The First Scripture is **HEBREWS 2:6-8** *(acronym: LL GH DO)*
     (Hint: Hebrew Cousin of Kenosis 431).

       1. The First Concept is **GOD MADE ME LITTLE LOWER THAN HIMSELF.**
       2. The Second Concept is **HE CROWNED ME WITH GLORY AND HONOR.**
       3. The Third Concept is **GOD GAVE ME DOMINION OVER ALL THE EARTH.**

     B. The Second Scripture is **JEREMIAH 29:11-13.**
       1. The concept is **GOD HAS A PLAN TO PROSPER ME AND TO GIVE ME A HOPE AND A FUTURE.**

     C. The Third Scripture is **ROMANS 8:28-29**.
       1. The concept is **ALL THINGS WORK TOGETHER FOR MY GOOD BECAUSE I LOVE GOD AND I AM CALLED ACCORDING TO HIS PURPOSE.**

       2. The Second concept is **GOD'S PURPOSE FOR ME IS TO BE CONFORMED TO THE IMAGE OF HIS SON.**

6 D S P

Sample Fellowship Format

Disciple's reply is in **bold type**

What is the third seed in the sixth pod?
Sense of Worthiness

Great. What is the first concept of Sense of Worthiness?
Every person has two critical needs:
The First Need is... To be loved and accepted with a perfect love and acceptance.
The Second Need is... To have a strong sense of purpose.

What is the second concept?
The only way to perfectly meet these two important needs is through an intimate relationship with Jesus.

What is the first Scripture for Sense of Worthiness?
Hebrews 2:6-8

Very good. What are the three concepts of this Scripture?
God made me a Lower than Himself
God crowned me with Glory and Honor
God gave me Dominion Over all the Earth

Excellent. What is the Second Scripture for Sense of Worthiness?
Jeremiah 29:11-13.

Great. What is the concept?
God has a plan to prosper me and to give me a hope and a future

That is correct. What is the Third Scripture this seed?
Romans 8:28-29

Good. What are the two concepts?
All things work together for the good for my good because I love God and I am called according to His purpose
God's purpose for me is to be conformed to the image of His Son
Excellent.

6 D **S** P

END OF SEED 361   Sense of Worthiness
REVIEW SEED UNTIL MASTERED

6 D **S** P

Seed 361 Further Information – Sense of Worthiness

The 3rd Seed in the 6th Pod of the 1st Year

Much of the psychology in today's world emphasizes a belief in the importance of self-esteem. But self-esteem misses the essence of what is actually needed for successful godly living. What is actually needed is a sense of worthiness which is not based on what a person thinks about himself, but rather is based on faith in what God says about him. No man is equipped with righteousness for godly living simply because he says or thinks he is, but he is righteous by faith as the result of the Gift of God *(Romans 5:17)*. This is the way that grace works.

For example, there are many "religious" beliefs that reject Jesus Christ the Messiah as the only Way to salvation. Those who reject Jesus in this way may, by all outward appearances, do more "good works" than some true believers in Jesus. However, they have no eternal life in them. And though they may think well of themselves, the Bible truth is, apart from regeneration *(being born again)*, all they do has no eternal value and is nothing but filthy rags in the sight of God *(Isaiah 64:6)*.

There are two seed concepts for "Sense of Worthiness". The first concept is "Every person has two essential needs. The first essential need is to be loved and accepted *(with a perfect love and acceptance)*. The second essential need is to have a strong sense of purpose. The second concept is "The only way these two essential needs can be PERFECTLY met is through a genuine and intimate relationship with Jesus".

Too often in our lives, we foolishly search for another human being who we imagine will love us with a perfect love and accept us with a perfect acceptance to meet that first essential need. Such a search is an endeavor totally lacking godly wisdom and puts an unfair burden on those closest to us. For no human being can love us perfectly. While a spouse, family member, friend, or partner may be able to meet our relational needs to a certain degree, it is only the Lord Jesus Himself who perfectly loves us and perfectly accepts us at all times. This is the outcome of the miracle of the work of our Savior at the Cross.

6 D S P

Additionally, we each need to see that our primary and ultimate purpose according to God's point of view *(the reality)*, is to be transformed and conformed to the very image of Christ that He might be the Firstborn of many brothers *(Romans 8:29)*. Christ is the Prototype, we are the type. Only when this truth is completely rooted, grounded, and established *(written)* on our hearts can we begin to live a truly abundant and fulfilled life.

6 D S P

Seed 461 – Prayer

*(In fellowship Seed 461 is referred to as the
4th Seed in the 6th Pod of the First Year)*

Simple format

IV. The Fourth Seed in the Sixth Pod is **PRAYER**.

    1. The concept for Prayer is **THE BEST PRAYER IS THE PRAYER LED BY THE HOLY SPIRIT.**

        A. The Scripture for Prayer is **JAMES 5:16.**
            1. The concept is **THE EFFECTUAL FERVENT PRAYER OF A RIGHTEOUS MAN ACCOMPLISHES MUCH.**

6 D S **P**

Sample Fellowship Format

Disciple's reply is in **bold type**

What is the Fourth Seed in the Sixth Pod?
Prayer.

Very good. What is the concept?
The best prayer is the prayer led by the Holy Spirit.

Great. What is the Scripture for Prayer?
James 5:16.

That is right. What is the concept?
The effectual fervent prayer of a righteous man accomplishes much.

Excellent.

END OF SEED 461   Prayer

REVIEW SEED UNTIL MASTERED

6 D S P

Seed 461 Further Information – Prayer

The 4th Seed in the 6th Pod of the 1st Year

Scripture instructs believers to pray in the Spirit on all occasions with all kinds of prayers and requests. We are to be alert and keep praying for all the saints *(Ephesians 6:18)*. We are also told to make requests, prayers, and intercessions and thanksgivings for everyone, especially those in governmental authority *(1 Timothy 2:1, 2)*. Other kinds of prayers would include prayers of: agreement, confession, contemplation, deliverance, impartation, unknown tongues, warfare, travail, praise, and worship.

But whatever kind of prayer the believer prays, the most important factor is to pray in the Spirit of God with alertness. The believer should not struggle trying to think of what to pray according to his own creative thinking, but rather he should develop the ability to feel and hear in his spirit the impressions, leadings, burdens, and speakings given to him by the Spirit of God that resides in him. When the believer prays in such a way, he is praying "diamonds" and is praying according to God's perfect will.

When praying with or among other believers, beware not to make the common error of thinking that a long prayer is the best prayer. Indeed, the longer you pray during fellowship with others, the more likely you are to lose the attention of those who increase the power of your prayer through their agreement. Do your best not to be at all self-conscious. Also, you should not have any concerns about the impression that others have regarding your "skill" in praying. You can simply pray out of your spirit by the Holy Spirit fully trusting God. Often, the most effective prayer is the one that is short in length, but long in passion and Holy Spirit power. Always remember, it is the fervent, not the long or fancy prayer of the believer that is powerful and effective *(James 5:16)*.

Finally, consider this, the more you spend time in prayer with any person by the Spirit, the stronger your relationship will grow to be with that person. When others ask you to pray for them, it is best, when possible, to offer to pray with them immediately. To involve them personally in such a prayer will serve to minister to them in a way that is higher and more powerful than simply praying for them.

6 D S P

Overview of the Sixth Pod

I. **6 Elementary Principles of Christ** *(RooFeD LoRE)*
   1. REPENTANCE from dead works
      a. I am totally persuaded there is nothing I can do to EARN righteousness.
   2. FAITH toward God
      a. I am who God says I am.
      b. God is who He says He is.
      c. God always keeps His Word.
   3. DOCTRINE of Baptisms
      a. Putting off something old and immersion into something new.
   4. LAYING on of Hands
      a. An outward physical ritual that signifies an inward spiritual reality.
   5. RESURRECTION from the Dead
      a. The fuel *(Power)* of all salvation.
   6. ETERNAL Judgement
      a. Judgement of sin at the Cross.
      b. Judgement of self as just and innocent in Christ.
      c. Judgement of the believers' works at the Judgement Seat of Christ.
      d. Judgement of the unbelievers at the Great White Throne.

   A. Hebrews 5:11-6:3
      1. The 6 Elementary Principles outlined above.

II. **Doctrine of Christ**
   1. Building up others by dispensing Christ.
      A. 1 Timothy 1:3, 4
         1. Teach no other doctrine rather than godly edification which is in faith.

III. **Sense of Worthiness**
   1. Every person has 2 critical needs.
      a. To be perfectly loved and accepted.
      b. To have a strong sense of purpose.
   2. The ONLY way these 2 needs can be PERFECTLY met is through an INTIMATE relationship with Jesus Christ.
      A. Jeremiah 29:11-13
         1. God has a plan to prosper me and give me a hope and a future.

6 D S P

    B. Hebrews 2:6-8
        1. God made man a little lower than Himself *(Elohim)*.
        2. God crowned man with glory and honor.
        3. God gave man dominion over the earth.
    C. Romans 8:28, 29
        1. All things work together for the good of those who love God and are called according to His purpose. God's purpose for us is that we be conformed to the image of Jesus.

IV. Prayer
    1. The best prayer is the prayer led by the Spirit.
        A. James 5:16
            1. The fervent prayer of a righteous man accomplishes much.

6 D S P

Epilogue for Chapter Six

One of the major challenges when discipling one another is staying perfectly consistent with the Word of God. It is no secret that there are some genuine differences of understanding of the Word, even among mature men of God, of whom few of us would doubt their love for God or their seriousness in their seeking of God. We should learn to be grateful for the many men that have gone before us who literally have spent decades seeking God and studying His Word. These men have received much revelation. Without these forerunners, it is likely none of us believers would be where we are today in our understanding and application of God's Word. However, even someone who has spent decades walking with God can lack light regarding certain Bible teachings. As you move into the 7th pod, Most Effective Discipleship Seeds *(MEDS)* starts to deal with subjects such as baptisms and gifts. There is often significant differences in understanding even among some mature men of God, and certainly among the various denominations.

The goal of Most Effective Discipleship Seeds *(MEDS)* is to be thorough and organized to cover all the main topics of scripture in a prioritized order. So then, while some believers may not agree with the Seeds at every point, Most Effective Discipleship Seeds' *(MEDS')* simple goal is to stay as consistent as possible with the Word and with the leading of the Holy Spirit. As I mentioned in the Introduction of this book, if a teaching is inconsistent with your personal revelation, remain open to the Holy Spirit. But at the same time, recognize that there always has been, and likely always will be genuine differences of understanding even among serious students of the Word, at least until Christ returns.

For this reason, the position of this Discipleship is one of flexibility, which allows each sincere believer to be fully persuaded in his own mind according to the progressive revelation received by him through faith from our Lord Jesus. While what is presented in this book represents our best Spirit-led understanding of God's Word, we recognize that there may be different views by some other sincere believers. The MEDS approach of learning *(we are convinced)* was given to us, not for a part *(denomination)* or division of the Body of Christ, but rather was given for the entire Church *(all genuine Christians)*. For this reason, we encourage you to take the liberty to change any Seed or Seeds where you are persuaded by the Word and the Spirit that you need to do so to continue on in the Seeds

6 D S P

with a good conscience. It is with humility that these Seeds were developed. Our only request is if you do change the order or content of any Seed, please do it with the same humility. Thank you.

7 W F S F

CHAPTER SEVEN

THE SEVENTH POD - ACRONYM: 7WFSF

POD CLUE: 3'S AND 6'S

Seed 171 – 7 Baptisms of the New Testament

(In fellowship Seed 171 is referred to as the
1st Seed in the 7th Pod of the First Year)

Simple format

I. The first seed in the Seventh Pod is **7 BAPTISMS OF THE NEW TESTAMENT**. *(Acronym: RiBbeD Single White FeMale)*.

  1. The first Baptism is **BAPTISM OF REPENTANCE** *(from dead works)*. This baptism is also referred to as "John's Baptism".
  The concept of John's Baptism is **I AM TOTALLY IMMERSED IN THE TRUTH THAT THERE IS NOTHING I CAN DO TO EARN RIGHTEOUSNESS**. This baptism is closely related to the first elementary principle "Repentance from Dead Works". Review the "Further Explanation" of Seed 161 for greater insight into this baptism.

  2. The Second Baptism is **BAPTISM INTO THE BODY OF CHRIST**. The concept of Baptism into the Body is **THE INFILLING OF THE HOLY SPIRIT FOR LIFE AND GROWTH**. It takes place when a person through genuine heart belief receives the Lord Jesus as the Messiah *(Anointed)* Savior".

  3. The Third Baptism is **BAPTISM INTO THE DEATH AND RESURRECTION** of Jesus.
  The concept of Baptism into Death **is AT THE MOMENT OF NEW BIRTH, I SPIRITUALLY DIED WITH CHRIST AND WAS RAISED WITH HIM**. *(Baptism into Death occurs simultaneously with Baptism into His Body)*.

  4. The Fourth Baptism is **BAPTISM INTO THE HOLY SPIRIT**.
  The concept for Baptism into the Spirit is **THE OUTPOURING OR CLOTHING GIVEN FOR THE PURPOSE OF EMPOWERMENT AND WITNESSING**

(This Baptism is often called 'The infilling of the Holy Spirit' by some. This has often caused the Baptism into the Holy Spirit to be confused with the New Birth Baptism into His Body and Death. Therefore, it is best to refer to the Baptism into the Holy Ghost as an Outpouring or Clothing of the Holy Spirit. This is consistent with the vast majority of Scripture passages that refer to the Baptism into the Holy Spirit).

5. The Fifth Baptism is **BAPTISM INTO WATER.**
   The concept of Water Baptism is "A picture *(a playing out in the physical realm)* of what happened when we were born again in the spiritual realm. We were **BURIED WITH JESUS IN BAPTISM AND RAISED UP WITH HIM** to walk newness of life
   (This baptism is an 'after type of the 3rd Baptism (the reality of the death and resurrection with Him) and contributes to the salvation of the soul (progressive sanctification) of Christ and into His Resurrection which was already completed at the time of his baptism into Death, the Third Baptism. Because as human beings we have a strong consciousness of our physical bodies. Christ instructs that all should be baptized into water in order to experience in the physical realm what has already been accomplished in the Spiritual Realm when we first believed in our hearts unto eternal life. When the believer goes down into the baptismal water it signifies dying with Christ; when the believer comes out of the water it signifies his resurrection with Christ).

6. The Sixth Baptism of the New Testament is **BAPTISM INTO FIRE**.
   The concept of Baptism into Fire is **THE CLEANSING OF FELLOWSHIP** which occurs as believers in Christ speak God's Word into one another's lives.

7. The Seventh Baptism of the New Testament is **BAPTISM INTO MOSES**.
   The concept is the **BIRTH FROM OUR MOTHER'S WOMB INTO THE WORLD** *(under the bondage of the Law of Sin which is activated and strengthened by Moses' Law).*

   OR

   It could be referring to having a strong sensitivity to God's current movement at any point in time *(metaphorically speaking where the cloud and fire are)* from a natural point of view it

7 W F S F

A. The first Scripture is MATTHEW 3:11.
The concept is, "There comes one after me who is mightier than I, HE WILL BAPTIZE WITH THE HOLY SPIRIT AND FIRE.

B. The Second Scripture is ROMANS 6:3.
The concept is "Know you not that so many of us as were BAPTIZED INTO HIS DEATH were BAPTIZED INTO HIS RESURRECTION.

C. The third Scripture is ACTS 19:1-6.
The concept is "John's Baptism was a baptism of repentance, and after Paul baptized them in water, he laid hands on them and they were baptized with the Holy Ghost.

7 WFSF

Sample Fellowship Format

Disciple's reply is in **bold type**

What is the first seed in the seventh pod?
7 Baptisms of the New Testament.

That is correct! What is the first baptism and its concept?
I am totally IMMERSED in the truth that there is nothing I can do to earn righteousness.

Very good. What is the second baptism and its concept?
Baptism into the Body of Christ. This Baptism takes place when I first believed And was born again. I received an infilling of the Spirit for life and growth.

That is correct. What is the third baptism and its concept?
Baptism into the Death and Resurrection of Jesus. At the moment of New Birth, I spiritually died with Christ and was raised with Him.

That is right. What is the fourth baptism and its concept?
Baptism into the Holy Spirit. This baptism is an OUTPOURING or clothing given for the purpose of empowerment and witnessing.

Very good. What is the Fifth Baptism and its concept?
Baptism into Water. This baptism is an important outward ritual that symbolizes the reality of our having been baptized into the death and resurrection of Christ.

Excellent. What is the sixth baptism and its concept?
Baptism into Fire. The cleansing of our souls which takes place as believers in Christ speak God's Word into one another's lives.

Very good. What is the seventh baptism and its concept?
Baptism into Moses. Being sensitive to and subject to God's current movement *(Present truth)* in the church today or it could refer to the fact that all people are born into the natural world confined under the law until the time of their New Birth in Christ.

7 W F S F

That is correct, good job. What is the first Scripture and its concept?
Matthew 3:11. There comes one after me who is mightier than I, He will baptize with the Holy Spirit and fire.

Very good. What is the second Scripture and its concept?
Romans 6:3. The concept is if I'm baptized into His Death I'm baptized into His Resurrection.

Great. What is the third Scripture and its concept?
Acts 19:1-6. The concept is "John's Baptism was a baptism of repentance, and after Paul baptized them in water, he laid hands on them and they were baptized with the Holy Ghost.

Excellent. What is the seventh baptism and its concept?
Baptism into Moses. Being sensitive to and subject to God's current movement *(Present truth)* in the church today or it could refer to the fact that all people are born into the natural world confined under the law until the time of their New Birth in Christ.

That is correct, good job. The first Scripture is **MATTHEW 3:11.** The concept is, "There comes one after me who is mightier than I, **HE WILL BAPTIZE WITH THE HOLY SPIRIT AND FIRE.**

What is the first Scripture and its concept?
Matthew 3:11. There comes one after me who is mightier than I, He will baptize with the Holy Spirit and fire.

Very good.

END OF SEED 171   7 Baptisms of the New Testament

REVIEW SEED UNTIL MASTERED

7 WFSF

Seed 171 Further Information – 7 Baptisms of the New Testament

The 1st Seed in the 7th Pod of the 1st Year

The word "Baptism" means to be immersed, covered, or enveloped". Just as Naaman dipped himself in the Jordan 7 times as directed by the Man of God *(2 Kings 5:14)*; respectively, there are 7 Baptisms spoken of in the New Testament, each baptism being an important type or reality for our progressive life growth in Christ Jesus. These 7 Baptisms can be properly distinguished from one another in four important ways:

1. The teaching, preaching, or message associated with the baptism.
2. The person, or element into which the disciple is being baptized.
(In this seed, as in the Bible, the Baptism will always be named according to "Who is the Person" or "What is the Element" into which the believer is being baptized.)
3. The conditions/prerequisites required for the Baptism.
4. The agent performing the Baptism.

Much of the confusion and disputation that exists among various teachers and believers regarding baptisms is due to a lack of applying the four listed above distinguishing factors. Many individuals, anytime they read or hear the word baptism immediately assume it is referring to Water Baptism.

The words "Baptism, Baptizing, and Baptized" are used approximately 100 times in the New Testament and refer at different times to each of the 7 Baptisms that are carefully outlined below according to the 4 explained above distinguishing factors.

40 times the Immersion of Baptism is referring to:
THE FIRST BAPTISM - *(John's)* Baptism of *(into)* Repentance.
The four distinguishing features of this Baptism are:

1. The message of this Baptism is "Repent, the Kingdom is near" *(Matthew 3:2)*.

2. The element of this Baptism is Repentance *(the Greek word for repentance is "metanoia" which literally means "change of mind)*.

3. The condition/prerequisite for John's Baptism was to "bear fruits worthy of repentance" *(Matthew 3:8)*. This fruit had to be something that could be evidenced as being bore immediately as John was immediately baptizing the harlots and the tax collectors as they came to Him. Therefore, it is highly likely that the fruit spoken of was the confession of one's own inability to achieve righteousness through maintaining the "works of the law" *(perfectly)* and a "change of mind" *(repentance)* to trusting and relying on The Way of the Messiah Jesus, for whom John was preparing the way *(Acts 19:4; Hebrews 6:1; 10:9-10; John 14:6)*. The Pharisees and Sadducees' were not about to put to put their trust in any teaching other than that of Moses; as their identity and power was strongly linked to the fact that they were the "stewards" of Moses' Law, and they perceived any move away from dependence on law-keeping as disloyalty to Moses, to whom they were totally dedicated *(Matthew 21:32; Luke 7:29-30; John 9:28, 29)*.

4. The agents of this Baptism were John, his Disciples, as well as the Disciples of Jesus *(John 4:2)*. In today's dispensation of grace, we receive this Baptism into Repentance by yielding to a "change of mind" from "works of the law" and IMMERSING ourselves in the Spiritual Truth that there is nothing we can do to EARN righteousness; fully understanding that it is our genuine faith in Jesus Christ which allows us to receive the Gift of Righteousness *(right standing with God) (Romans 5:16, 17)*. The Baptism of Repentance, because it involved water, is often incorrectly understood to be the same as the Water Baptism. However, it was only after His resurrection that Jesus commanded the Water Baptism that John's Disciples later received, even though they had already undergone John's Baptism *(Acts 19:1-6)*. Therefore, with careful investigation, it is clear that each of these two Baptisms *(into Repentance, and into Water)* has a different message and a different prerequisite than the other. John's Baptism into Repentance signifies a turning away from a "trying to earn it self-righteousness through a "keeping of the law mentality", and instead completely trusting in Christ's Life, Death, and Resurrection as the only Way to Eternal Life. To receive the Baptism of Repentance after Christ's Resurrection requires no water. It can be carried out by the believer simply "Repenting from Dead Works" and receiving "A cleansing of the conscience from dead works *(Hebrews 6:2; 9:17)*".

So then, John's Baptism into Repentance *(from Dead Works)* can be summed up as follows: The believer receives the proper Bible teaching and is able to honestly confess, "I am totally immersed in the truth *(concept)* that there is nothing I can do to earn righteousness." In this baptism, the believer comes to fully believe that it is only the Spirit that gives life, and the flesh counts for nothing *(John 6:63)*. When we cease from our own work and enter into the Accomplishment and Person of Jesus Christ as our rest *(Hebrews 4: 9-11; Matthew 11: 28-30)* then we have truly Repented from Dead Works and undergone John's Baptism of Repentance, even as Jesus did *(Matthew 3:14, 15)*. Obviously, this Baptism, which was taught at the beginning of Jesus' Ministry on earth *(both by John the Baptist and Jesus)* is closely related to the First Elementary Principle: "Repentance from Dead Works. See Seed 161 for a more complete explanation of John's Baptizing of Jesus and the proper understanding of the reason for it.

22 times the Immersion of Baptism is referring to
THE SECOND BAPTISM - Baptism of *(into)* Death of Christ *(the Spiritual Reality)*.
The four distinguishing features of this Baptism are:

1. The message is "You have become dead to the law" and as a result were "raised up together in Christ Jesus" and "But now we have been delivered from The Law, having died to what we were held by" *(Romans 7:4-6; Ephesians 2:6)*.
2. The element is the Death of Christ on the Cross *(Romans 6:3)*.
3. The condition/prerequisite is "believing in the heart" *(Romans 10:10)*.
4. The agent is Father God *(Acts 2:24)*.

In Matthew 20:20-23 the mother of James and John tries to persuade Jesus to give her two sons the preeminence of being seated directly next to Jesus in eternity. Jesus then asked James and John if they were able to drink the cup that He was going to drink and be baptized with the Baptism with which He was going to be baptized. Both Disciples replied that they were able. Jesus then confirmed that they would indeed drink the same cup and be baptized with the same baptism as Jesus. This passage shows that each believer drinks the same cup of suffering as Jesus did *(the dying to self)* and has indeed spiritually died with Christ at the Cross of Calvary.

When a convert believes in his heart *(not just mental assent)* in Christ Jesus, he is spiritually reckoned to have died with Jesus and to have been spiritually risen up and seated with Him in the heavenlies *(Ephesians*

2:1-7 and John14:20). The Baptism into Death is simultaneous with the New Birth. This baptism should be followed as soon as possible with Water Baptism which is an "after type", that is a "playing out" in the physical realm what has already been miraculously accomplished in the Spiritual Realm. The Baptism into Jesus Death is seldom emphasized in the Church as it should be; for it is the baptism that actually cleanses the believer eternally from sin and causes him to be one with Christ Jesus in the Spirit. 1 Peter 3:20,21 clearly speaks of the Baptism into Death, yet is often misused to exalt Water Baptism above the other baptisms, which ought not be. This is, to a certain degree because of the translation of this particular passage in the King James Version of the Bible. Verse 20 refers to the days of Noah as a type and shadow, pointing out God's patience during the time of the preparation of the Ark *(a type of Christ)* where 8 souls were saved "by water". At first glance, it may seem as if they were saved by "anointed water". However, rightly dividing the Word shows us the water is NOT what saved the them *(the water was a judgment, the Ark is what saved them (a type of Christ)*.

Most reputable Bible versions are translated to show that the eight souls were saved "THROUGH water". This is a much better rendering of the original Greek, as it is clear, in this case, that water was the element used by God to judge and destroy those not in the Ark. It was not the water that saved the eight souls but rather the fact that they were in the Ark, just as we are saved by being in Christ Jesus.

In verse 21, the KJV Bible says that it is the "like figure", even Baptism that saves us. But in the original Greek language, the word that the KJV Bible translates "like figure" is "antitupon" which literally means "not the type or like figure, but the reality." Therefore, correctly understood, the Ark is a type *(which cannot save us)* but it is the Essential Baptism into the Death of Christ which actually saves us. Indeed, this verse goes on to explain that this Baptism does NOT cleanse our flesh, but rather give us a good *(clear)* conscience toward God by the Resurrection of Jesus. We should keep in mind that nothing "fixes" or "cleanses" our flesh, only as we walk by the Spirit is the flesh annulled and put to death experientially.

3 times the Immersion of Baptism is referring to
THE THIRD BAPTISM - Baptism of *(into)* the Body of Christ
The four distinguishing features of this Baptism are:

1. The message is, you have all "been baptized by One Spirit into One Body *(1 Corinthians 12:13)*.
2. The element is the Body of Christ *(the Church)* with Jesus as the Head and each believer as a member of His Body *(1 Corinthians 12:12; Colossians 2:19,20)*.
3. The condition/prerequisite is "heart belief" *(Romans 10:10; 1 Timothy 1:5)*.
4. The agent is the Holy Spirit *(1 Corinthians 12:13; Ephesians 1:13)*.

The Baptism into the Body brings an infilling of the Holy Spirit for life and growth. As with the Baptism into Death, Baptism into the Body of Christ is automatic and miraculous, taking place the moment, the convert believes in his heart that Jesus is the Messiah *(1 John 5:1)*. At that very moment, the believer becomes one with Christ and a part of His Body *(the Church)*. There is no outward ritual taught or required for this even to take place, simply genuine heart belief. Indeed, this Baptism should ALWAYS properly take place before a convert is eligible for Water Baptism in Jesus Name. Every true believer has already, by definition *(of being a believer)*, been baptized into the Body of Christ by the Spirit and into Christ's death by the Father at the moment of true conversion. So then, it would be technically correct to say that a believer must be baptized to be saved, when it is understood that the Baptism into the Death and the Body of Christ are automatic and spontaneous at the miraculous moment of New Birth of the believer.

19 times the Immersion of Baptism is referring to
THE FOURTH BAPTISM -Baptism of *(into)* Water *(An important spiritual type, shadow, or ritual)*.
The four distinguishing features of this Baptism are

1. The message is "make Disciples of all the nations, baptizing them in the Name..." *(Matthew 28:18)*.
2. The element is Water" *(Acts 8:38)*.
3. The condition/prerequisite is "if you believe with all your heart you may be baptized in water" *(Acts 8:37)*.
4. The agent is a human minister *(Acts 8:38, 39)*.

7 W F S F

Water Baptism is commanded by Jesus Himself and should be undergone by every true believer in Christ at the earliest opportunity. However, it is important to understand that Water Baptism is a symbol of the Death with Christ *(going down in the water)* and the resurrection with Christ *(coming out of the water)*. Water Baptism is an important act because it allows the believer to experience in the Physical and Soulish Realm what has already taken place in the Spiritual Realm. While the water does not literally accomplish eternal salvation *(in the Spiritual Realm)*, it is a proper part of the believer's experience of his salvation in his natural *(soul)* man and in his physical man *(the fact that he has died with Christ and has been raised with Him)*.

There is some controversy among some denominations about the proper speaking "formula" for Water Baptism. Some say it must be done "in the Name of the Father, the Son, and the Holy Spirit" as commanded by Jesus in Matthew 28:18. Others claim that it must be carried out "in the Name of Jesus" which was clearly the practice of the apostles in the book of Acts *(2:38; 8:12; 19:5)*, It is likely, that since the Name of Jesus is the One Name above every name *(Philippians 2:9-11)*, it is the name that best fully and properly represents the Father, the Son, and the Holy Spirit *(Colossians 2:9,10)*. Both "formulas" seem to be supported by Scripture. However, once we understand that Water Baptism, while it is important and commanded, is only the picture and type of the reality *(and not the actual Death of Christ that it symbolizes)* then we can realize the folly of Christians separating themselves or even strongly disputing over such points of disagreement *(Romans 14:1)*. It is always important to remember that it is only our genuine faith in Jesus and His sacrifice that makes us righteous in God's sight; not any ritual or work on our part, even though such acts are commanded and scripturally proper to carry out.

11 times the Immersion of Baptism is referring to
THE FIFTH BAPTISM - Baptism of *(into)* the Holy Spirit
The four distinguishing features of this Baptism are:

1. The message Is "And you will be endued *(clothed)* with power when the Spirit comes ON you" *(Luke 24:49)*.
2. The element is the Holy Spirit *(Acts 1:8)*.
3. Usually the conditions/prerequisites are asking for this Baptism and receiving this Baptism *(Luke 11:11-13)*.
   Normally, hands are laid on the recipient *(Acts 8:17))*, although, this is not a requirement.

4. The agent is Jesus Christ *(Matthew 3:11)*.

The Baptism of *(into)* the Holy Spirit seems to be the one Baptism that has aroused the most controversy among different groups of believers. There are three primary reasons for this. The first reason is pride. Those who have received this outpouring sometimes wrongly see themselves as "better" or "more spiritual" than those who have not. Those who do not understand this baptism as a separate act sometimes take pride that they do NOT participate in what they see as unnecessary or perhaps even false teaching. In both cases, where such pride exists, it is due to the second reason for the controversy; which is ignorance! Ignorance is simply not knowing, that is, not having the correct understanding or adequate revelation of God's Word regarding baptisms. The third reason for the controversy is a confusion of terminology. For example, the Baptism into the Body *(which is an infilling)* at the New Birth is done by the Holy Spirit *(1 Corinthians 12:13)*; however, this infilling is not the Baptism of *(into)* the Holy Spirit. The Baptism of *(into)* the Holy Spirit is not done by the Holy Spirit, but rather by Jesus Christ *(Matthew 3:11)*. Baptism of *(into)* the Holy Spirit is not an infilling, but rather is an enduement, that is a clothing, and it is also referred to in scripture as an outpouring on the believer *(Acts 1:8)*.

There are two automatic baptisms *(at New Birth)*, into the Body and into Death, which are initially signified in scriptures by an act of Jesus on the Day of Resurrection breathing into His Disciples. By comparing John 20:19-22 with Luke 24:49 we can better understand the Baptism into the Body. Both of these scriptures are describing the event that took place on the evening of Resurrection Day *(John 20:19; Luke 24:29, 33)*. Luke 24:45 is describing the fulfillment of what Jesus had prophesied before His death *(The Holy Spirit living IN them to help them)* - John 14:17) At that moment, He "opened their understanding, that they might comprehend the Scriptures". In John 20:22 Jesus "breathed on" them and said, "Receive the Holy Spirit". Both of these passages are describing the moment of the New Birth of the Disciples. The breathing "on" actually would be properly translated breathed "into" *(Greek word "emphusao", according to Young's Concordance "breathed into")*. When they received the Spirit *(the infilling)*, the Spirit "opened their understanding".

Then after 50 days, at which time they were "tarrying" in Jerusalem, the Spirit came on them, which is the Baptism of *(into)* the Holy Spirit. This was prophesied by Jesus in Luke 24:49 and Acts 1:8. Jesus' promise in these verses is not for an infilling *(which already happened)* but rather was for an outpouring, that is to be clothed or endued with Holy Spirit power. In Acts 2:2, the house was "filled" *(which is the Greek word "pleroo" meaning "to be filled inwardly")* with "a sound from heaven, as of a rushing mighty wind" In verse 3, Fire *(the Spirit)* sat <u>on</u> each of the believers. In verse 4, "they were all "filled" *(which is the Greek word "pletho" meaning "outwardly filled or covered")* and "they began to speak with other tongues, as the Spirit gave them utterance". Of course there is only one Holy Spirit, so each of these, the essential infilling during the New Birth on the Day of Resurrection, and the subsequent outpouring/clothing on the Day of Pentecost are closely related. The outpouring can probably be correctly understood as an overflow or release *(cup running over of Psalms 23:5)* of the infilling. Normally, the clothing of the Spirit "<u>on</u>" is accompanied by a speaking in tongues. *(Tongues is dealt with in Seed 463)*. There is no scripture that says speaking in tongues is "the evidence" of or proof of Baptism *(into)* the Holy Spirit *(as some teach)*. However, if there is no tongue speaking when this Baptism is received it is likely due to a lack of full biblical revelation regarding the spiritual manifestation of speaking in tongues.

In Acts 18:12-18, Phillip is preaching "concerning the Kingdom of God and the Name of Jesus Christ," and many were baptized in the Name of Jesus *(which is Water Baptism)*. When the apostles in Jerusalem had heard that the Samarians had received the Word, they sent them two apostles to minister further to them. John and Peter then ministered to them the Outpouring of the Baptism of *(into)* the Holy Spirit, for as of yet the Spirit had not fallen upon any of them, though they were already clearly born again evidenced by the fact they had been Water Baptized. This clearly shows two separate Baptism experiences, that is the infilling that takes place at the time of genuine heart belief *(into the Body and Death of Christ)* and the Outpouring, which is the Baptism of *(into)* the Holy Spirit, normally associated with the Laying on of Hands. Note that in this passage there is no specific mention of "Speaking in Tongues".

In Acts 10:34-43 Peter preaches, "Whoever believes in Him will receive remission of sins". While Peter is still preaching, the Holy Spirit fell "upon all" due to the Spirit being "poured out on" them. Peter then explained it would be improper to forbid Water Baptism since they were clearly Born Again, evidenced in this case, by the Holy Spirit coming on them. This passage demonstrates clearly that Water Baptism is not a prerequisite to be born again, or even to receive the Baptism of *(into)* the

Holy Spirit. For here, clearly they were clothed with the Spirit before they were Water Baptized.

3 times the Immersion of Baptism is referring to
THE SIXTH BAPTISM -The Baptism of *(into)* Fire
The four distinguishing features of this Baptism are:

1. The message is "He will thoroughly purge His floor and gather the wheat, but will burn up the chaff" *(Matthew 3:12)*.
2. The element is the Cleansing Fire of the Holy Spirit which always burns away any evil dross of sin through genuine fellowship in the Word. *(Malachi 3:2-3 Ephesians 5:26)*
3. The condition/prerequisite is "to walk in the light *(truth)* and have fellowship" *(1 John 1:1-7)*.
4. The agent is Jesus Christ ministering through the believer by the Holy Spirit *(Matthew 3:11)*.

The Baptism of Fire is a cleansing of the soul *(part of soul salvation)* that takes place as believers fellowship with one another, speaking the Word *(Christ)* to each other by the Spirit. Hence, the Word cleanses the soul from the filth it has been exposed to and tainted by from being daily exposed to the world. John the Baptist first prophesied about this cleansing that would come through Jesus by Fire *(Matthew 3:11, 12)*. And then, Jesus Himself prophesied about the Fire Baptism in Luke 12: 49. In this verse, Jesus is looking forward to the day when He would reside in and be one with each believer in order to accomplish more perfectly this cleansing of fellowship.

In John 13, Jesus' washing of the disciples feet was much more than a simple demonstration of humility, but was additionally an excellent picture *(type)* of Fire Baptism. In verses 6 and 7 Peter asks Jesus, "Lord, are You washing my feet?" Jesus replied, "What I am doing you do not understand now, but you will know after this. Certainly Peter already understood the humility of a servant washing the feet of another person. But what Peter did not understand was the spiritual meaning and significance of washing feet. For that reason Peter tried to prevent the washing of his feet by Jesus. But Jesus retorted with a strong rebuke of Peter saying, "If I do not wash you, you have no part with Me". To have "no part" here does not mean no Eternal Life, but rather no participation in the genuine fellowship that cleanses.

7 W F S F

This is because true fellowship in Christ takes place through the Washing of the Word *(Ephesians 5:26)*. Peter, in his characteristic zeal proclaimed, "Lord, not my feet only, but also my hand and my head!" But Jesus calmed Peter explaining to him, "He who is bathed needs only to wash his feet, but is completely clean, and you are all clean, but ".The previous "bath" here signifies the cleansing *(of the spirit of man)* of regeneration that takes place at New Birth *(Titus 3:5)*. As believers, even though each of us has been already perfectly sanctified in our spirit man *(Hebrews 10: 10)*, each day as we walk in the world we are soiled by the influence of the world and its agents. This makes it needful to have a regular washing of our feet" *(souls)*. This cleansing of the soul takes place through fellowship in Jesus *(The Word)*. When Jesus had finished washing the disciples feet he asked them in verse 12, "Do you know what I have done to you?"

It is likely, because they did not yet possess the Spirit or the Mind of Christ, they could not begin to completely understand the spiritual significance of what Jesus had done. However, Jesus went on to explain that even as he set the example of "washing their feet", they ought to follow the example and wash one another's feet. Churches today rarely, if ever, practice the "literal washing of feet". To practice a literal washing of feet would be okay, but it would only be the symbol, not the reality. The reality of foot washing takes place when the believers, in Christ, by the Fire of the Spirit, speak the Word *(Christ)* to one another in fellowship which results in a cleansing of their natural *(soul)* man.

In John 1:1-7, John writing to the Church, focuses their attention to the importance of fellowship in verses 3 and 7, and proclaims in verse 4 that such a fellowship is required "that your joy may be full". In verses 5 and 6, John goes on to explain that God is light *(here meaning truth)* and in Him there is no darkness *(no deception)*. Verse 8 brings out the specific truth that is critical to this passage, which is that we still have sin in our lives. If we deny this, we are still in darkness *(deception)*. Verse 7 explains, "But if we walk in the light *(the truth that being exposed daily to the world, we are always in need of additional cleansing in our souls)* as He is in the light *(the same truth)*, we have fellowship *(with Him in fellowship with each other)* and *(as a result of this light and fellowship)* the blood cleanses us from all sin." So while essentially we are already clean *(having had the bath of regeneration)* we still need regular cleansing *(our soul "feet" washed "by the blood")*. This allows us to maintain a good and clean conscience before God, even though we fall short of His perfect standard *(His glory)*. However, if we deceive ourselves into believing we have arrived *(no longer having any sin in us)*, then we cut ourselves off from the daily cleansing that is needed and which comes through "foot washing" fellowship.

1 time the Immersion of Baptism is referring to
THE SEVENTH BAPTISM - Baptism into Moses *(in the Cloud and Sea)*

Because there is only one clear scripture reference in the New Testament to this Baptism, it is difficult to say with certainty what its proper application is to the believer, if there is any. However, it may be that this Baptism represents the Baptism of each human being into the world *(from the mother's womb)* to be confined under the bondage of The Law until that person is born again *(Romans 3:19-22; Galatians 3:19; 22-25)*; Hence, it may be a Baptism prior to New Birth, and hence a pre-Christian Baptism experienced by each person, whether he knows it or not. A second possible alternative is that it could signify a believer's discerning of a current "move of God". So, just as the cloud led the Israelites and showed them where to go or stay from day to day, now by God's grace the believer can discern where the Holy Spirit would have him go or stay from day to day.

Acts 19: 1-6 is the best single passage to show a panoramic view of the multiple Baptisms of the New Testament. By rightly dividing this scripture and comparing it with other Baptism scriptures we can uncover, to a certain degree, all seven Baptisms which are taught in this seed. The ministry of Paul which is being described at the beginning of Acts 19 took place about 26 years after the death of Jesus. In verses 1 and 2, after arriving at Ephesus, Paul ministered to 12 men who are referred to in this passage as being Disciples having believed in Christ Jesus. By definition, they had *(of necessity)* already undergone the Baptism into Christ *(the Body)* and Baptism into Christ's death and resurrection *(Romans 6:3)*.

Verses 2 and 3 teach us that they had also already undergone John's Baptism of Repentance *(from dead works)*, but had no revelation concerning the Baptism of *(into)* the Holy Spirit. In verse 5 they are Water Baptized in the Name of Jesus. In verse 6, they receive the Baptism of *(into)* the Holy Spirit, which came UPON them, resulting in them speaking in tongues and prophesying. Their prophesying, as well as the Word that was being ministered to them, certainly had a cleansing power; hence, the Baptism of Fire through fellowship took place. And as all people are, they

7 WFSF

were born into the world to be confined by The Law until they were Born Again INTO ONENESS WITH CHRIST JESUS.

7 W F S F

ADDENDUM TO 7 BAPTISMS OF THE NEW TESTAMENT
MINISTERING THE BAPTISM OF *(INTO)* THE HOLY SPIRIT TO A BELIEVER OR TO YOURSELF

First, the candidate must be a born-again believer in Jesus Christ as those of the world cannot receive this Baptism *(John 14:16, 17)*. This Baptism is available to all believers who are willing to ask for it and receive it *(Luke 11:13)* as God is no respecter of persons.

Second, it is very helpful if the believer seeking this baptism understands the difference between the "Infilling" of the Spirit of Christ *(Romans 8:9) (the Infilling is for Eternal Life and Growth, which the believer receives at time of his New Birth)* and the "Outpouring" of the Baptism of *(into)* the Holy Spirit. The Outpouring of the Holy Spirit is for power and witness and usually comes by asking for and receiving it. The Outpouring can be best understood as an increase and overflow of the original Infilling.

Third, the following four questions should be ministered to the disciple seeking the Baptism of *(into)* the Holy Spirit.

1. Do you firmly believe that when you ask the Father for the Baptism *(Outpouring)* of the Holy Spirit that He will most assuredly give it to you immediately? *(Luke 11:9-13)*
2. Do you promise to be faithful and to immediately receive this Baptism by faith after you ask for it? *(Acts 19:2)*
3. Do you firmly believe that the Holy Spirit will give you an utterance *(sounds or syllables to speak)* immediately after you receive the Baptism of the Holy Spirit? *(Acts 2:4)*
4. Will you commit right now to speak whatever utterance *(words of a language you will not understand)* the Holy Spirit gives you without doubting or judging by your flesh? *(Acts 2:4)*

If there is NOT a confident answer of "Yes" by the disciple to each and every one of these four questions, it may be advisable to have further teaching ministry in the problem areas in order to build up the disciples faith *(be led by the Holy Spirit)*.

Fourth, after the believer can honestly answer "Yes" to the above four questions, he is ready to receive the GIFT of the Baptism of *(into)* the Holy

Spirit. Now, he should ask for and receive by faith the Outpouring *(clothing)* of the Holy Spirit. As he asks for the Gift, it is the proper time for the person ministering to him to Lay Hands On him as in Acts 8:17. Next, the disciple should speak all sounds or words *(utterances)* that he is able to sense coming forth from his spirit man. It is important that he understands that the Spirit will not force him to speak, or even necessarily cause him to speak in tongues, but the Spirit will faithfully give him the utterance, enabling the disciple to speak in tongues.

The disciple must initiate and speak in tongues by faith. Failure to understand how the Holy Spirit normally works in this process is the cause of many people failing to operate in the Manifestation of Tongues, even though the gift is freely and fully available to them. A disciple may speak in unknown tongues with the words flowing like a river or he may only speak a single syllable. In either case he should resist the natural *(soulish)* tendency to judge his "speaking in tongues". He should just receive the Gift by faith. He should remember, when he asks for an "egg" *(something good)*, God will NOT give him a scorpion *(something bad) (Luke 11:12)*.

Finally, the disciple should continue to praise God and thank Him for The Gift of the Baptism *(Outpouring)* of *(into)* the Holy Spirit for power and witness. The disciple/receiver should understand that he can now speak in tongues whenever he wants to by simply yielding to the utterance of the Holy Spirit which is continuously available to him after he has operated in the Gift of Tongues, even if it has only been one time. It is highly recommended that he continue to operate in the Gift of Tongues at least once per day. This practice will edify him spiritually and build him up in the most holy faith *(1 Corinthians 14:4; Jude 20)*. Remember, the adversaries *(the devil, the world, and The flesh)* will always do their best to get the disciple to question and doubt every wonderful thing that God has freely given to him. The disciple should not be ignorant of Satan's devices. He will need to stand strong in the faith without wavering, totally trusting on the Word of God and on His promises.

7WFSF

Seed 271 – Witnessing

(In fellowship Seed 271 is referred to as the 2^{ndt} Seed in the 7th Pod of the First Year)

Simple format

II. The second Seed in the Seventh Pod is **WITNESSING**.

1. The concept for Witnessing is **"HP+ CP +CC= MI."**
   HP stands for **"HIGH POTENCY WALK"** which means "The Christian walks after the Spirit setting a good example in his life for others".
   CP stands for **"CLOSE PROXIMITY"** which is "Developing first a relationship with the unbeliever before attempting to witness to him".
   CC stands for **"CLEAR COMMUNICATION"** which is "Presenting the gospel *(Good News)* message in a plain and concise manner using illustrations/example to make it clear and to win the attention of others".
   MI stands for "Maximum Impact" *(The best possible results)*.

   A. The scripture for Witnessing is **ACTS 10:34-43** *(acronym: IF PRAD JR)*.
      1. The First Concept is **"GOD IS IMPARTIAL"**.
      2. The Second Concept is **"FAITH WORKS RIGHTEOUSNESS"**.
      3. The Third Concept is **"CHRIST IS OUR PEACE"**.
      4. The Fourth Concept is **"REPENTANCE FROM DEAD WORKS"**.
      5. The Fifth Concept is **"JESUS IS OUR ANOINTING"**.
      6. The Sixth Concept is **"THE DEATH AND RESURRECTION OF CHRIST"**.
      7. The Seventh Concept is **"JESUS IS THE JUDGE OF THE LIVING AND THE DEAD"**.
      8. The Eighth Concept is **"THE REMISSION OF SIN TO THOSE WHO BELIEVE"**.

7WFSF

Sample Fellowship Format

Disciple's reply is in **bold type**

What is Second Seed in the Seventh Pod?
Witnessing

That is right. What is the concept of Witnessing
The concept is HP+ CP +CG= MI which stands for I have a high potency walk through walking after the spirit, I develop close proximity with unbelievers before attempting to evangelize them, I practice clear communication by speaking the truth to them in a clear and concise manner by using examples and illustrations where possible to win their attention. This threefold approach results in a maximum impact!

Very Good! What is the scripture for Witnessing?
Acts 10:34-43

That is correct. What are the Eight Concepts for Acts 10:34-43?
The first concept: God is impartial
The second concept: faith works righteousness
The third concept: Christ is our peace
The fourth concept: repentance from dead works
The fifth concept: Jesus is our anointing
The sixth concept: death and resurrection of Christ
The seventh concept: Jesus is the judge of the living and the dead
The eighth concept: remission of sins to those who believe.

Excellent Job!

END OF SEED 271   Witnessing

REVIEW SEED UNTIL MASTERED

7 W F S F

Seed 271 Further Information – Witnessing

The 2nd Seed in the 7th Pod of the 1st Year

Why Witness? Because people matter to God! Indeed, you never have and never will lock eyes with another human being who is not valuable to God.
What is the reward of Witnessing? Witnessing will bring you purpose, give you fulfillment, bring you adventure, cause you to grow, and establish you with a godly confidence and rejoicing.
What is the cost? Possibility of rejection, likely some persecution, a risk of embarrassment, a consumption of your time and energy.

3 ESSENTIAL WITNESSING FACTORS can be recalled by
HP + CP + CC = MI
HP stands for the believer having a HIGH POTENCY walk, which includes three aspects.

The First Aspect is "The Attractiveness of Authenticity". When a witness has a genuine intimate relationship with Jesus Christ, and is truly rooted in his identity with Christ, his authentic convictions and emotions will come through in many non-verbal ways. This is simply the radiant Life of Christ working its way in, though, and out of the believer/witness.

The Second Aspect is "The Pull of Compassion". There is an old saying, "People need to know that you care, before they care what you know". When we are able to see others through God's eyes, and truly care for them with God's love, others can sense it and are drawn to us *(to the Christ in us)*.The more we are at peace and fulfilled in Jesus, the more others will recognize that we have something better than most. All glory to God!

The Third Aspect is the "Strength of Sacrifice". This aspect is simply a willingness to give of your time and resources. As you progressively die to self and learn to yield completely to the Holy Spirit, putting others first becomes an easy yoke.

CP stands for CLOSE PROXIMITY. Normally, people are not comfortable talking to a person they do not know, particularly concerning matters as important and as personal as their faith. It is of great help to get to know and develop a working relationship with a person before approaching the matter of faith with him. This is simply a guideline, not a hard-fast rule. You need to be led by the Holy Spirit in all things.

7**W** F S F

CC stands for CLEAR COMMUNICATION. The idea here is to clearly explain the gospel *(good news)* of how a person can receive Eternal Salvation in a simple and succinct manner *(short and to the point)*.

It is very helpful to use illustrations and examples to "paint the picture" of how salvation works. Learning to communicate our faith is important, as becoming Born Again is truly the greatest actual need of every unbelieving person on the face of the earth.

MI stands for MAXIMUM IMPACT which means to influence the person to whom you are witnessing in the strongest way possible to move them toward a decision for Christ.

HP *(High Potency)* walk plus
CP *(Close proximity)* plus
CC *(Clear Communication* equals
MI *(Maximum Impact*

4 PROVEN WITNESSING METHODS
The "Roman's Road" Approach

In this approach you take the potential convert through seven scriptures from the book of Romans.

1. Romans 3:23, 24 - This scripture shows that every single person needs to be saved. Praise be to God, the salvation needed is freely given to those who are willing to receive The Gift.
2. Romans 3:10-19 - These ten verses prove it is not possible to obtain reconciliation with God by our works or attitudes.
3. Romans 6:23 This scripture teaches two important truths.
First, sin brings serious negative consequences. Second, God gives us Eternal Life as a free gift. It does not have to be, nor can it be earned.
4. Romans 5:12 - This scripture teaches us that the unconverted person is irrefutably Identified with sin because he is descended from Adam. Mankind is not of Adam because they sin. They sin because they are of Adam.
5. Romans 5:8 - This scripture shows us that God's love for us is not based on our behavior, but rather on God's character.
6. Romans 10:9, 10 - This scripture proves it is heart belief that makes a man righteous.
7. Romans 10:13 - This scripture clearly shows that salvation is freely available to all who are willing to trust in the Lord.

The "Do versus Done" Approach

In this method, you start with a question to discover if the potential convert understands what makes true Christianity so greatly different from all religion.

1. You ask, "Do you understand the difference between religion and Christianity?" Now listen carefully to the answer.
Seldom, if ever, will you get the correct answer, according to God's point of view (as expressed by the Bible).
2. Explain that religion is spelled "D-0" and consists of all the things a person must "do" to receive or earn God's approval or an eternal reward. The problem with the "do" teaching is that the "victim" of this teaching never really knows for sure if he is doing enough to meet God's requirement.
3. The truth is, no matter how much a person DOES, he cannot meet God's perfect standard (James 2:10).
4. Thankfully, true Christianity is spelled D-O-N-E•••Done! God's offer of salvation is never based on "who man is" or on "what man has done" or "will do", but rather salvation is based completely on what Jesus Christ has DONE for us, which we freely inherit through our faith in Christ Crucified and Resurrected, the only WAY to Eternal Life.
5. Then, after being Born Again and receiving God's gift of righteousness (Romans 5:15, 17), as we choose to continue to follow after God's Spirit, He changes us progressively from the inside out. And all glory goes to God!

The "Bridge" Approach

In this third method of evangelizing, we use an allegory *(an expression that uses symbolism)*. If you have at least some minimal drawing skills, it helps to illustrate this allegory on paper as you explain it verbally.

1. Every person matters a great deal to God, and He strongly desires a personal and intimate relationship with every human being (Draw a picture of a simple cliff and write the words "Loving God" above it.
2. But there is a problem, God is Holy. All of mankind is sinful. Consequently, man is separated from God by a great gulf (While you are explaining this draw a second cliff across from the first cliff and put the words "Sinful Man" above the second cliff. Add the word "Holy" above the words "Loving God" on the first cliff).

3. It is not possible for man's efforts or works to ever bridge this gap (point to the gap between the two cliffs). No matter how hard man tries, he cannot make the jump.
4. The result of trying to gain salvation through our own work or effort is death (Write the word "Death" at the bottom of the valley, between the two cliffs). Any effort to please God by works is futile, as man has not, and cannot meet God's standard of perfection.
5. (Now explain the gospel which is Good News.) Because God loves each of us so much, and because we matter so much to Him, He did for us what we could never do for ourselves.
He built a Bridge. He built the Bridge by coming to earth to live as one of us, and then· died to pay the death penalty we owed (Draw a Cross shaped Bridge from God's cliff to Sinful Man's cliff. Bridge). Write the words "Death of Christ" on the bridge.
6. What is Man's part in true salvation? Just knowing about the Good News or just agreeing with it is not enough. We need to act on this Great Truth. God requires us to BELIEVE in our heart who He is and what He has done for us. We do this by humbly admitting before God that we are far from perfect and need His LIFE and leadership in us (This is True Repentance). Our simple act of trusting Him and obediently believing in our heart results in full reconciliation with God. All of our sins are blotted out and we are immediately and eternally placed as genuine sons in His family (Scratch out the words "Sinful Man" from the second cliff, and put the words "Reconciled Man" over the first cliff with the words "Holy Loving God").

The "Good News" Approach

This is the fourth and most elaborate method of evangelism. In this approach, seven truths are shared by the person witnessing to the potential convert. The Evangelist here should use scriptures and be led by the Holy Spirit. Here are the truths you will share *(not necessarily in this exact order)*.

1. All of your sins are forgiven: past, present, and future (1 John 2:2; Hebrews 9:26).
2. God is not mad at you NO MATTER WHAT! (Colossians 1:21; Isaiah 54:9, 10).
3. In our earthly lives, God is the giver of all good things and is never the source of tragedy or trouble. You matter to God dearly! (James 1:17; 1 Corinthians 4:5).

7 **W** F S F

4. On the Cross of Calvary, Jesus received and bore ALL the punishment and wrath for sin that mankind deserved (Hebrews 10:12; 1 Peter 2:24).
5. God has a great desire and would be greatly pleased to give you your Greatest Need in life which is Eternal Life (which is of Himself) and the Greatest Treasure a man could have which is The Spirit of Jesus Christ living in you (Romans 5:8; 2 Corinthians 4:7)!
6. You can completely eliminate ANY and ALL possibility of ever experiencing any of God's wrath by making one important decision (Romans 5:9; 1 Thessalonians 5:9)!
7. Are you willing to put away your pride and freely receive through a sincere heartfelt believing, God's multi-faceted Gift? When you receive this Free Gift, always remember it includes "Blamelessness in His sight", "Eternal Salvation", and the "All Inclusive Christ in you" (Ephesians 2:8-10; 2 Corinthians 4:7).

FIVE WITNESSING TEMPERAMENTS

Each of us are fearfully and wonderfully made according to God's Word. However, we each differ in our personalities and temperaments. Nevertheless, God can and does use all personalities and temperaments when they are yielded to Him, for the carrying out of His purposes. So, while there are many things we may have in common as we witness to others, there will also be some major differences. God designed these differences and revels in them. We are not called to be "cookie cutter Christians", rather He uses each of us in accordance with the Unique Masterpiece into which He made each of us to be *(Ephesians 2: 10)*. Here are a few of the possible "Different Approach Temperaments" that we may be called to use when Witnessing.

I. John 4:29 - First is the Invitational Approach of the Samaritan woman. She said, "Come see a Man" as she invited the townspeople to come out to see the Messiah and to drink of the Living Water that wells up to Eternal Life. Not every believer feels "qualified" to evangelize or disciple others. But all believers are qualified, for Christ in them is their qualification. They simply need to gain confidence to witness to others as well as to teach them. This comes mostly from simply witnessing and teaching by faith. Confidence will grow with each experience. Meanwhile, even the most inexperienced believers can continue to invite others to come to Church or to meet with those with more experience in Witnessing.

2. John 4:9, 10 -Second is the Compassionate Approach of Jesus.
Jesus said "If you knew the Gift of God ••• you would have asked and He

would have given you Living Water". Each believer carries within himself a well of this Living Water to give to others to drink. We need to learn to operate in the compassion of Jesus Christ caring enough to reach out to touch and bless those who may desire the Living Water *(The Spirit)*.

3. John 9: 25 - Third is the Testimonial Approach of the Blind Man. He said "One thing I know, I was blind, and now I see". One of the most powerful witnesses of our faith is what the Lord has done for us personally. Others may resist or argue a doctrinal teaching, but it is impossible to argue with a genuine personal experience.

4. Acts 2:22, 23 - Fourth is the Confrontational Approach of Peter. Peter said, "By the foreknowledge of God you have taken Jesus of Nazareth and crucified and put Him to death" Sometimes the unconverted person needs someone to come to them with a stronger approach. But keep in mind when using a Confrontational Approach that witnessing still always needs to be done with a motive, an attitude, and with actions consistent with God's Love.

5. Acts 17:2, 3 - Fifth is the Intellectual Approach of Paul.
Paul said, "•••Christ had to suffer, and rise again from the dead" and "This Jesus whom I preach to you is the Christ". Paul would spend weeks *(Acts 17:2)*, months *(Acts 19:8)*, and sometimes even years *(Acts 19:10)* in one location to reason with the people in order to persuade them of the truth of "The Only WAY" to salvation *(Jesus Christ)*. Some doubters need to be persuaded with a lot of God's Word as well as historical proofs and other Bible evidence to reverse and defeat their natural and ungodly logic and philosophy. At times, the Holy Spirit requires us to exercise great patience and persistence until the person is won to Christ always, ALL GLORY GOES TO GOD!

7 W **F** S F

Seed 371 – Foundational Ministries

(In fellowship Seed 371 is referred to as the
3rd Seed in the 7th Pod of the First Year)

Simple format

III. The Third Seed in the Seventh Pod is **FOUNDATIONAL MINISTRIES** *(Acronym: PM-TEL GM).*

1. The First Foundational Ministry is "**PROPHECY**".
   The concept of Prophecy is "**SPEAKING FOR GOD** *(God speaking through me)* **IN SEASON WITH ACCURACY AND CLARITY**".

2. The Second Foundational Ministry is **MINISTRY**.
   The concept of Ministry is "**I UNSELFISHLY SERVE OTHERS BY THE SPIRIT**".

3. The Third Foundational Ministry is "**TEACHING**".
   The concept of Teaching is "**I HELP OTHERS TO UNCOVER TRUTH BY THE SPIRIT**".

4. The Fourth Foundational Ministry is "**EXHORTATION**".
   The concept of Exhortation is **I ENCOURAGE** *(build up)* **OTHERS BY THE SPIRIT**".

5. The Fifth Foundational Ministry is "**LEADING**".
   The concept of Leading is "**I SET AN EXAMPLE FOR OTHERS BY THE SPIRIT**".

6. The Sixth Foundational Ministry is "**GIVING**".
   The concept of Giving is "**I GENEROUSLY BLESS OTHERS BY THE SPIRIT**",

7. The Seventh Foundational Ministry is "**MERCY**".
   The concept of Mercy is "**I EMPATHETICALLY COMFORT OTHERS BY THE SPIRIT**".

   A. The scripture for Foundational Ministries is **ROMANS 12:6-8**.
      1. The concept is the Seven Foundational Ministries **AS OUTLINED IN THE SEED CONCEPTS ABOVE**.

7W F S F

Sample Fellowship Format

Disciple's reply is in **bold type**

What is the Third Seed in the Seventh Pod?
FOUNDATIONAL MINISTRIES.

Yes, that is correct! What is the acronym for this seed?
PM TEL GM

Very Good. What is the First Foundational Ministry and its concept?
PROPHECY. I SPEAK FOR GOD IN SEASON WITH ACCURACY AND CLARITY

Very Good! What is the Second Foundation Ministry and its concept?
MINISTRY. I UNSELFISHLY SERVE OTHERS BY THE SPIRIT.

Correct! What is the Third Foundational Ministry and its concept?
TEACHING. I HELP OTHERS UNCOVER TRUTH BY THE SPIRIT.

Excellent. What is the Fourth Foundational Ministry and its concept?
EXHORTATION. I ENCOURAGE OTHERS BY THE SPIRIT.

That's right! What is the Fifth Foundational Ministry?
LEADING. I SET A GOOD EXAMPLE FOR OTHERS BY THE SPIRIT.

That is correct! What is the Sixth Foundational Ministry?
GIVING. I GENEROUSLY BLESS OTHERS BY THE SPIRIT.

That is correct! What is the Seventh Foundational Ministry?
MERCY. I PRACTICE EMPATHY IN COMFORTING OTHERS BY THE SPIRIT.

Excellent! What is the scripture for Foundational Ministries?
ROMANS 12:6-8 That is right!

What are the concepts of this scripture?

7 W F S F

THE CONCEPTS ARE 7 FOUNDATIONAL GIFTS I CAN RECALL BY
"PM TEL GM". *(Already given in the Seed Concepts)*

END OF SEED 371   Foundational Ministries
REVIEW SEED UNTIL MASTERED

7w F s F

Seed 371 Further Information – Foundational Ministries

The 3rd Seed in the 7th Pod of the 1st Year

There are various and differing lists of gifts in the New Testament. In Romans 12: 6-8, seven gifts are listed which are foundational for every believer. These gifts are imparted to all converts at the moment of New Birth. They are received according to the Grace given to us through the Infilling of the Holy Spirit. These 7 Foundational Gifts become more and more active for the Lord's practical use in proportion to the increase of our experience and maturity in Christ Jesus. God's Grace is simply the Reality of Christ as the Divine Person coming into our being to be our Life and our Everything for His use and our enjoyment.

Generally, due to our individual temperaments and preferences, one or more of these seven gifts will flow with an ease that could lead us to believe that we have received only that *(those)* particular gift*(s)* to the exclusion of the rest of them. However, since the fullness of the Godhead is in Christ, and Christ is in us, we are complete in Him *(Colossians 2:9, 10)*. All that the Lord has in us and for us is through our being in Him. Keep in mind that all of God's gifts are of no profit unless they are used in His Love *(1 Corinthians 13:1-3)*. Below are the 7 Foundational Ministries *(along with a brief explanation of each one)*:

1. **Prophesying** - In the Old Testament, prophesying was for a select few men who God used both to foretell future events and to tell forth God's view and instructions. However, in this Age of Grace, every believer is encouraged to Prophesy *(1 Corinthians 14:1, 5, 24, 31)* which is defined in the New Testament as speaking edification *(to build)*, exhortation *(to encourage)*, and comfort *(1 Corinthians 14:3)* to others by yielding to the lead of the Holy Spirit allowing the Lord to speak His word through each believer. The Gift of Prophecy should be desired by believers above every other gift *(1 Corinthians 14:1, 39)*.

2. **Ministry** -"Ministry" simply means "to serve". Generally, many think of a Minister as one who preaches the Word of God to others. However, Ministry includes any kind of service to others which is done unselfishly out of love as led by the Holy Spirit. The scripture teaches that God has made all believers sufficient as Ministers of the New Covenant and of

reconciliation *(2 Corinthians 5:18, 19; 2 Corinthians 3:6)*.

3. **Teaching** - In the highest spiritual sense, believers need no one to teach them because they all have received the Anointing *(active Holy Spirit)* and He teaches the believers all things *(1 John 2: 27)*. In Christ, Christians know all things *(1 John 2:20)* and need no one to instruct them because they have the Mind of Christ" *(1 Corinthians 2:15, 16)*. However, teaching by believers is listed more than once as properly belonging in the Body of Christ. So then, in the Church the servant's teaching is not supplying to another believer what he does not know, but rather it is helping the believer who is being "taught" to discover and uncover God's Truth which they have in Christ.

4. **Exhortation** - This gift is when a believer simply encourages other people and builds them up by his words, attitudes, and actions as led and empowered by the Holy Spirit. The most basic way for a believer to exhort to other people is through releasing and expressing the same love that God has freely given to him *(1 Corinthians 8:1)*.

5. **Leading** - The primary idea of this gift is not that of ruling or lording over the life of other believers. Jesus Christ is the only proper Ruling Head. "Leading" has the basic meaning of "going before or in front of". The concept is the Leader is the person who "sets the example". Because believers see and discern the Leader knows "where he is going" and "what he is doing", that they follow him and learn from his example. That is the meaning of true Leadership. A Leader may or may not have a title or an official position, but it is never the title or position that qualifies him to lead, but rather it is the Gift of Leading operating in and through the Leader by the Holy Spirit in accord to the believer's willingness and experience. The true Leader always sets the example and oversees his fellow believers by pointing them to Christ, Who is the only Head of the Church. The scripture instructs us to give double honor to those who lead with excellence *(1 Timothy 5:17)*.

6. **Giving** - The Gift of Giving is a readiness and willingness to freely and generously bless people by the Spirit out of the Giver's own possessions and life. A man has nothing unless it is given to him from heaven *(John 3:27)*. Each believer is called to be a faithful steward with all that the Lord has blessed Him *(1 Corinthians 4:1, 2; 2 Corinthians 9:7, 8)*.

7.Mercy - The Gift of Mercy allows the believer to feel genuine compassion for those who are hurting or suffering in any way. Out of this godly empathy, the believer has the Spiritual capacity to console and comfort other persons by the Spirit of God with the same comfort that God makes available to each believer *(2 Corinthians 1:3,4)*

Remember, it is likely each believer will flow more easily in one or more of these 7 Foundational Gifts. Nonetheless, it is important to realize that all of these gifts are available to each believer through and in Christ Jesus. Out of God's love, the believer needs to continue to use those gifts which come easier to him and learn to operate in those gifts which are not yet fully developed.

7 W F **S** F

Seed 471 – Sowing and Reaping

*(In fellowship Seed 471 is referred to as the
4th Seed in the 7th Pod of the First Year)*

Simple format

IV. The Fourth Seed in the Seventh Pod is **SOWING AND REAPING** *(471)*.
1. The concept is "**IF A PERSON SOWS TO THE FLESH THEY WILL REAP DEATH AND DESTRUCTION, BUT I SOW TO THE SPIRIT AND REAP LIFE AND BLESSINGS**".

    A. The First Scripture for Sowing and Reaping is **GALATIANS 6:7, 8.** *(Read now)*
    The concept is "God is not mocked; whatever a man sows, that he will reap".

    B. The Second Scripture for this seed is **GENESIS 8:22.** *(Read now.)*
    The concept is "The Law of Seedtime and Harvest will remain forever".

7 W F **S** F

Sample Fellowship Format

Disciple's reply is in **bold type**

What is the Fourth Seed in the Seventh Pod?
Sowing and reaping.

Yes! What is the concept of Sowing and Reaping?
If a man sows to the flesh he'll reap death and destruction, but I sow to the spirit, and reap life and blessings.

What is the First Scripture for Sowing and Reaping?
GALATIANS 6:7, 8.

Yes! What is the concept of this scripture?
GOD IS NOT MOCKED. WHAT I SOW I WILL REAP.

Yes! What is the Second Scripture for Sowing and Reaping?
GENESIS 8:22.

That is right! What is the concept for this scripture?
The law of seedtime and harvest will remain forever.

Very good!

END OF SEED 471   Sowing and Reaping

REVIEW SEED UNTIL MASTERED

7 W F **S** F

Seed 471 Further Information – Sowing and Reaping

The 4th Seed in the 7th Pod of the 1st Year

Man's fall brought on the curse *(Genesis 3:17)* But the offering of Christ to God through the Cross redeems us from the curse bringing in blessings as we trust in God. God promised through Noah that as long as the earth existed that the Law of Seedtime *(Sowing)* and Harvest *(Reaping)* would be in effect *(Genesis 8:22)*. This law, affecting both the natural and spiritual realms, allows us to understand how to "Plant Seed" {God's Word) and be able to Reap the Harvest *(Blessings)* by the application of the Sowing and Reaping Principle. God's ultimate plan and purpose is, in submission to Him that we *(believers)* would increase in Christ. The ultimate goal is that the Kingdom of God would be established on the earth, and that progressively Christ would-be ALL-in ALL *(Daniel 2:35, 44, 45; Ephesians 1:23)*.

God's Word is Seed. In addition, all of our beliefs, thoughts, words and actions are seeds. As seeds are sown *(planted)* in our own heart, in the world, or in the lives of other people they produce a corresponding return in the way of either godly or ungodly fruit. All of God's blessings, in this Age of Grace, are freely given and are never earned. There is a spiritual path to walk which is the place where God's move and blessings come into our experience. This path includes what the Scripture refers to as "Abiding in the Vine" and "Walking after the Spirit". Consistently operating in those 2 godly practices will empower each of us believers to continually sow godly seeds and will always produce the return of an Abundant Life. However, if we walk after the flesh *(our own fallen human ability)*, we will sow ungodly seeds which will produce many kinds of death and its fruits: fear, worry, depression, sickness, etc. and all kinds of destruction will enter into our lives and the lives of those whom we love.

As Born Again Believers our regenerated human spirit has been made one with and also is indwelt by the Holy Spirit *(1 Corinthians 6:17)*. The Holy Spirit as the Source with our human spirit as the vessel is the means of inheriting all the promised blessings of the Scripture. As believers, we need to understand that all sin and corruption is related to the flesh *(not referring here to the physical flesh)*, indicating that the flesh itself is corrupt. Eternal Life is of the Spirit and is the Life of Jesus Christ

Himself. The flesh is the uttermost expression of fallen man; the Spirit is the Reality of Christ as our life.

We need to *(and always should) Walk after the Spirit. The successful Christian Life is a matter of dying to the ways of the flesh and walking according to the Spirit. The flesh is the expression of the Old Man Adam. Everything the flesh does results in "dead works" which means it is absent of any "zoe" God Life and consequently has NO value in God's sight. The Law of the Old Testament, having only a shadow of the Good Things to come was intended for and is related to our flesh (Hebrews 7:16; 10:1; Galatians 4:3-5)*, and was given to be a temporary regulator and exposer of the flesh of the unbeliever, until the Reality *(Jesus Christ)* was received by faith. The Spirit is related to Grace. Consequently, when we walk by the Spirit, we are no longer under The Law *(Galatians 5:18)*, and as a result, we gain dominion over sin *(Romans 6:14)*. The Spirit, when yielded to, always brings forth the Fruit of the Spirit *(Galatians 5:22, 23)* which results in Grace reigning through Righteousness unto Eternal Life, now and forever *(Romans 5:21)*.

7 W F S **F**

Seed 571 – Faith Additives

(In fellowship Seed 571 is referred to as the 5th Seed in the 7th Pod of the First Year)

Simple format

V. The Fifth Seed in the Seventh Pod is **FAITH ADDITIVES** *(acronym: ViKings PiG Blue).*

1. The First Faith Additive is **VIRTUE**.
   The concept of Virtue is **THE MORAL GOODNESS OF GOD**.

2. 2, The Second Faith Additive is **KNOWLEDGE**.
   The concept of Knowledge is **INTIMACY WITH GOD THROUGH INCREASED UNDERSTANDING AND WISDOM"**.

3. The Third Faith Additive is **SELF CONTROL**.
   The concept of Self Control is **BALANCED LIVING BY THE SPIRIT**.

4. The Fourth Faith Additive is **PERSEVERANCE**.
   The concept of Perseverance is **"PATIENT ENDURANCE AND PERSISTENCE"**.

5. The Fifth Faith Additive is **GODLINESS**.
   The concept of Godliness is **INFUSED HOLY LIVING BY THE SPIRIT**.

6. The Sixth Faith Additive is **BROTHERLY KINDNESS**.
   The concept of Brotherly Kindness is **PHILIA LOVE UPLIFTED BY THE SPIRIT**.

7. The Seventh Faith Additive is **LOVE**.
   The concept of Love is **GOD'S UNCONDITIONAL AGAPE LOVE**.

   A. The First Scripture for-Faith Additives is **2 PETER 1:5-7**.
      1. The concept is THE **7 THINGS WE NEED TO ADD TO OUR FAITH: VIRTUE. KNOWLEDGE, SELF-CONTROL, PERSEVERANCE, GODLINESS, BROTHERLY KINDNESS, AND LOVE.**

   B. The Second Scripture is **JOHN 3:27**.
      1. The concept is **A MAN CAN RECEIVE NOTHING UNLESS IT HAS**

7WFS F

**BEEN GIVEN TO HIM FROM HEAVEN.
FAITH ADDITIVES?**

C. The Third Scripture is **JOHN 3:30.** Yes, very good!
   1. The concept **is I MUST DECREASE, AND HE MUST INCREASE.**

7 W F S **F**

Sample Fellowship Format

Disciple's reply is in **bold type**

What is the Fifth Seed in the Seventh Pod?
Faith Additives.

Correct! What is the 1st Faith Additive and its concept?
Virtue. Virtue is the moral goodness of God that resides in me by the Spirit.

That is right. What is the 2nd Faith Additive and its concept?
Knowledge. Knowledge is the intimacy I gain with God through wisdom and understanding,

Very good! What is the 3rd Faith Additive and its concept?
Self-control. Self-Control is the balanced life I live by the spirit.

Right. What is the 4th Faith Additive and its concept?
Perseverance. Perseverance is the patient endurance and persistence I practice by the Spirit.

That's correct. What is the 5th Faith Additive and its concept?
Godliness. Godliness is an infused holy living through the spirit.

Okay. What is the 6th Faith Additive and its concept?
Brotherly Kindness. Brotherly Kindness is my natural philia love which is uplifted and refined by the Spirit.

Very Good! What is the 7th Faith Additive and its concept?
Love. Love refers to the unconditional love *(agape)* of God Which I freely receive from Christ and pay forward by the spirit.
Excellent!

What is the First Scripture for Faith Additives?
2 Peter 1:5-7

What is the concept of 1 Peter 1:5-7?
I add to my faith: virtue, knowledge, self-control, perseverance, godliness, brotherly kindness, and love

7 W F S **F**

That is right. What is the Second Scripture for this seed?
JOHN 3:27.

Yes. What is the concept of John 3:27?
I CAN RECEIVE NOTHING UNLESS IT IS GIVEN TO ME FROM HEAVEN.

What is the Third Scripture for Faith Additives?
John 3:30.

What is the concept?
He must increase, I must decrease".

END OF SEED 571 Faith Additives

REVIEW SEED UNTIL MASTERED

7 W F S F

Seed 571 Further Information – Faith Additives

The 5th Seed in the 7th Pod of the 1st Year

The Apostle Peter, in his first letter to the Church, told the believers that Jesus had redeemed them from their old ways and that they should now rest fully upon the Grace of God that would come to be experienced by them in proportion to their revelation of Jesus Christ *(1 Peter 1:13,18,19)*. Additionally, Peter explained to the saints that they should abstain from fleshly lusts *(that warred against their souls)*, and should no longer live according to the flesh *(1 Peter 2:11; .4:2)*. In Peter's second epistle to the Church, he reveals to his readers the Source of the Power and Strength that would enable them to escape the corruption of lust. That Source comes through taking part in God's Divine Nature through an intimate knowing of Him who called us *(the Father)*. Through this Divine Knowledge, He *(Christ)* has already provided us everything we need for Life and Godliness *(2 Peter 1:3, 4)*.

God's precious and wonderful blessings have already been bequeathed to the believer but are actually experienced through inheritance. Therefore, it is necessary to diligently cooperate with the Holy Spirit in order to fully participate in the promised practical benefits of God's Divine Promise. To this end, Peter goes on in his second epistle to list a ladder of attributes that each believer is called to experientially add to his faith. As each believer takes hold of his promised inheritance, he will be able to confidently abound in the Graces of God that are freely bestowed on Him.

The 7 Additives to Faith are as follows:

I. **Virtue** - Virtue is the excellency of God's goodness which flows by the Power of the Divine Life, which will result in a passionate and moral living which will bring the believer enjoyment and growth *(Philippians 4:8)*.

2. **Knowledge** - Knowledge is closely related with wisdom and understanding. Increased experiential knowledge of Christ will always result in a closer intimacy with the Lord *(Philippians 1:9)*.

3. **Self-Control** - The source of genuine Self Control is not self, but rather is the Leading and Power of the Spirit of God in us. As we yield to the

Spirit, a perfectly balanced life is the result. The fruit of such a life, on one side of the scale, is great confidence, surety, and peace. On the other side of the scale is a Stronghold of Christ like humility with a clear revelation of how completely blind and naked we are apart from our identification and oneness with Him *(I Timothy 3:2)*.

4. **Perseverance** - Perseverance is "Patient Endurance and Persistence" which includes a "never give up" attitude, not only regarding our own walk with Christ, but also expressed through a genuine love toward all people.

5. **Godliness** - Godliness is the believer's development in taking the very nature and character of God. This development is expressed through the Life of Christ being released from the inmost part of the believer *(his spirit)*.

6. **Brotherly Kindness** - Brotherly Kindness is a human feeling or affection that is bathed in the power of the Spirit of God, and that has been up-lifted by God's Unconditional Love. *(1 Peter 3:8, 9)*.

7. **Love** - Love here is the "Agape" Love of God Whose Source and Substance is always God Himself. As His elect, by the power of the Holy Spirit, believers are able to progressively understand, receive, contain, and express such a Love. This Love always wants the best for others and consistently displays it in both attitude and actions *(1 John 4:6-11)*.

7 W F S F

Overview of the Seventh Pod

I. 7 Baptisms of the New Testament *(RBD SWFM)*

1. Baptism of *(into)* Repentance *(from dead works)*
   a. I am immersed in the truth that there is nothing I can do to earn righteousness.
2. Baptism of *(into)* the Body *(of Christ)*
   a. Joined to Church, Received INFILLING for LIFE and GROWTH.
3. Baptism of *(into)* Death *(of Christ)*
   a. Died with Christ and was raised up with Him *(born again)*.
4. Baptism of *(into)* the Holy Spirit
   a. An OUTPOURING of the Holy Spirit for POWER and WITNESS *(Spirit comes ON the believer)*
5. Baptism of *(into)* Water
   a. An acting out in the physical realm *(as an after type)* the Death and Resurrection that already took place at new birth *(at the time of the 3rd baptism)*
6. Baptism of *(into)* Fire
   a. The cleansing of the Word *(of our soul)* that takes place *(by Christ in us)* as we fellowship speaking God's Word to one another.
7. Baptism of *(into)* Moses
   a. Being born into the world under the Law.
   b. *(Or it could be)* An ability to be sensitive to a current movement or activity of God.

   A. Matthew 3:11
   2. The One who comes after me will baptize you with the Spirit and with fire.

   B. Romans 6:3
   1. If you have been baptized into *(the Body of)* Christ, you have been baptized into His death.

   C. Acts 19:1-6
   1. Explains John's Baptism of Repentance *(related primarily to trusting in Jesus)* and Water Baptism *(here in the name of Jesus)*.

7 W F S F

II. Witnessing

1. HP + CP + CC = MI
2. HP stands for "High Potency" which refers to practicing a strong walk with the Lord.
3. CP stands for "Close Proximity" which refers to developing relationship *(getting to know)* with another person before witnessing to him about Christ.
4. CC stands for "Clear Communication" which refers to speaking the truths of the Gospel in a simple, clear way and using illustrations, allegories, or parables when doing so.
5. MI stands for "Maximum Impact" which means the witnessing will result in a successful outcome.

   A. Acts 10:34-43 *(IF PRAD JR)*
   1. God is IMPARTIAL
   2. FAITH produces works by righteousness
   3. Christ preached peace and is our PEACE
   4. REPENTANCE from dead works *(John's Baptism)*
   5. Christ is the ANOINTED one and He anoints me.
   6. The DEATH and resurrection of Jesus
   7. Jesus is the JUDGE of the living and the dead
   8. Those who believe receive REMISSION of sins.

III. Foundational Ministries *(PM TEL GM)*

1. PROPHECY is speaking God's Word in season with accuracy and clarity.
2. MINISTRY is unselfishly serving others by the Spirit.
3. TEACHING is helping others uncover the truth.
4. EXHORTATION is encouraging others by the Spirit.
5. LEADING is setting the example for others by the Spirit.
6. GIVING generously blessing others by the Spirit.
7. MERCY is empathetically comforting others by the Spirit.

   A. Romans 12:6-8
   1. The concept is the 7 foundational ministries outlined above.

7 W F S F

IV. Sowing and Reaping

1. If a man sows to the flesh, he will reap death and curses, but I sow to the Spirit and I reap Life and Blessings.

    A. Genesis 8:22
    1. God has established forever the Law of Seedtime and Harvest.

    B. Galatians 6:7, 8
    1. God is not mocked. Whatever a man sows, that he will also reap.

V. Faith Additives *(VKS PG BL)*

1. VIRTUE is the moral goodness of God.
2. KNOWLEDGE is gaining intimacy with God through wisdom and understanding.
3. SELF CONTROL is balanced living by the power of the Spirit.
4. PERSEVERANCE is patient endurance and persistence *(PEP)*.
5. GODLINESS is infused holy living by the Spirit.
6. BROTHERLY KINDNESS is Philia love uplifted by the Spirit.
7. LOVE is the unconditional love of God.

    A. 2 Peter 1:5-7
    1. The 7 Faith Additives as outlined above.

    B. John 3:27
    1. A man has nothing except it be given to him from heaven.

    C. John 3:30
    1. I must decrease, Christ must increase.

7 W F S F

Epilogue for Chapter Seven

Now that you have mastered the first 30 seeds, your heart is well on its way to being wholly established in the Truth that *(as a believer in Jesus Christ)* you are always forgiven and righteous in God's sight. As you continue to line up your "point of view" with God's, the Fruit of Righteousness will flow from you more easily and spontaneously... "For as a man thinks in his heart, so he is" *(Proverbs 23:7)*.

Always keep in mind that your standing with God is not based on how good your behavior is, but rather is predicated on God's love, goodness, and generous giving of His righteousness as a gift to you. As you believe in your heart, and learn to yield to this Truth, you will find that you are more holy "by accident" than you could ever be through striving by your flesh *(your own ability)*. A mature man of God once said, "The life of the mature Christian is as easy as lying down in a boat and letting it carry you down the stream". Jesus is that boat.

GALATIANS PHASE

Galatians Phase

Chapter One

The First Pod – Acronym: DNRP *(DiNneR·Plate)*

SUBJECT OF GALATIANS
CHRIST REPLACES THE LAW AND CHRIST IN ME REPLACES RELIGION AND TRADITION.

PRINCIPLE for Chapter One
GOD'S SON VERSUS MAN'S RELIGION.

I. The First Seed *(11G)* in the First Pod of the Galatians Phase is **D**IFFERENT GOSPEL *(vs.9-11)*.
The concept is **I DO NOT RECEIVE OR PREACH A DIFFERENT GOSPEL THAN THE ONE I RECEIVED** *(as Jesus gave it to Paul)*.

II. The Second Seed *(21G)* is **N**OT OF MAN *(v. 12)*.
The concept is Paul writing that **I DID NOT RECEIVE THE GOSPEL FROM MAN BUT BY THE DIRECT REVELATION OF JESUS CHRIST.**

III. The Third Seed *(31G)* is **R**EVEALED IN ME *(v. 16)*.
The concept is **THE SON IS REVEALED IN ME FROM THE INSIDE-OUT.**

IV. The Fourth Seed *(41G)* is **P**REACHED THE FAITH *(v.23)*.
The concept is **PAUL WAS PREACHING THE FAITH THAT HE HAD ONCE TRIED TO DESTROY.**

   A. NO SPECIALS in POD 1

Note: A Special is a scripture that is also already used in another seed in a different Phase other than the Galatians Phase. All six chapters/pods in the Galatians Phase has specials except for Chapter/Pod 1.

SRNM/CF

Chapter Two

The Second Pod – Acronym: SRNM *(SiR NaMe)*

PRINCIPLE for Chapter Two
GOD'S SON VERSUS MAN'S RELIGION *(same as Chapter One)*

I. The 1ˢᵗ Seed *(12G)* of the Second Pod is **S**PY OUT LIBERTY *(v.4)*.
   The concept is **FALSE BROTHERS CAME IN BY STEALTH TO ATTEMPT TO SPY OUT** *(steal)* **OUR LIBERTY IN CHRIST** *(by teaching religion instead of Christ)*.

II. The 2ⁿᵈ Seed *(22G)* is **R**IGHT HAND OF FELLOWSHIP *(v.9)*.
    The concept is **PAUL AND BARNABAS RECEIVED THE RIGHT HAND OF FELLOWSHIP FROM JAMES, CEPHAS, AND JOHN WHO SEEMED TO BE PILLARS** *(leaders of the Church in Jerusalem)*.

III. The 3ʳᵈ Seed *(32G)* is **N**OT UPRIGHT *(v. 14)*.
     The concept is **PAUL DESCRIBING PETER'S BEHAVIOR REGARDING PETER NOT BEING WILLING TO EAT WITH THE GENTILES ONCE CERTAIN JEWISH BROTHERS HAD ARRIVED IN GALATIA..**

   The 4ᵗʰ Seed *(42G)* is **M**INISTER OF SIN *(v. 17)*.
IV. The concept is **IF A BELIEVER SINS AFTER COMING TO CHRIST THAT DOES NOT MAKE CHRIST A MINISTER OF SIN.**

SRNM/C F

SPECIALS for Chapter 2   Acronym: CF *(ConFess)*

Note: A Special is a scripture that is also used in another seed in a Phase other than the Galatians Phase.

A. The 1st special is **GALATIANS 2:20.**

   The name of the Seed is **Crucified with Christ**.

   > The concept is **I HAVE BEEN CRUCIFIED WITH CHRIST AND I NO LONGER LIVE; THE LIFE I LIVE, I LIVE BY FAITH IN THE SON OF GOD, WHO LOVED ME AND GAVE HIMSELF FOR ME.**

B. The 2nd special is **GALATIANS 2:21**

   The name of the seed is **Frustrate Grace**.

   > The concept is **I DO NOT FRUSTRATE THE GRACE OF GOD, FOR IF RIGHTEOUSNESS IS BY THE LAW THEN CHRIST DIED IN VAIN.**

P S L C / BRF IFLC.A GAA

Chapter Three
The Third Pod – Acronym: PSLC *(PS LoCk)*
Acronym for Specials: BRF/IFLC.A/GAA *(BRieF/IFLac.Aye/GAA)*

PRINCIPLE for Chapter Three
CHRIST VERSUS THE LAW

I. The First Seed *(13G)* is **P**ROMISED BEFOREHAND *(vs. 8, 9)*.
The concept is **THE GOSPEL WAS GIVEN TO ABRAHAM BEFORE THE LAW WAS GIVEN TO MOSES; PROMISING ABRAHAM THAT HIM** *(his Seed)* **ALL NATIONS** *(people)* **WOULD BE BLESSED.**

II. The Second Seed *(23G)* is **S**EED IS CHRIST *(vs. 16, 17)*.
The concept is **THE PROMISE OF GOD WAS NOT TO ABRAHAM'S SEEDS, AS OF MANY, BUT TO ABRAHAM'S SEED WHO IS CHRIST.**

III. The Third Seed *(33G)* is **L**AW WAS ADDED UNTIL THE SEED SHOULD COME *(v. 19)*.
The concept is **THE LAW WAS ADDED TO REGULATE THE BELIEVER UNTIL CHRIST JESUS CAME.**

IV. The Fourth Seed *(43G)* is **C**ONFINED ALL *(v.22)*.
The concept is **THE LAW CONFINED EVERY PERSON UNDER SIN** *(proving everyone to needs the Savior Jesus Christ)*.

PSLC/ BRF IFL C.A GAA

SPECIALS for Chapter 3 Acronyms: BRF
(BRieFcase) / IFLC.A (IF LaCk.Aye) / GAA

A. The First Special is **GALATIANS 3:1-3** *(BRF)*.

   1. The First Seed is **B**EWITCHED YOU.
      The concept is **WHO BEWITCHED YOU BEFORE WHOM CHRIST WAS CLEARLY PORTRAYED TO YOU AS THE WAY OF SALVATION** *(through faith in His crucifixion and resurrection)*?

   2. The Second Seed is **R**ECEIVED SPIRIT.
      The concept is **DID YOU RECEIVE THE SPIRIT BY THE HEARING OF FAITH OR BY THE WORKS OF THE LAW?**

   3. The Third Seed is **F**OOLISH.
      The concept is ARE **YOU SO FOOLISH HAVING BEGUN IN THE SPIRIT THAT YOU ARE NOW TRYING TO BE MADE PERFECT BY YOUR FLESH?**

B. The Second Special is **GALATIANS 3:10-14** *(IFLC)*.

   1. The First Seed is **I**F UNDER THE LAW.
      The concept is **IF I PUT MYSELF BACK UNDER THE LAW I AM UNDER A CURSE.**

   2. The Second Seed is **F**AITH JUSTIFICATION.
      The concept is **THAT NO ONE IS JUSTIFIED BY THE LAW IN THE SIGHT OF GOD IS EVIDENT, FOR THE JUST SHALL LIVE BY FAITH.**

   3. The Third Seed is **L**AW NOT OF FAITH.
      The concept is **MY RIGHTEOUSNESS IS ONLY BY FAITH, THE LAW CAN NOT ADD ANYTHING TO MY RIGHTEOUSNESS.**

4. The Fourth Seed is **C**HRIST REDEEMED.
   The concept is **CHRIST HAS REDEEMED ME FROM THE CURSE OF THE LAW.**

5. The Fifth Seed is **A**BRAHAM'S BLESSINGS.
   The concept is **I WAS REDEEMED AND AM RECEIVING THE BLESSINGS OF ABRAHAM.**

C. The Third Special is **GALATIANS 3:24, 25, 28** *(GAA)*.

   1. The First Seed is **G**UARDIAN.
      The concept is **THE LAW WAS MY GUARDIAN TO BRING ME TO CHRIST THAT I MIGHT BE JUSTIFIED BY FAITH.**

   2. The Second Seed is **A**FTER FAITH.
      The concept is **AFTER FAITH** *(in Christ)* **HAS COME I AM NO LONGER UNDER A GUARDIAN** *(The Law)*.

   3. The Third Seed is **A**LL ONE.
      The concept is **WE ARE ALL ONE IN CHRIST.**

HFSS. B E. Z L / T B C C

Chapter Four *(Specials Only)*
Note: A Special is a scripture that is also used in another seed in a Phase other than the Galatians Phase.

The Fourth Pod – Acronyms: HFSS.BE.ZL *(HalFSS.BE.ZeaLous)* TBCC *(To-BaCCo)*

PRINCIPLE for Chapter Four *(Two Specials)*
YIELDING TO THE SPIRIT BY FAITH VERSUS YIELDING TO THE FLESH BY THE WORKS OF THE LAW

A. The First Special is **GALATIANS 4:1-20** *(HalFS BE ZeaLous)*

1. The First Seed is **H**EIR UNDER GUARDIAN *(vs. 1-3)*.
   The concept is **AS LONG AS THE HEIR IS A CHILD** *(under the law)* **HE IS NO DIFFERENT THAN A SLAVE. THE HEIR IS UNDER GUARDIANS UNTIL THE TIME** *(of maturity)* **APPOINTED BY THE FATHER.**

2. The Second Seed is **F**ULLNESS OF TIMES *(v. 4)*.
   The concept is **WHEN THE FULLNESS OF TIME HAD COME GOD SENT HIS SON TO REDEEM ME FROM THE LAW.**

3. The Third Seed is **S**ON, NOT SLAVE *(v. 7)*.
   The concept is **I AM NO LONGER A SLAVE, BUT A SON, AND AN HEIR WITH CHRIST.**

4. The Fourth Seed is **S**PIRIT CRIES OUT.
   The concept is **THE SPIRIT IN ME CRIES OUT ABBA FATHER.**

HFSS. BE. ZL / TBCC

HalFSS.**BE.ZeaLous**) TBCC *(ToBaCCo)*

5. The Fifth Seed is **BEGGARLY ELEMENTS** *(v.9)*.
   The concept is **NOW THAT I BELONG TO GOD WHY WOULD I TURN AGAIN TO THOSE BEGGARLY ELEMENTS** *(the keeping of The Law for the gaining of righteousness)*.

6. The Sixth Seed is **ENEMY BECAUSE** *(v. 16)*.
   The concept is **HAVE I** *(Paul inspired by Spirit)* **BECOME YOUR ENEMY BECAUSE I TELL YOU THE TRUTH?**

7. The Seventh Seed is **ZEALOUS FOR THEM** *(v. 17)*.
   The concept is **THEY** *(the legalists)* **ZEALOUSLY COURT YOU THAT YOU MAY BE ZEALOUS FOR THEM** *(who depend on law keeping for righteousness)*.

8. The Eighth Seed is **LABOR IN CHILDBIRTH** *(v. 19)*.
   The concept is **I** *(Paul inspired by Spirit)* **LABOR IN CHILDBIRTH UNTIL CHRIST IS FORMED IN YOU.**

HFSS. BE.ZL / TBCC

HalFSS.BE.ZeaLous) **TBCC** *(ToBaCCo)*

B. The Second Special is GALATIANS 4:21-31 *(TBCC)*

The First Seed is **T**WO COVENANTS *(vs. 11-26)*.
The concept is **HAGAR** *(A TYPE OF THE OLD COVENANT)* **BORE ISHMAEL** *(A TYPE OF THE FLESH)* **WHICH HAGAR CORRESPONDS WITH MOUNT SINAI** *(SYMBOL OF THE LAW)* **WHICH RESULTS IN BONDAGE. SARAH** *(A TYPE OF THE NEW COVENANT)* **BORE ISAAC** *(A TYPE OF THE SPIRIT AND PROMISE)* **WHICH CORRESPONDS WITH MOUNT ZION** *(A SYMBOL OF THE CHURCH)* **WHICH RESULTS IN LIBERTY** *(FREEDOM)*

1. The Second Seed is **B**ARREN WOMAN *(v. 27)*
   The concept is **REJOICE O BARREN WOMAN, YOU WHO BARE NOT** *(SYMBOLIZES THE NEW COVENANT BELIEVER WHOSE ACTIONS ARE THE FRUIT OF THE SPIRIT, NOT THE WORKS OF THE FLESH)*. **BREAK FORTH AND SHOUT YOU WHO ARE NOT IN LABOR! FOR THE DESOLATE** *(HAGAR, OLD COVENANT)* **HAS MANY MORE CHILDREN THAN SHE** *(SARAH, NEW COVENANT)* **WHO HAS A HUSBAND** *(CHRIST TO WHOM THE BELIEVER IS BETROTHED)*.

2. The Third Seed is **C**URRENTLY THE SAME *(v.29)*.
   The concept is **EVEN AS HE WHO IS OF THE FLESH** *(ISHMAEL)* **PERSECUTED HIM WHO WAS BORN ACCORDING TO THE HOLY SPIRIT** *(ISAAC)*, **SO IT IS CURRENTLY** *(HE OR THAT WHICH IS OF THE FLESH/LAW PERSECUTES HE OR THAT WHICH IS OF THE SPIRIT/PROMISE)*.

3. The Fourth Seed is **C**AST OUT *(v. 30)*.
   The concept is **CAST OUT THE BONDWOMAN** *(LAW)* **AND HER SON** *(FLESH)* **FOR SUCH SHALL NOT BE AN HEIR WITH THE SON** *(PROMISE/GRACE)* **OF THE FREEWOMAN** *(NEW COVENANT)*.

S F C I / F HPLL.OL W.FB

Chapter Five
The Fifth Pod – Acronym: SFCI *(SaFe.CI)*
Acronym for Specials: F HPLL.OL W.FB *(Fine HePLLO.L With FullBack)*

PRINCIPLE for Chapter Five *(acronym: ESIS)*
No Longer **E**ntangled by the Yoke of The Law
No Longer **I**ndulging in the Flesh
No Longer **S**eparated from Christ
But **S**erving in Love by the Spirit

I. The First Seed *(1SG)* is **S**TAND FAST *(vs. 1-3)*
   The concept is **STAND FAST IN THE LIBERTY BY WHICH CHRIST HAS MADE YOU FREE.**

II. The Second Seed *(2SG)* is **F**AITH WORKS *(v. 6)*.
   The concept is **FAITH WORKS THROUGH LOVE.**

III. The Third Seed *(3SG)* is **C**UT OFF.
   The concept is **I WISH THAT THOSE WHO TROUBLE YOU WOULD CUT THEMSELVES OFF.**

IV. The Fourth Seed *(4SG)* is **I**F LED *(V. 18)*.
   The concept is **IF YOU ARE LED BY THE SPIRIT, YOU ARE NOT UNDER THE LAW.**

FINE HePLLO.L WITH

Fine HePLLO.L With

A. The First Special is **GALATIANS 5:4**.

   1. The Seed is **FALLEN FROM GRACE**.
      The concept is **YOU HAVE BECOME SEPARATED FROM CHRIST, YOU WHO ATTEMPT TO BE JUSTIFIED BY THE LAW, YOU HAVE FALLEN FROM GRACE**

B. The Second Special is **GALATIANS 5:7-9**.

   1. The First Seed is **HINDERED YOU**.
      The concept is **YOU RAN WELL! WHO HINDERED YOU FROM OBEYING THE TRUTH?**

   2. The Second Seed is **PERSUASION DOES NOT**.
      The concept is **THIS PERSUASION DOES NOT COME FROM THE ONE WHO CALLED YOU**.

   3. **The Third Seed** is a **LITTLE LEAVEN**.
      The concept is **A LITTLE LEAVEN LEAVENS THE WHOLE LUMP**.

C. The Third Special is **GALATIANS 5:11**.

   1. The Seed is **OFFENSE OF THE CROSS**.
      The concept is **THOSE WHO ARE OFFENDED BY THE TRUE GOSPEL OF GRACE ARE OFFENDED BY THE CROSS**.

D. The Fourth Special is **GALATIANS 5:13**.

   1. The Seed is **CALLED TO LIBERTY**.
      The concept is **I HAVE BEEN CALLED TO LIBERTY, BUT I DO NOT USE MY LIBERTY AS AN OCCASION TO SIN**.

E. The Fifth Special is **GALATIANS 5:16**.

   1. The Seed is **WALK AFTER THE SPIRIT**.
      The concept is **I WALK AFTER THE SPIRIT AND AS A RESULT DO NOT FULFILL THE LUST OF THE FLESH**.

S F C I / F HPLL.OL W. F B

a FullBack

F. The Sixth Special is **GALATIANS 5:22, 23.**

  1. The Seed is **FRUIT OF THE SPIRIT**. *(Long John's PLanK Grows FiGS)*
  The concept is **THE FRUIT OF THE SPIRIT IS LOVE, JOY, PEACE, LONGSUFFERING *(PATIENCE)*, KINDNESS, GOODNESS, FAITHFULNESS, GENTLENESS, AND SELF CONTROL *(TEMPERANCE)*.**

G. The Seventh Special is **GALATIANS 5:24, 25.**

  2. The Seed is **BELONG TO CHRIST.**
  The concept is **I BELONG TO CHRIST AND HAVE CRUCIFIED THE MY WITH ITS PASSIONS AND DESIRES** *(Spirit scripture)*.

BGGG OSN

Chapter Six
The Sixth Pod – Acronym: **BGGG** *(The B-Geesl)*
Acronym for Specials: **OSN** *(O'SoN)*

PRINCIPLE for Chapter Six
Crucified and Living as a New Creation

I. The First Seed is **B**EAR BURDENS *(vs. 2, 5)*.
   The concept is **I BEAR OTHER'S BURDENS AND I BEAR MY OWN BURDENS.**

II. The Second Seed is **G**ROW WEARY *(7. 9)*.
   The concept is **I DON'T GROW WEARY OF DOING GOOD. AS I HAVE OPPORTUNITY, I AM GOOD TO ALL, ESPECIALLY TO THOSE OF THE HOUSEHOLD OF GOD**

III. The Third Seed is **G**OOD SHOWING *(v.12)*.
   The concept is **THOSE WHO WANT TO MAKE A GOOD SHOWING IN THE FLESH TRY TO COMPEL ME TO "KEEP THE LAW" THAT THEY WILL NOT HAVE TO SUFFER PERSECUTION FOR THE CROSS OF CHRIST.**

IV. The Fourth Seed is **G**OD FORBID *(v. 14)*
   The concept is **GOD FORBID THAT I SHOULD BOAST EXCEPT IN OUR LORD JESUS CHRIST, BY WHOM I HAVE BEEN CRUCIFIED TO THE WORLD AND THE WORLD HAS BEEN CRUCIFIED TO ME.**

(O'SoN)

A. The First Special is **GALATIANS 6:1.**
   1. The seed is **OVERTAKEN.**

      The concept is **IF ANYONE IS OVERTAKEN IN A FAULT, YOU WHO ARE SPRITUAL RESTORE SUCH A ONE WITH A SPIRIT OF MEEKNESS.**

B. The Second Special is **GALATIANS 6:7, 8.**
   1. The Seed is **SOWING AND REAPING.**

      The concept is **GOD IS NOT MOCKED, I REAP WHAT I SOW** *(soul scripture)*.

C. The Third Special is **GALATIANS 6:15.**
   1. The Seed is **NEW CREATION.**

      The concept is **NOTHING MATTERS EXCEPT NEW CREATION** *(a high truth)*.

Most Effective Discipleship Seeds *(MEDS)*

APPENDIXES

for Book One

#1 Invitation Letter

#2. Most Effective Discipleship Seeds *(MEDS)* Synopsis

#3. Overview of Phase I *(Core Curriculum – for First 3 Years - 100 Seeds)*

#4. MEDS - 5 Years/Levels/Books Curriculums

#5. Little Child to Young Man Year/Level/Book One Seed Names

#6. Young Man to Father Year/Level/Book Two Seed Names

#7. Father to Mastercraftsman Year/Level/Book Three Seed Names

#8. Mastercraftsman to Masterbuilder Year/Level/Book Four Seed Names

#9. Masterbuilder to Advanced Masterbuilder Year/Level/Book Five Seed Names

#10. Consecration Plan Worksheet

#11. MEDS - Things We Say

#12. Essential Elements of MEDS: Philosophy, Structure, Process, and Results *(Phase IV)*

#13. Promotional Flyer

#14. Phase I, Year 1 Study Grid *(pegboard/map)*

#15. Galatians Grid *(pegboard/map)*

Appendix #1

Most Effective Discipleship Seeds *(MEDS)*
Invitation to Participate

Dear Brother/Sister in Christ,

May God's grace, peace, and love be multiplied to you and yours in the Name of our Lord Jesus Christ!

We invite you to participate in an outstanding and anointed Discipleship called. Most Effective Discipleship Seeds *(MEDS) (or the Seeds)*. MEDS is an informal, non-religious, Bible based and Christ centered Discipleship that has proven to be highly effective in assuring that each participant experiences a definite, solid, observable, and measurable growth in Spiritual Maturity in Christ.

MEDS is a curriculum of conceptual learning in which there is no condemnation, no pressure, no guilt trips, no unrealistic expectations, no tests, and no "lording over". Rather, you receive ongoing encouragement and the needed help for you to steadily and surely increase in intimacy with the Lord Jesus Christ. There may be no better way for you to redeem your time wisely than through this Discipleship. MEDS will benefit you for the rest of your natural life and throughout all of eternity; it will help you build up others in Christ as well.

A MEDS synopsis *(overview)* that explains more about this Discipleship is available to you. You can request it from the person who gave or sent you this invitation. It is our belief *(those who have participated in this Discipleship)* that MEDS is the simplest, yet most biblically sound and effective way to ensure a continual, well-rounded, efficient and practical growth in your walk with Christ.

Sincerely,

Current MEDS Servants

Appendix #2

Most Effective Discipleship Seeds *(MEDS)*
Synopsis

WHAT IS MEDS?

MEDS is a Discipleship of Jesus Christ with the central purpose and goal of edifying believers in the essential truths of God's Word through repetitive SPOKEN fellowship by which Bible Truths are learned in a priority order. This CHRIST CENTERED Discipleship has proven to be highly effective in assuring that each participant experiences a definite, organized, measurable, and enjoyable growth in spiritual maturity.

HOW DOES MEDS WORK?

MEDS is not the rote memorization of words or scriptures, but rather is a "CONCEPTUAL LEARNING" that takes place through spoken repetition of each important Bible Truth in, by, and through fellowship with another believer. Each Bible Truth passes through three stages of growth in the disciple:

GRAMMA KNOWLEDGE - The disciple can speak the "main idea" of the concept or scripture.

LOGOS UNDERSTANDING - the disciple has applied the concept to his own life and can explain the concept to another person in his own words.

RHEMA WISDOM - The disciple has become so filled and constituted with the Bible concept that it has been successfully and thoroughly assimilated into his life and living, and is producing much spiritual fruit.

As each believer learns the concepts of even a single seed, he is considered to be a servant-minister of MEDS qualified to teach to others the seeds he has learned as the Holy Spirit may lead him. So then the essence of this Discipleship is building up others through each servant-disciple speaking seed names, seed concepts, scripture locations, and scripture concepts repetitively until they are ROOTED, GROUNDED AND ESTABLISHED in the heart of each participating believer. There is likely no more valuable way to spend your time than through this unique Discipleship *(fellowship)*.

WHAT ARE THE RESULTS OF MEDS?

The remnant of current MEDS Disciples of Christ invariably testifies to:

A much greater UNDERSTANDING of God, His Word, and how to rightly divide it and understand it in its proper context.

A much closer RELATIONSHIP with Jesus Christ than ever before.

A much greater CONFIDENCE and effectiveness when ministering God's truths to others.

It is our belief *(current MEDS participants)* that MEDS is the simplest, yet most Biblically sound and effective way to ensure a continual, well-rounded, efficient and practical growth in maturity in your CHRIST LIFE.

Appendix #3
Overview of Most Effective Discipleship Seeds
(MEDS) Phase 1

These are the names of the 100 Root Curriculum Seeds *(Bible topics)* which represent an overview of the most important truths each believer should have rooted, grounded, and established in his heart to accomplish 3 years' worth of serious, solid and measurable Christian growth.

Year One of phase I. - 30 Seeds/ 50 Scripture Passages
(Seed Names)

POD 1
Faith-righteousness, Assurance, Clearance, Consecration

POD 2
Bible Reliability, Deity of Christ,
Spirit-Soul and Body, Rightly Dividing the Word

POD 3
3 Aspects of Salvation, Books of the New Testament,
2 or 3 Witnesses, Kenosis

POD 4
4 Laws / 4 Life's - SOSL, Pride vs Godly Humility,
Kingdom of God, 3 Aspects of Love, Kingdom Qualified

POD 5
5 Aspects of Obedience, Power of the Tongue,
Praise and Worship, Totally Equipped

POD 6
6 Elementary Principles of Christ, Doctrine of Christ,
Sense of Worthiness, Prayer

POD 7
7 Baptisms of the New Testament, Witnessing,
Foundational Ministries, Sowing and Reaping

Year two of phase I. - 30 Seeds / 75 Scripture passages
(Seed Names)

POD 1
Oneness and Unity, Loved Beyond Measure,
Promises of God, Forgiving Others

POD 2
2 Lines in the Bible, Faith And Works,
State of Astonishment, Christ and the Church

POD 3
3 Levels of Spiritual Growth, Entering the Rest,
Godhead, Grace-Glory-Hope and Life

POD 4
4 Kinds of Faith-4 Kinds of Unbelief, Righteousness Consciousness,
Divine Healing, Works of Patience

POD 5
5 Fold Ministry, Beatitudes,
Hot and Cold, Brotherly Kindness

POD 6
Fruit of the Spirit, Unforgivable Sin,
Fruit of Righteousness, Source of Pain, Corrective Discipline

POD 7
Armor of God, Defense of the Gospel, Pre-Adamite Theory,
Creationism Position, Eating Life

Year 3 of phase I. - 40 Seeds / 225 Scripture passages
(Seed Names)

POD 1
One Ministry, Anointing, Battle of Identity, Abba Intimacy, Great Faith

POD 2
Understanding God's Sovereignty, Progressive Faith and Unbelief, Comparing Two Loves, Waiting on God, Spiritual Maturity

POD 3
3 Aspects of Ministry, 3 Levels of Testimony,
Know-Reckon-Present and Reign, Biblical Deaths, Order of Melchizedek

POD 4
4 Aspects of the Flesh, At the Cross, Within the Veil,
Outside the Camp, Overcoming Degradation

POD 5
5 Much Mores, Wisdom from Above, Manifestations of Spirit,
Gifts-Ministries-Activities, Church Government

POD 6
Body Consciousness, Covet to Prophesy, One Bread Communion,
Two Tongues, Fasting

POD 7
House Divided, Calling on the Lord, Election and Free Will,
Division and Brokenness, Prayer Ministry

POD 8
Christ is All in All, Truth-Apostasy and Recovery,
God's Desire for Me, Name Above Every Name, Spiritual Liberty

Appendix 4
Most Effective Discipleship Seeds
Five *(5)* Books/Levels/Years
Overview

Seed 000 Shared Initiative and Shared Leadership *(SOSL) (A Floater/Implorer Seed)*. This Seed shared strategically when the servant-minister believes it is the best time as led by the Spirit. It is most commonly taught between the 1st and 2nd Pod of the First Year.

CONTENT OF BOOK ONE
88 Seeds /108 Scripture passages
Little Child to Young Man Level

Year One of phase I	30 Seeds/ 50 Scripture Passages
Galatians phase	58 Seeds/ 58 Scripture passages

CONTENT OF BOOK TWO
328 Seeds / 385 Scripture Passages
Young Man to Father Level

Year two of phase 1	30 Seeds / 75 Scripture passages.
Phase II God control of Body	12 Seeds/24 Scripture passages
John phase	155 seeds /155 Scripture passages
Romans phase	130 Seeds /130 Scripture passages

CONTENT OF BOOK 3
366 Seeds /576 Scripture passaged
Father to Master Craftsman Level

Year 3 of Phase I.	30 Seeds / 75 Scripture passages
Phase III – Christlikeness	16 Seeds / 40 Scripture passages
Ephesians Phase	64 Seeds / 64 Scripture passages
Hebrews Phase	145 Seeds / 145 Scripture passages
Philemon Phase	5 Seeds / 5 Scripture passages
James Phase	130 Seeds / 130 Scripture passages
1st, 2nd, and 3rd John Phase	52 Seeds / 52 Scripture passages

CONTENT OF BOOK FOUR
408 Seeds / 508 Scripture passages
Master Craftsman to Master Builder Level

Phase IV. Essential Elements of
Most Effective Discipleship

Seeds *(MEDS)*	18 Seeds / 33 Scripture passages
Acts Phase	164 Seeds / 164 Scripture passages
1 Corinthians Phase	140 Seeds / 164 Scripture passages
Philippians Phase	38 Seeds / 38 Scriptures passages
Colossians Phase	26 Seeds / 26 Scripture passages
1 Thessalonians Phase	17 Seeds / 17 Scripture passages
1 Timothy Phase	40 Seeds / 40 Scripture passages
1 Peter Phase	45 Seeds / 45 Scripture passages

CONTENT OF BOOK FIVE
953 Seeds / 1014 Scripture passages
Advanced Master Builder Level

Phase V. Healing	20 Seeds / 50 Scripture passages
2 Corinthians Phase	102 Seeds / 102 Scripture passages
2 Thessalonians Phase	11 Seeds / 11 Scripture passages
2 Timothy Phase	21 Seeds / 21 Scripture passages
Titus Phase	16 Seeds / 16 Scripture passages
2 Peter Phase	24 Seeds / 24 Scripture passages
Jude/Revelation Phase	284 Seeds / 284 Scripture passages
Genesis Phase *(blue)*	57 Seeds / 57 Scripture passages
Proverbs Phase *(blue)*	48 Seeds / 48 Scripture passages
Psalms Phase *(blue)*	100 Seeds / 100 Scripture passages
Synoptic Gospel Phase	300 Seeds / 300 Scripture passages

TOTAL FOR FIRST FIVE BOOKS
2235 Seeds / 2586 Scripture Passages

Appendix 5
MOST EFFECTIVE DISCIPLESHIP SEEDS
BOOK ONE *(Year One)*

88 seeds / 108 scripture passages
Little Child to Young Man Level

Content of Book 1 *(This Publication)*

BOOK ONE *(Year One)*
88 Seeds / 108 Scripture passages
* **Little Child to Young Man Level**

Year One of phase I 30 Seeds/ 50 Scripture Passages *(Seed Names)*

POD 1
Faith-righteousness, Assurance, Clearance, Consecration

POD 2
Bible Reliability, Deity of Christ,
Spirit-Soul and Body, Rightly Dividing the Word

POD 3
3 Aspects of Salvation, Books of the New Testament,
2 or 3 Witnesses, Kenosis

POD 4
4 Laws / 4 Life's - SOSL, Pride vs Godly Humility,
Kingdom of God, 3 Aspects of Love, Kingdom Qualified

POD 5
5 Aspects of Obedience, Power of the Tongue,
Praise and Worship, Totally Equipped

POD 6
6 Elementary Principles of Christ, Doctrine of Christ,
Sense of Worthiness, Prayer

POD 7
7 Baptisms of the New Testament, Witnessing,
Foundational Ministries, Sowing and Reaping

Galatians Phase 58 Seeds/ 58 Scripture passages
Subject of Galatians

CHAPTER AND POD 1 Principle
Different Gospel, Not of Man, Revealed in Me, Paul Preached

CHAPTER AND POD 2 Principle
Spied Out, Right Hand of Fellowship, Not Straightforward, Minister of Sin
Crucified With Christ, Frustrate

CHAPTER AND POD 3 Principle
Preached Beforehand, Seed is Christ, Law was Added, Confined All
Bewitched You, Receive, Foolish
If Under Law, Faith, Law Not of Faith, Christ Redeemed,
Abraham's Guardian, After Christ, All in All

CHAPTER AND POD 4 Principle
(all specials)
Heirs, Fullness of Time, Son-not Slave, Spirit Cries Out, Beggarly Elements, Enemy, Zealous for You, Labor in Pains Two Covenants, Barren Woman, Currently, Cast Out

CHAPTER AND POD 5 Principle
Stand Fast, Faith Works by Love, Cut Off, If Yield Fallen from Grace, Hindered, Persuasion, Little Leaven, Offense of the Cross, Liberty, If Walk, Fruit of the Spirit, Crucified Flesh

CHAPTER AND POD 6 Principle
Bears, Grow Weary, Good Showing, God Forbid Overtaken in Fault, Sowing and Reaping, New Creation

Appendix 6

BOOK TWO *(Year Two)*
328 seeds / 385 scripture passages
* Young Man to Father Level

Year Two of Phase 1 30 Seeds / 75 Scripture passages.

POD 1
Oneness and Unity, Loved Beyond Measure, Promises of God, Forgiving Others

POD 2
2 Lines in the Bible, Faith And Works, State of Astonishment, Christ and the Church

POD 3
3 Levels of Spiritual Growth, Entering the Rest, Godhead, Grace-Glory-Hope and Life

POD 4
4 Kinds of Faith-4 Kinds of Unbelief, Righteousness Consciousness, Divine Healing, Works of Patience

POD 5
5 Fold Ministry, Beatitudes, Hot and Cold, Brotherly Kindness

POD 6
Fruit of the Spirit, Unforgivable Sin, Fruit of Righteousness, Source of Pain, Corrective Discipline

POD 7
Armor of God, Defense of the Gospel, Pre-Adamite Theory, Creationism Position, Eating Life

Phase II God Control of Body 12 Seeds / 24 Scripture passages

POD 1
Standard is Holiness, Place is the Body, Enemy is Never, Goal is Purity

POD 2
Method is Sanctification, Choice is to Abstain Submission: Soul to Spirit, Submission: Body to Soul

POD 3
Means is Abiding, Sacrifice is Dying to Self-Freedom from Do To Be, Assurance of the Way

John Phase 155 seeds / 155 Scripture passages

CHAPTER AND POD 1 Principle
Came to Own, No One Has Seen, Preferred Before, Behold the Lamb, You are the Son

In the Beginning, Fullness Received

CHAPTER AND POD 2 Principle
Beginning of Signs, Zeal Consumed, Destroy This Temple, Commit

CHAPTER AND POD 3 Principle
Unless Born Again, Born of Spirit, How Can This Be, Ascended/As Moses, Is not Condemned, He Who Believes Man can Receive, Must Decrease

CHAPTER AND POD 4 Principle
Water Springing, I have Food, White for Harvest, Prophet No Honor, You Son Lives Worship in Spirit

CHAPTER AND POD 5 Principle
Do You Want?, Sees the Father, Dead Will Hear, Bear Witness, Honor that Comes
Myself, Search the Scriptures

CHAPTER AND POD 6 Principle
About Five Thousand, Because You Ate, True Bread, No One Can, Spirit Gives Life Bread of Life

CHAPTER AND POD 7 Principle
World Hates Me, If Anyone Will, Where I Am, Rivers of Living, No One Ever Judge With

CHAPTER AND POD 8 Principle
He Who is Without, I Judge No One, Die in Your Sin, If God, I Am Condemn You?, Light of the World

CHAPTER AND POD 9 Principle
Who Sinned, Anointed Eyes, Does Not Keep, Ask Him I Was Blind Say, "We See"

CHAPTER AND POD 10 Principle
By the Door, Hireling Flees, My Sheep Hear, I and My Father, Cannot Be Broken Thief Does Not, No One Takes

CHAPTER AND POD 11 Principle
Twelve. Hours, Die With Him, Wept-Jesus, Lifted Up Eyes, Expedition for Us, Resurrection and Life

CHAPTER AND POD 12 Principle
Anointed the Feet, Blessed is He, Gone After Him, Grain of Wheat, If I am Lifted, Blinded Eyes, Praise old Men, Follow Me, Judge the World

CHAPTER AND POD 13 Principle
He Who Receives, Disciple Jesus Loved, Satan Entered Him, New Commandment, Peter Said, Do You Know, Know My Disciple's

CHAPTER AND POD 14 Principle
Heart Be Troubled, Show Us the Father, Spirit of Truth, Our Home, Teach You All Way-Truth and Life, Greater Things

CHAPTER AND POD15 Principle
Takes Away, Abide in Me, Called You Friends, Servant Not Greater, When Helper, Nothing-Can Do, Greater Love, Were of World

CHAPTER AND POD 16 Principle
Have Not Known, Little While, Sorrow Turn, Speak Plainly, You May Have Peace, Convict the World, Ask the Father

CHAPTER AND POD 17 Principle
Your Name, I Pray for Them, World-Take Them Out, Sanctify Them, May Be One, Eternal Life

CHAPTER AND POD 18 Principle
I Am He, Cut Off, I Am Not He, Struck Jesus, For This Cause

CHAPTER AND POD 19a Principle
Pilate Scourged Him, Son of God, Unless From Above, Pace of Skull, Cast Lots

CHAPTER AND POD 19b
Behold Your Mother, It is Finished, Pierced His Side, Joseph of Arimathea, New Tomb

CHAPTER AND POD 20 Principle
Stone From Tomb, Folded Together, Not Yet Ascendend, Breathed on *(into)* Them, My Lord

CHAPTER AND POD 21 Principle
Showed Himself, Cast the Net, Third Time, What is That?

Romans Phase 130 Seeds / 130 Scripture passages
CHAPTER AND POD 1 Principle
Power of Resurrection, Not Ashamed, Unseen by Seen, Gave Over, Approved of Them Believing is Obedience

CHAPTER AND POD 2 Principle
Same Things, No Partially, Accusing and Excusing, God Blasphemed, Circumcision of Heart, Goodness of God

CHAPTER AND POD 3 Principle
Without Effect, Slanderous Report, None Righteous, Knowledge of Sin, Righteousness of God, All Have Sinned

CHAPTER AND POD 4 Principle
Abraham Believed, Heirs by Faith, Blessed Is, Call Things, Wavered Not

CHAPTER AND POD 5 Principle
(all specials)
Access by Faith, Glory in Tribulation, Justified by Blood, Reconciled by Death, Death by One, Death Reigned, Sin Abounded, Commended Love, Sin Entered, Grace Reigns

CHAPTER AND POD 6 Principle
Sin not Okay, Once for All, Slaves of Righteousness, Baptized in Christ, Walk in Newness, Crucified with Christ, Resurrection Power, Dominion Over, Freed from Sin, Reckon Myself, Present Members, Dominion Over, Wages of Sin

CHAPTER AND POD 7 Principle
Passion of Sin, Law is Holy, Sin in Me, Spiritual Laws, Dead to Law, Ability of Self, Nothing Good, Wretched Man

CHAPTER AND POD 8 Principle
Joint Heirs, Creation Groans, Spirit Intercedes, God for Us, No Condemnation, Righteous Requirement, Carnally Minded, Live by Spirit, Abba Father, Purpose, Freely Give, Nothing Can Separate
POD 9 Principle
Myself Accursed
Jesus is God
Israel is Israel, Seed, Works, Elder Serves Younger, Jacob I Loved, Mercy On, Potter has Power
Faith Righteousness

CHAPTER AND POD 10 Principle
Zeal for God, Gospel Report, Lost and Found, Confess with Mouth, Faith by Hearing

CHAPTER AND POD 11 Principle
Spirit of Stupor, Provoke to Jealousy, Broken Off, Blinded in Part, Gifts Irrevocable
Grace
Disobedience, Riches of Wisdom, Counsel Him, Repay Him, All Things

CHAPTER AND POD 12 Principle
Abhor Evil, Fervent in Spirit, Distribute to Saints, Rejoice with Those, Associate with Humble
Present Body
PM TEL GM *(foundational ministries)*
PROVED *(repay no one passage)*

CHAPTER AND POD 13 Principle
Subject to Authorities, Owe No One, Fulfillment of Law, Salvation is Nearer, Put on Christ

(no specials)

CHAPTER AND POD 14 Principle
He Will Stand, Fully Persuaded, Judgment Seat, All Things Pure, Whatever is Not
Kingdom of God

CHAPTER AND POD 15 Principle
Receive One Another, Abound in Hope
Scriptures are Written

CHAPTER AND POD 16 Principle
Cause Division, God of Peace, Obedience of Faith
(no specials)

Appendix 7
BOOK THREE *(Year Three)*
366 Seeds / 576 Scripture passages
* Father to Master Craftsman Level

Year 3 of Phase 1 40 Seeds / 225 Scripture passages

POD 1
One Ministry, Anointing, Battle of Identity, Abba Intimacy, Great Faith

POD 2
Understanding God's Sovereignty, Progressive Faith and Unbelief, Comparing Two Loves, Waiting on God, Spiritual Maturity

POD 3
3 Aspects of Ministry, 3 Levels of Testimony,
Know-Reckon-Present and Reign, Biblical Deaths, Order of Melchizedek

POD 4
4 Aspects of the Flesh, At the Cross, Within the Veil,
Outside the Camp, Overcoming Degradation

POD 5
5 Much Mores, Wisdom from Above, Manifestations of Spirit,
Gifts-Ministries-Activities, Church Government

POD 6
Body Consciousness, Covet to Prophesy, One Bread Communion,
Two Tongues, Fasting

POD 7
House Divided, Calling on the Lord, Election and Free Will,
Division and Brokenness, Prayer Ministry

POD 8
Christ is All in All, Truth-Apostasy and Recovery,
God's Desire for Me, Name Above Every Name, Spiritual Liberty

Phase III Christlikeness Phase 16 Seeds / 40 Scripture passages
(Seed Names)

POD 1
Power Over Death, Equipped for Victory, Gentle Demeanor and Solemn Dignity, Earnest and Compassionate

POD 2
Individuality and Sufficiency, Virtue and Integrity, Temperance Mastered, Love of Wisdom

POD 3
Empathetic and Entreatable, Meek But Powerful
Peaceful and Patient, Non-Judgmental Teacher

POD 4
Discerning and Authoritive, Wholesome Character,
Hospitable and Charming, Pure and Conscientious

Ephesians Phase 64 Seeds/ 64 Scripture passages

CHAPTER AND POD 1 Principle
Spiritual Blessings, Accepted in the Beloved, Dispensation of Fullness, Sealed with Holy Spirit
Chose Us, Spirit of Wisdom
Understanding Enlightened, Power Toward Us, Seated in Heavenlies, Put All Things, All in All
Name Above

CHAPTER AND POD 2 Principle
Made Alive, He Himself, Preached Peace, Built on Foundation
Seated Together
Saved by Grace, God's Workmanship
Without Christ, Brought Near
Abolished Emnity

CHAPTER AND POD 3 Principle
Whole Family, Rooted and Grounded
Dispensation of Grace
Revelation of Mystery, Mystery of Christ, Not Made Know

Unsearchable Riches, Fellowship of the Mystery, Intent that Now, According to Purpose
Access, Passes Knowledge, Exceedingly Abundantly
Access,

CHAPTER AND POD 4 Principle
Walk Worthy, Equipping of Saints, Futility of Mind
APE.PeT *(fivefold ministry)*, Unity of Faith
Wind of Doctrine, Speaking the Truth, Joined and Knit
Put Off, Renewed in Spirit, Put On
Put Away, Angry, Let No, Grieve Not

CHAPTER AND POD 5 Principle
Not Fitting, Wrath of God, Be Filled, Church is Subject, Glorious Church
GReaT *(goodness)*
Awake from Dead, Walk Circumspectly, Great Mystery
CHAPTER AND POD 6 Principle
Honor Your Parents, As to Christ, Whatever Good, Open My Mouth
Strong in Lord, Put On Armor, We do not Wrestle, Take Up Whole
MUD.LeTteR.M *(armor of God)(middle, up, down, left, top, right, mouth)*

Hebrews Phase 145 Seeds / 145 Scripture passages

CHAPTER AND POD 1 Principle
Various Times, Word of Power, Angels Worship, Oil of Gladness
Inherited Name

CHAPTER AND POD 2 Principle
Great Salvation, Captain of Salvation, Power of Death, Aid to Seed, Suffered Temptation
Mindful of Man, Little Lower, Dominion
Jesus Little Lower, Declare Father's Name

CHAPTER AND POD 3 Principle
Consider the Apostle, More Honor, Whose House, Confidence Steadfast, Because of Unbelief
Evil Heart, Deceitfulness of Sin
Because of Unbelief

CHAPTER AND POD 4 Principle
Promise Remains, We Who Believe, Since It Remains, If Joshua, Hold Fast

Because of Disobedience, Labor to Enter, Living and Powerful, Boldly to Throne

CHAPTER AND POD 5 Principle
Compassion on Those, No Man, Ought to Be, Unskkilled in Word, Solid Food
Begotten You, Obedience Learned, Author of Salvation

CHAPTER AND POD 6 Principle
Impossible to Renew, Better Things, Assurance of Hope, High Priest Forever
Elementary Principles, Inherit Promises
Covenant Blessing, Immutable Things, Sure and Steadfast
Anchor for Soul

CHAPTER AND POD 7 Principle
Lesser by Better, Loins of Father, Fitting for Us, After the Law
King of Righteousness, Genealogy
According to Order, Change of Law, Endless Life, Annulled Because
Better Covenant, Save to Uttermost, Lives to Intercede

CHAPTER AND POD 8 Principle
Copies and Shadows, More Excellent Ministry, If First Faultless, None Shall Teach, First Obsolete
(no specials)

CHAPTER AND POD 9 Principle
Holiest of All, Mediator of New, Death of Testator, Copies of True
Not Without Blood, Way Into, Symbolic For, Only with Types, Greater Tabernacle, Own Blood, Animal Sacrifice, Much More
Without the Shedding, Put Away Sin

CHAPTER AND POD 10 Principle
Law a Shadow, Body Prepared, Takes Away, Sin Willfully, Need or Endurance
No More Consciousness
Sanctified Once, One Offering
Covenant I, Remember Their Sins, Remission of These, Boldness to Enter, Veil/Flesh, True Heart
Assembling Ourselves, Cast Away, Just Shall Live

CHAPTER AND POD 11a Principle
Framed by Word, Waited for City, Died in Faith, Not Ashamed, Figurative Sense
Faith is Substance, Without Faith
Pod 11b
Beautiful Child, Choose to Suffer, Through Faith, World was Not, Perfect Apart

CHAPTER AND POD 12a Principle
Cloud of Witnesses, Without Holiness, Root of Bitterness, No Place
Do Not Despise
Pod 12a
Mont Zion, Spirits Made Perfect, Cannot be Shaken

CHAPTER AND POD 13 Principle
Entertaining Angels, Remember the Prisoners, Bed Undefiled, Good Conscience, Great Shepherd
Never Leave You
Christ the Same, Established by Grace, Privileged Altar, Outside the Camp, Praise to God

James Phase 44 Seeds / 44 Scripture passages

CHAPTER AND POD 1 Principle
Gives Liberally, Double Minded, Endures Temptation, Swift to Hear, Religion is Useless
Count it All, Every Good Gift
Save Soul, Doer of Word, Immediately Forgets, Law of Liberty

CHAPTER AND POD 2 Principle
Chosen the Poor, Keep Law, Mercy Triumphs, One God, Justified by Works
Faith without Works

CHAPTER AND POD 3 Principle
Stricter Judgment, Small Rudder, Set on Fire, Tame the Tongue, Ought Not Be
Perfect Man
Bitter Envy, Earthly/Sensual/Demonic
Wisdom from Above
Fruit of Righteousness

CHAPTER AND POD 4 Principle
War in Members, Ask Amiss, Speak No Evil, If the Lord Wills, Knows to Do
Spirit Yearns Jealously, Draw Near
CHAPTER AND POD 5 Principle
Perseverance of Job, Yes and No, Call for Elders, Nature Like Ours, Save a Soul
Confess Trespasses, Fervent Prayer

1, 2, 3 John Phase 52 Seeds / 52 Scripture passages

CHAPTER AND POD 1 Principle
Hands Have Handled, Say No Sin
Fellowship with Us, God is Light, Blood of Christ
Confess our Sins

CHAPTER AND POD 2 Principle
Says in Light, Deny the Son, Abide in Him
Advocate With, Propitiation for Sin
Little Children, Young Men, Fathers
Love of World, Lust of Flesh
Antichrists Have Come
Know All Things, Anointing Teaches

CHAPTER AND POD 3 Principle
Manner of Love, Whoever Sins, Of the Devil, Whoever Hates, God is Greater
Revealed, Purifies Self
Born of God, Deed and Truth

CHAPTER AND POD 4 Principle
Test the Spirits, He Who Knows, Ought to Love, Love Perfected, First Loved Us
Antichrist Coming, Overcome Them, Love *(God is)*, Fear in Love, Loves God

CHAPTER AND POD 5 Principle
Begot loves Begotten, Commandments not Burdensome, Whatever is Born, Whoever is Born, True God
Three Bear Witness, Eternal Life, Leads to Death

2 John Phase

CHAPTER AND POD 1 Principle
Many Deceivers, Doctrine of Christ

3 John Phase

CHAPTER AND POD 1 Principle
Loves Preeminence, Putting Them Out
You May Prosper

Appendix #8
BOOK FOUR *(Year Four)*
488 Seeds / 508 Scripture passages
* Master Craftsman to Master Builder Level

Phase IV MEDS Essential Elements *(for Complete Phase IV content see Appendix 12)*
18 Seeds / 33 Scripture passages

POD 1
Mutual Cooperative Fellowship, Christ-Grace and Relationship Centered, Planting and Engrafting, Learning Through the Enjoyment of Fellowship, Shared Initiative and Leadership

POD 2
Seeds, Levels, Format, Special Addendum Phases

POD 3
One Seed at a Time Permanently Rooted, Balanced Conversational Fellowship, Repetitive and Persistent Mutual Feeding, Edification Through Dispensation

POD 4
Understanding Greater, Intimacy Greater
Confidence Greater, Insightful Wisdom

Acts Phase 164 Seeds / 164 Scripture passages

CHAPTER AND POD 1 Principle
Infallible Proofs, Like Manner, One Accord, Cast Lots
Receive Power

CHAPTER AND POD 2 Principle
This is That, Not Possible, Not Leave,
Continued Daily
Day of Pentecost, Call on Name
Both Lord and Christ, Cut to Heart, Repent and Be Baptised
Apostle's Doctrine

CHAPTER AND POD 3 Principle
Silver and Gold, Men of Israel, Faith in Name, Blotted Out, Raise Up
(no specials)

CHAPTER AND POD 4 Principle
Heard the Word, What Power, Sight of God, One Accord, Shaken and Filled
No Other Name, Boldness of

CHAPTER AND POD 5 Principle
Ananias and Sapphira, Shadow of Peter, Opened Doors, Gameliel, Counted Worthy
Holy Spirit is God

CHAPTER AND POD 6 Principle
Good Reputation, Dispute Stephen
(no specials)

CHAPTER AND POD 7 Principle
Moses Learned, Cut to Heart, Do Not Charge
(no specials)

CHAPTER AND POD 8 Principle
Made Havoc, What Hinders
Phillip Preached, Heard of Samaritans, Receive Holy Spirit, On Any of Them, Received Holy Spirit, Simon Saw

CHAPTER AND POD 9 Principle
Breathing Threats, Immediately Fell, Tabitha Arise
(no specials)

CHAPTER AND POD 10 Principle
Rise Peter, Myself Also
Impartial God, Faith Works, Preached Peace, Repentance From, Anointed One, Death and Resurrection, Judge of, Remission of Sins

CHAPTER AND POD 11 Principle
Grant Repentance, Hand of Lord, Called Christians
(no specials)

CHAPTER AND POD 12 Principle
Killed James, Constant Prayer, Struck Peter, Beside Yourself
(no specials)

CHAPTER AND POD 13 Principle
Son of Devil, Man After Own, Today Begotten, Forgiveness of Sins, Judge Yourselves
Ministered to Lord

CHAPTER AND POD 14 Principle
Seeing Faith, Why Are You?, Without Witness, Supposed Dead, Enter Through Tribulation
Witness to Word

CHAPTER AND POD 15 Principle
Certain Men, Test God, Rebuild Tabernacle, Sharp Contention
(no specials)

CHAPTER AND POD 16 Principle
Well Spoken, Come Over, Come Out, Midnight Prayer, Beaten Openly
(no specials)

CHAPTER AND POD 17 Principle
Reasoned With Them, Upside Down, Spirit Provoked, Epicurean and Stoic, Poets Have Said
Searched Scriptures

CHAPTER AND POD 18 Principle
Occupation Tentmaker, Compelled by Spirit, Night Vision, Continued a Year, Vigorously refuted
(no specials)

CHAPTER AND POD 19 Principle
Reasoned and Persuaded, Handkerchiefs and Aprons, Seven Sons of Sceva, Purposed in Spirit, Confused Assembly
Disciples Baptisms

CHAPTER AND POD 20 Principle
Fell on Him, Elders/Bishops, Blessed to Give
Testify to Grace Gospel

CHAPTER AND POD 21 Principle
Told Through Spirit, Virgin Daughters, Zealous for Law
(no specials)

CHAPTER AND POD 22 Principle
Taught by Gamaliel, Why Persecuting Me, Why Are You Waiting, Consenting to Death
(no specials)

CHAPTER AND POD 23 Principle
Paul Perceived, Testified For Me
(no specials)

CHAPTER AND POD 24 Principle
Called a Sect, Judged For Resurrection
(no specials)

CHAPTER AND POD 25 Principle
Appeal to Caesar, Certain Jesus
(no specials)

CHAPTER AND POD 26 Principle
Judged For Hope, Open Their Eyes, Much Learning
(no specials)

CHAPTER AND POD 27 Principle
No Loss, Unless Stay
(no specials)

CHAPTER AND POD 28 Principle
Fastened On, Laid Hands, Persuaded Them, Preaching the Kingdom
(no specials)

1 Corinthians Phase 140 Seeds / 140 Scripture passages

CHAPTER AND POD 1 Principle
Come Short, Not Many
Called Saints
Speak the Same, Perfectly Joined, Christ not Divided
Message of Cross, Written, Made Foolish, Wisdom of World, Jews Request, Christ Crucified, Called Both

Wisdom from God

CHAPTER AND POD 2 Principle
Demonstration of Power, Eye Has Not, Spiritual with Spiritual
Christ Crucified
Speak Wisdom, God in a Mystery, Had They Known
Natural Man
Spiritual Man, Mind of Christ

CHAPTER AND POD 3 Principle
Temple of God, Wisdom of World
Carnal Babes, God Gives, Christ not Divided
Masterbuilder, Foundation is Christ, Gold/Silver/Precious Stones, Fire, Reward, Suffer Loss

CHAPTER AND POD 4 Principle
Beyond What is Written, Ten Thousand Instructors, Word but Power
Stewards of God, Required That, Small Thing, Judges Me, Judge Nothing

CHAPTER AND POD 5 Principle
Puffed Up, Delivered to Satan, Christ our Passover, Judge Those
NO SPECIALS for chapter 5

CHAPTER AND POD 6 Principle
Judge World, Utter Failure, Joined to Harlot, Body is Temple
All Things Lawful, Joined to Lord, Flee Immortality

CHAPTER AND POD 7 Principle
Render to Wife, Better to Marry, Willing to Live, Keeping the Commandments, Things of World
Do Not Deprive

CHAPTER AND POD 8 Principle
Knowledge Puffs Up, Idol Is Nothing, Food Does Not, Wound Conscience
Anything Known

CHAPTER AND POD 9 Principle
Muzzle an Ox, Sow Spiritual, Woe is Me, Became a Jew
Body into Subjection

CHAPTER AND POD 10 Principle
Baptized Into Moses, For our admonition, Eat Whatever, Give No Offense
Lest He Fall, No Temptation
Cup of Blessing, All Things Lawful

CHAPTER AND POD 11 Principle
Keep the Traditions, Head Covered, Long Hair, Must be Factions
Not to Eat, Thanks, Cup is New, Proclaim Lord's Death, unWorthy Manner, Examine Himself, Discerning Lord's Body
Weak and Sick

CHAPTER AND POD 12 Principle
No One Speaking, If One Suffers
Ignorant, Gifts/Ministries/Activities
Manifestations of Spirit
Many Members, All Baptised, Because I am Not, No Need of You, No Schisms
Apostles First, Earnestly Desire

CHAPTER AND POD 13 Principle
Know in Part, When I Was, See in Mirror
Tongues of Men
Love is Patient...
Abide These Three

CHAPTER AND POD 14 Principle
(all specials)
Pursue Love, Tongues Does Not, Prophesies Edification, Tongues Edifies, Wish You All
Zealous for Gifts, All Prophesy, Come Together
2 or 3 Speak, Revealed to Another, All Prophesy
Covet to Prophesy, Decently and in Order
Interpret, Spirit Prays
Thanks Well, Thank My God
Understanding as Babes, Prophecy, Sign to Unbelievers, Out of Your Mind
Spirits of Prophets, Author of Confusion

CHAPTER AND POD 15 Principle
a) Seen By, Least of Apostles, Preaching in Vain, Enemies Under Feet, Baptized for Dead
Gospel I Preach, Hold Fast, Delivered to You, Buried and Rose

By the Grace, Death by Man, Die Daily
b) Unless it Dies, Kind of Flesh, Natural First, Flesh and Blood, Behold a Mystery
First Man Adam, Strength of Sin, Victory Through Christ

CHAPTER AND POD 16 Principle
First Day, Great and Effective, Devoted to Ministry, Be Accursed
(no specials)

Philippians Phase 38 Seeds / 38 Scripture passages

CHAPTER AND POD 1 Principle
Love May Abound, Pretense or Truth, Supply of Spirit, Terrified by Adversary
Saints/Bishops/Deacons, Confident of This, Defense and Confirmation

CHAPTER AND POD 2 Principle
All Seek Own, Hold in Esteem
Selfish Ambition, Kenosis, Name Above
Work Out, God Who Works, No Complaining, Blameless and Harmless, Holding Fast

CHAPTER AND POD 3 Principle
Enemies of Cross, Citizenship in Heaven
Tedious Not
No Confidence, Gain Christ, Resurrection/Fellowship, Attain To, Press On, Forgetting Those Things

CHAPTER AND POD 4 Principle
Book of Life, Rejoice Again, Seek the Fruit, Supply All
Rejoice in the Lord, Let Your Gentleness, Anxious For Nothing, Whatever is True
Learned to be Content

Colossians Phase 26 Seeds / 26 Scripture passages

CHAPTER AND POD 1 Principle
Hope Laid Up, Filled With Knowledge, Forgiveness of Sins, Present Every Man
Strengthened with Might, Delivered Us
All Things, Before All, Church Head

Reconcile All Things, Enemy in Own Mind, Fill Up in Flesh, Christ in Me, According to His Working

CHAPTER AND POD 2 Principle
Absent in Flesh, Without Hands
Rooted and Built, Beware Lest Cheated
Complete in Him, Shadow of Things
Cheat You, Holding Fast, Basic Principles, Perish with Use, Appearance of Wisdom

CHAPTER AND POD 3 Principle
Put on Love, Do it Heartily
Above Things, Life is Hidden
New Man, Forgiving One Another
Let the Word, Whatever You Do

CHAPTER AND POD 4 Principle
Continue Earnestly, Walk in Wisdom, Beloved Physician, Take Heed
(no specials)

1 Thessalonians Phase 17 Seeds / 17 Scripture passages
(Seed Names)

CHAPTER AND POD 1 Principle
Work of Faith, Word Only
Delivers Us

CHAPTER AND POD 2 Principle
Nursing Mother, Welcomed Word
Flattering Words

CHAPTER AND POD 3 Principle
Establish and Encourage, Pray Exceedingly
(no specials)

CHAPTER AND POD 4 Principle
Quiet Life, Not Ignorant, Caught Up
(no specials)

CHAPTER AND POD 5 Principle
Day of Lord, Be Sober, Recognize Those, Exhort You

Appointed Not, Quench the Spirit, Spirit/Soul/and Body

1 Timothy Phase 40 Seeds / 40 Scripture passages
(Seed Names)
Subject of 1 Timothy

CHAPTER AND POD 1 Principle
Purpose of Commandment, Formerly a Blasphemer, Me First, King Eternal
Teach No Other, Teachers of Law, Faithful Saying, Wage Good Warfare

CHAPTER AND POD 2 Principle
First of All, One Mediator, Propriety and Moderation, Silent Submission, Woman Deceived
Lift Holy Hands

CHAPTER AND POD 3 Principle
Rules His Own, Not a Novice, One Wife, Without Controversy
Bishop Position

CHAPTER AND POD 4 Principle
Doctrine of Demons, Received With Thanksgiving, Bodily Exercise, Give Yourself
(no specials)

CHAPTER AND POD 5 Principle
Rebuke Not, Provide for Own, Double Honor, Lay Hands
(no specials)

CHAPTER AND POD 6 Principle
Wholesome Words, Godliness With Contentment, Love of Money, Who Alone, Falsely Called
(no specials)

1 Peter Phase 45 Seeds/ 45 Scripture passages
(Seed Names)
Subject of 1 Peter

CHAPTER AND POD 1 Principle
Living Hope, More Precious, Manner of Time, Born Again, Flesh as Grass
Elect According To, Joy Inexpressible, Salvation of Soul, Gird Up Loins, Redeemed With, Purified Your Soul

CHAPTER AND POD 2 Principle
Newborn Babes, Living Stones, Free not Using, Commendable Before, Deceit in Mouth
Chosen Generation, Abstain from Fleshly, Stripes Healed, Shepherd and Overseer

CHAPTER AND POD 3 Principle
Hidden Person, Heirs Together, Eyes of Lord, Just for Unjust, Preached to Spirits
Of One Mind, Defense Ready, Baptism Antitype

CHAPTER AND POD 4 Principle
Ceased from Sin, Think it Strange, Preached to Dead, Reproached for Name, Judgment Begins
Love Covers, Received Gift, Oracles of God

CHAPTER AND POD 5 Principle
Exhort Elders, Not Lording Over, Crown of Glory, Perfect-Established, Mark-My Son, God Resists, Resist Devil

Appendix #9

BOOK FIVE *(Year Five)*
953 Seeds / 1014 Scripture passages
* Advanced Master Builder Level

Phase V. Healing 10 Seeds / 50 Scripture passages

POD 1
Source of Sickness-Source of Healing, God Heals and Forgives, Sickness Borne, Isaiah's Prophecy Fulfilled, Reason for Sickness

POD 2
God Sends His Word, Word Gives Like,
Healing is the Children's Bread, Eating the Lamb, Keeping the Passover

POD 3
Names of God, High Priest of our Confession, No Weapon-No Plague and No Feebleness, Looking to Be Healed, Healing Now and Future

POD 4
First Consideration, Established in Grace, Lying Vanities, Seated in the Heavenlies, Inner Cause Greater

2 Corinthian Phase 102 Seeds / 102 Scripture passages

CHAPTER AND POD 1 Principle
Delivered Us, Conducted Ourselves, Yes and No, Fellow Workers, Blessed Be, Sentence of Death, Promises of God

CHAPTER AND POD 2 Principle
Punishment Sufficient, Lest Satan, Fragrance of Knowledge, Not Peddling
(no specials)

CHAPTER AND POD 3 Principle
(Specials Only)
Epistle Read, Sufficiency Not, Sufficient as Ministers, Letter Kills, Ministry of Death, Glory Exceeds, Boldness is Speech,
Lord is Spirit, Transformed by Same

CHAPTER AND POD 4 Principle
Renounced Hidden, Minds Blinded, Hard Pressed, Always Delivered, Preach Ourselves, Light to Shine, Treasure in Vessels
Same Spirit, Outward Man, Light Affliction, Look at Unseen

CHAPTER AND POD 5 Principle
Building From God, Absent From Lord, Must All Appear, Beside Ourselves, If One Died, Walk by Faith, Regard No One
New Creation, Reconciled Us, Imputing Not, Ambassadors for Christ, Righteousness of God

CHAPTER AND POD 6 Principle
Acceptable Time, Commend Ourselves, Spoken Openly, Unequally Yoked, Come Out
(no specials)

CHAPTER AND POD 7 Principle
No One Wronged, Spirit Refreshed, Let Us Cleanse, Godly Sorrow

CHAPTER AND POD 8 Principle
Deep Poverty, Though Rich, By Equality, Beyond Ability, Imploring You, Gave Themselves

CHAPTER AND POD 9 Principle
Zeal Stirred Up, Supplies Seed, Generous not Grudging, Sows Sparingly, Purposes in Heart, God is Able

CHAPTER AND POD 10 Principle
For Edification, Letters Weighty, Glory in Lord, Walk in Flesh, Weapons of Warfare, Casting Down
Compare Ourselves

CHAPTER AND POD 11 Principle
Godly Jealousy, Different Spirit, Trained in Speech, Brings Bondage, Are They?
False Apostles, Satan Himself, Transform Themselves

CHAPTER AND POD 12 Principle
Visions and Revelation, Inexpressible Words, When Weak, Seek Yours, Humble Me, Grace is Sufficient

CHAPTER AND POD 13 Principle
Mighty in You, Examine Yourselves, Become Complete, Holy Kiss, 2 or 3 Witnesses, Grace of Jesus

2 Thessalonians Phase 11 Seeds / 11 Scripture passages
(Seed Names)

CHAPTER AND POD 1 Principle
God to Repay, Faith Grows Exceedingly

CHAPTER AND POD 2 Principle
Gathering Together, Mystery of Lawlessness, Strong Delusion
(no specials)

CHAPTER AND POD 3 Principle
Disorderly Busybodies, Faith *(not all have)*

2 Timothy Phase 21 Seeds / 21 Scripture passages
(Seed Names)

CHAPTER AND POD 1 Principle
Holy Calling, Know Whom I, Spirit of Fear

CHAPTER AND POD 2 Principle
Endure Hardship, Faithful Saying, Solid Foundation, Rightly Dividing, Flee Lusts
Servant of Lord, Humility Correcting, Come to Their Senses

CHAPTER AND POD 3 Principle
Know This, Always Learning, All Scripture, Equipped for Every

CHAPTER AND POD 4 Principle
Preach The Word, Good Fight, First Defense
(no specials)

Titus Phase 16 Seeds / 16 Scripture passages

CHAPTER AND POD 1 Principle
Rebuke Them, All Things Pure
(no specials)

CHAPTER AND POD 2 Principle
Speak Proper, Showing Yourself, Blessed Hope, Grace of God, Teaching Us, Redeems Us

CHAPTER AND POD 3 Principle
Speak No Evil, Washing of Regeneration, Good and Profitable, Meet Urgent Needs
(no specials)

2 Peter Phase 24 Seeds / 24 Scripture passages

CHAPTER AND POD 1 Principle
Precious Faith, Call and Election, Present Truth, Eyewitnesses of His, Word Confirmed, Life and Godliness, Add to Faith

CHAPTER AND POD 2 Principle
False Teachers, Down to Hell, Righteous Lot, Greater in Power, Heart Trained
(no specials)

CHAPTER AND POD 3 Principle
Stir Up, Fervent Heat, Hasten Coming, Hard to Understand, Grow in Grace, Willfully Forget, World Then, World Now
None Should Perish

Jude Phase 8 seeds / 8 Scripture Passages

CHAPTER AND POD Principle
Reserved in Chains, Michael the Archangel, Way of Cain, Lord Comes, Building Yourselves Up, Alone is Wise
Contend Earnestly, Able to Keep

Revelation Phase 284 Seeds/ 284 Scripture passages
(Seed Names)

CHAPTER AND POD 1 Principle
a) Revelation of Christ, Blessed is He, Faithful Witness, Coming With the Clouds, Kingdom and Patience
(no specials)

b) Write in Book, Son of Man, Feet Like Fine Brass, Fell As Dead, You Have

Seen
(no specials)

CHAPTER AND POD 2 Principle

a) Church of Ephesus, Remove Your Lampstand, Tree of Life, Church in Smyrna, Tribulation and Poverty, Second Death
Labored for Name, Left First Love, Promised Crown, Synagogue of Satan Antipas Faithful, Hold Fast, Satan Dwells, Teaching of Balaam, Teaching of Nicolaitans

b) Church in Pergamos, Will Fight, Hidden Manna, Church in Thyatira, Into Great Tribulation, Power Over Nations
Last More, Depths of Satan, Teaching of Jezebel

CHAPTER AND POD 3 Principle

a) Church in Sardis, Watchful and Strengthen, White Garments, Church in Philadelphia, Open Door, Pillar in Temple
Few Names, Name Alive, Open and Shut, Little Strength, Kept My Word, Keep You From

b) Church in Laodicea; Wretched, Miserable; Buy From Me; Be Zealous; Sit With Me
Stand at Door, Lukewarm, Wretched/Miserable

CHAPTER AND POD 4 Principle
a) Come Up Here, In the Spirit, Jasper and Sardius, Twenty-four Elders, Seven Spirits
(no specials)

b) Glass, Sea of; Four Living Creatures; Holy, Holy, Holy; Cast Their Crowns; Glory and Honor
(no specials)

CHAPTER AND POD 5 Principle
a) Who Is Worthy, Lion of Judah, Lamb was Slain, Eyes are Seven, Bowls of Incense
(no specials)

b) New Song, Kings and Priests, Thousands of Thousands, Worthy is the Lamb, Elders Fell Down
(no specials)

CHAPTER AND POD 5 Principle
a) Who Is Worthy, Lion of Judah, Lamb was Slain, Eyes are Seven, Bowls of Incense
(no specials)

b) New Song, Kings and Priests, Thousands of Thousands, Worthy is the Lamb, Elders Fell Down
(no specials)

CHAPTER AND POD 6 Principle
a) White Horse, Red Horse, Black Horse, Pale Horse, Souls Under Alter
(no specials)

b) Great Earthquake, Stars Fell, Sky Receded, Fall on Us, Wrath Has Come
(no specials)

CHAPTER AND POD 7 Principle
a) Four Angels; Another Angel; Do not Harm; Sealed 44,000; Twelve Sealed
(no specials)

b) Great Multitude, Loud Voice, Angels and Elders, Washed Their Robes, Wipe Every Tear
(no specials)

CHAPTER AND POD 8 Principle
a) Seventh Seal Silence, Prayer of Saints, Smoke of Incense, Threw to Earth, Prepared to Sound
(no specials)
b) First Angel; Second Sounded; Third Angel; Fourth Sounded; Woe, Woe, Woe
(no specials)

CHAPTER AND POD 9 Principle
a) Key to Pit*(s)*, Locusts Came, Torment for Five, Faces Like Men, Breast-plates of Iron
(no specials)

b) King Abaddon *(Apolyon)*, Sixth Angel, Release the Four, Two Hundred Million, Did Not Repent
(no specials)

CHAPTER AND POD 10 Principle
a) Another Mighty Angel, Foot on Sea, Cried as Lion, Seal Up, Raised Up Hand
(no specials)

b) Delay No Longer, Mystery Finished, Take Little Book, Sweet in Mouth, Prophesy Again
(no specials)

CHAPTER AND POD 11 Principle
a) Measure Temple, Two Olive Trees, Fire From Mouth, Beast Will Kill, Three and a Half, Two Witnesses
b) Ascended to Heaven, Seven Thousand Killed, Seventh Sounded, Kingdoms of This World, Temple Opened
(no specials)

CHAPTER AND POD 12 Principle
a) Great Sign, Great Red Dragon, Third of Stars, Male Child, Woman Fled
(no specials)
b) Now Salvation, Dragon Persecuted Woman, Two Wings, Water Out of Mouth, Enraged With Woman
Overcame Him

CHAPTER AND POD 13 Principle
a) Beast Out of Sea, Mortally Wounded, Worshiped Dragon and Beast, Blasphemes for Forty-two, Granted to Make War
(no specials)

b) Another Beast, Great Signs, Image of Beast, Mark Hands and Foreheads, Number of Beast
(no specials)

CHAPTER AND POD 14 Principle
a) One Hundred and Forty-four, Sang as New Song, Everlasting Gospel, Fallen Babylon, Wine of Wrath
(no specials)

b) Patience of Saints, Die in Lord, Sharp Sickle, Grapes Fully Ripe, Blood Came Out *(no specials)*

CHAPTER AND POD 15 Principle
a) Seven Last Plagues; Glass, Sea Of; Song of Moses; All Nations Worship

b) Tabernacle of Testimony, Seven Angels and Plagues, Bowls of Wrath, Smoke From Glory

CHAPTER AND POD 16 Principle
a) First Bowl, Second Angel, Third Bowl, Fourth Angel, Fifth Bowl

b) Sixth Angel; Mouth of Dragon, Beast + False; Gathered to Armageddon; It Is Done; Earthquake Great

CHAPTER AND POD 17 Principle
a) Great Harlot, Woman on Scarlet Beast, Mystery Babylon, Woman Drunk, Was and Is Not

b) Mind Has Wisdom, Seven Kings, Also the Eighth, War With Lamb, Ten Horns

CHAPTER AND POD 18 Principle
a) Another Angel; Drunk of Wine; Come Out of Her; Double, Double

b) One Hour; No One Buys; Soul Longed; Alas, Alas; Dust on Heads

CHAPTER AND POD 19 Principle
a) Voice of Multitude, Many Waters, Marriage of the Lamb, Fine Linen, White Horse

b) Robe Dipped, Sharp Sword, King of Kings, Eat the Flesh, Two Cast Alive

CHAPTER AND POD 20 Principle
a) Key to Bottomless Pit, Bound Him, Released for Little While, First Resurrection, Satan Will Be Released

b) Gog and Magog, Devil Cast, Earth and Heaven, Book of Life, Death and Hades

CHAPTER AND POD 21 Principle
a) New Heaven and Earth, New Jerusalem, Loud Voice, All Things New, Water of Life

b) Cowardly Unbelieving, Show the Bride, Jasper Stone, Twelve Gates, Twelve Foundations
c) Gold Reed, Pure Gold, Gates Were Pearl, Lamb is Its Light, No Night

CHAPTER AND POD 22 Principle
a) River of Water, Tree of Life, No More Curse, See His Face, Reign Forever

b) I Am Coming, Do Not Do That, Do Not Seal, Let Him, Reward With Me

c) Alpha and Omega, Outside Are Dogs, Root and Offspring, Thirsty Come, Takes Away, Come Lord Jesus
Genesis phase *(blue)* 57 Seeds / 57 Scripture passages

Proverbs Phase *(blue)* 48 Seeds / 48 Scripture passages

POD 1
Lean Not, Strength to Bones, Health to Flesh, Keep Your Heart, Six Things
Mercy and Truth, Get Wisdom, Give Attention

POD 2
Makes Rich, Wins Souls, Tongue of Wise, Anxiety in Heart, Hope Deferred, Hand of Diligent

POD 3
Idle Chatter, Soft Answer, Due Season, Enemies At Peace, Pleasant Words
True Witness, Strong Confidence, Pride Goes, There's a Way

POD 4
Rules His Spirit, Repeats a Matter, Man Accepts, Answer a Matter, Who Can Say
Merry Heart, Name of Lord, Gift Makes Room, Power of Tongue, Counsel in Heart, Spirit of Man

POD 5
Little Sleep, As A Door, Do Not Boast, Open Rebuke, Word Is Pure
Good Name, Thinks in Heart, By Wisdom, Righteous Man, Plant the Field, Glory of God, Iron Sharpens Iron, Vision, Fear of Man

Genesis Phase *(blue)*
(Seed Names)
Subject of Genesis

POD 1
Our Image, Here for Food, Very Good, Living Being, Surely Die
In the Beginning, Earth Became, Let There Be
Tree of Life

POD 2
More Cunning, Will Not Surely Die, Fig Leaves, Cursed More, Tunics of Skin
(no specials)

POD 3
Brother's Keeper, Mark on Cain, Enoch Was Not, Strive With Flesh, Fountains and Windows
Call on Name

POD 4
Animals for Food, Rainbow Covenant, Noah's Nakedness, Mighty Nimrod, Brick for Stone
Seedtime and Harvest

POD 5
Abram Get Out; Shield and Reward, Abram/Sarai/Hagar, Return and Submit, Sign of Covenant
Melchizedek Priesthood

POD 6
Abraham Visited, Abraham Intercedes, Pillar of Salt, Israel Bore, Ishmael Mocks
(no specials)

POD 7
God Will Provide, Wife for Son, Babies Jostle, Despised Birthright, Covenant Confirmed
(no specials)

POD 8
I Am Esau, Ladder Set Up, Wrestled God, Joseph's Dream, Joseph Sold
(no specials)

POD 9
Great in House, Put Into Prison, Butler and Baker, Pharaoh's Dream, Over My House
(no specials)

POD 10
Governor Over Land, Ephraim Before Manasseh, Sons Blessed, Scepter Shall Not Depart, Meant Evil
(no specials)

Psalms phase *(blue)* 100 Seeds/ 100 Scripture passages

POD 1
Nations Rage, Kiss the Son, How Excellent, Out of Mouth, Foundations Destroyed, Know Your Name

POD2
Words Pure, Fool has Said, My Goodness, Always Before Me, Fullness of Joy

POD 3
Heavens Declare Glory, Chariot Trust, Enthroned in Praises, Poured Out Like Water, Pierced My Hands
(no specials)

POD 4
Lord My Shephard, Goodness and Mercy, One Thing, Seek My Face, Anger for Moment
(no specials)

POD 5
Hiding Place, Bless the Lord, Angel of Lord, Pleasure in Prosperity, Righteous Begging
Good Courage, Acknowledging My Sin, Delight Yourself, Many Works

POD 6
Deep Unto Deep, Tongue is Pen, Throne Forever, River Whose Streams, Thought Was Like You, Very Present Help, Be Still

POD 7
Create In Me, Rock is Higher, Let God Arise, Solitary Set in Families, Deep

Mire
Truth Inward Parts, Broken Spirit, Fixed Heart, Wait For God

POD 8
Hate Without Cause, More And More, Sea to Sea, Earth be Filled, Until I Went
(no specials)

POD 9
Arrows Flashed, Utter Dark Sayings, You Are Gods, Even the Sparrow, Better One Day
Limited Holy One, Mercy and Truth

POD 10
Days of Our Lives, He Who Dwells, Nothing Wicked, Enemies Reproached Me, Grow Old
Plague Not Near, Called on His Name, God Who Forgives *(El Nasa)*, Enter His Gates

POD 11
Bless the Lord, You His Angels, Wicked No More, Do Not Touch, Soon Forgot
Forgives All, East from West, Laid the Foundation, None Feeble

POD 12
Stood in Breach, Let the Redeemed, Rewarded Me Evil, Lord Said to My Lord, Order of Melchizedek
Cried Out to God, Sent His Word

POD 13
Rising of Sun, Praise the Lord, Word is Lamp/Light, Slumber Nor Sleep, Let Us Go
Heaven is the Lord's, Young Man, Hidden in Heart

POD 14
Filled With Laughter, Quieted My Soul, Magnified Your Word, If I Ascend, Set a Guard, Unless the Lord, Behold How Good, Perfect that Which, Formed My Inward, Search Me, Teach Me, Executes Judgment, Let Everything

TOTAL FOR FIRST FIVE BOOKS

2235 SEEDS / 2586 SCRIPTURE PASSAGES

Appendix #10

(Informal) Personal Consecration Plan Worksheet

Promises and Characteristics of This Discipleship *(The Seeds)*:

1. ○ This Discipleship is NOT a competition. We do not practice any fleshly judging, pressuring, guilt trips, or lording over amongst ourselves.

2. ○ In this Discipleship, we do not practice religiosity. Our focus is NOT on outward behavior modification, law keeping, or "trying harder", but rather "MEDS" is highly effective by inward transformation *(the work of God, not man)* through relationship with Jesus Christ, writing God's Word on our hearts and abiding in His presence.

3. ○ Our aim in this Discipleship is NOT to memorize words, but rather our aim is to learn God's Word "conceptually" through the enjoyment of mutual fellowship *(balanced conversation)*.

4. ○ In this Discipleship there is NO writing or reading is REQUIRED, however, personal study is encouraged.

5. ○ This Discipleship we have NO practice of rank, status, or titles... we recognize Jesus Christ as the only Head of the church and understand that all believers are brothers.

○ My goal is to learn at least _____ Seed*(s)* per day.
○ My goal is to learn at least _____ Seed*(s)* per week.
○ My goal is to learn at least _____ Seed*(s)* per month.
○ I intend to take the initiative to attain the goal I have indicated above.
○ I understand that there are three primary enemies to accomplishing my above indicated godly objective:

1. The Laziness of my own flesh.

2. An unbalanced distraction of worldly things such as watching TV, "working out", playing games, or the desire for the approval of men.

3. The deception and the confusion of the enemy.

- Mastering each scripture and applying it personally in my life is much more important than learning a large number of scriptures. Nonetheless, I always strongly desire to continue to have an increase of God's Word in my heart.

- My intent fellowshipping in "MEDS" *(The Seeds)* is that each seed I learn is to be rooted, grounded, and established in my heart so that I will always be able to automatically and spontaneously apply the truths of God to my own life and will always be thoroughly equipped to dispense these truths to others as the Spirit leads me.

_____

Sign or print name *(optional)*

Appendix 11

Most Effective Discipleship Seeds
Thing We Say

MEDS *(formerly SOD)* is an informal Discipleship which brings about significant and measurable growth which has been proven to be of great benefit to all participants regardless of their current Christian experience or Spiritual maturity level, supplying both the "milk" and the "meat" of the Word through the use of dozens of phases of seeds *(Bible truths with scriptures to support them)*.

1. In this Discipleship there is NO competition, no pressure, no judging, no lording over by rank, status, or titles. Just patient encouragement with each disciple progressing according to his own desire, hunger, and ability. A mutual fellowship where we say,
"If you don't know a seed *(an important Bible truth)* it is because you have not heard it enough and said it enough... The Solution: Hear it again and say it again until it is mastered."

2. MEDS is not a monologue with one person preaching or dominating the fellowship, but the Disciples alternately speaking important Bible truths and scriptures until they are written on the heart or engraved deep in the heart. This results in growth through a balanced conversational fellowship where we say,
"Don't believe any spiritual 'truth' based solely on man's opinion or tradition, believe it only when you see it for yourself in the Scriptures (rightly divided and in context)."

3. Each disciple is responsible to take the initiative according to his own personal spiritual goals to pursue and receive his next seed when he is ready and also to take up a leadership role to encourage and plant seeds in others as needed and as led by the Holy Spirit. In this shared initiative and leadership we say,
"A servant brings the food to the table and the master eats it. the one 'leading' by teaching the seed is the servant and the receiver is the master. When the receiver speaks it back the roles change."

4. Advantages of MEDS over traditional Discipleship.
   a. The learning style is not rote memory but rather "conceptual learning" which is a much faster way to learn and much more effective as it engraves the Word on the heart of the believer.

   b. Every seed is learned with the intent that it becomes permanently engraved in the heart, meaning the disciple will forever be able to apply it to himself and give it to others including his friends and family.

   c. The learning in this Discipleship is in the context of fellowship which makes it very enjoyable and allows God's Word to spread exponentially among the local Body of Christ and beyond.

   d. Promotes a Body of Christ "Jesus" consciousness and unity in Him where we say,
   "When we speak God's Word, we always make it Personal, Positive and Present tense. We also speak it Prophetically *(by the Spirit)* and Poetically *(with passion)*.

5. The result of MEDS are outstanding. Each person who has participated in "The Seeds" for at least a couple of months testify...
   First, to a much greater understanding of God's Word and how to rightly divide it.
   Second, a much greater intimacy with Christ through the fellowship and in revelation and understanding of God's Word.
   Third, a much greater confidence to minister God's Word to others.
   We say,
   "MEDS is not intended to replace any kind of current Bible study you are currently doing but rather is designed to enhance and add to it."

NOTE: MEDS makes no practice of division or separation of or from the actual Body of Christ *(every believer)*. The ultimate goal is for each believer to "see Jesus" in a much greater way, to be a vessel that contains Christ to express Christ!

ALL GLORY AND THANKS FOR THE EXTRAORDINARY RESULTS GOES TO GOD ALONE!

Appendix 12

Most Effective Discipleship Seeds *(MEDS)*
Phase IV
ESSENTIAL ELEMENTS OF DISCIPLESHIP

INTRODUCTION POD

1st intro seed * VISION
concept TO SIGNIFICANTLY AID A MULTITUDE OF BELIEVERS
TO CONCEPTUALLY ENGRAFT GOD'S WORD ON THEIR HEARTS THROUGH THE ENJOYMENT OF SPIRITUAL FELLOWSHIP.
TO FACILITATE A MORE INTIMATE RELATIONSHIP WITH CHRIST AND TO HELP EACH PARTICIPANT UNCOVER THEIR OWN ABILITY TO "PAY IT FORWARD" IN THIS LIFESTYLE

scripture PROVERBS 29:18
concept WHERE THERE IS NO VISION THE PEOPLE PERISH

2nd intro seed * HOUSE
concept MOST EFFECTIVE DISCIPLESHIP SEEDS *(MEDS)* IS THE MOST EFFICIENT AND EFFECTIVE CHRIST-CENTERED WAY TO MATURE AS A DISCIPLE OF CHRIST OF WHICH WE ARE AWARE.

scripture PSALMS 127:1
concept UNLESS THE LORD BUILDS THE HOUSE THE LABORERS LABOR IN VAIN .

After the Introduction there are 4 Pods *(PSPR)* covering the Philosophy, Structure, Process, and Results of Most Effective Discipleship *(MEDS)*.

POD 1 - Philosophy *(MC.PLuS)*
seed 1 concept NOT COMPETITIVE, NO PRESSURE, NO FLESHLY JUDGING, NO GUILT TRIPS, BUT RATHER AN ABUNDANCE OF PATIENT ENCOURAGEMENT MAKING IT A...
seed 1 * MUTUAL COOPERATIVE FELLOWSHIP

1st scripture 2 CORINTHIANS 10:12
concept IT IS NOT WISE TO COMPARE OURSELVES WITH OURSELVES.

2nd scripture 1 CORINTHIANS 2:6-8
concept 1 WE SPEAK WISDOM AMONG THE MATURE
concept 2 WE SPEAK WISDOM IN A MYSTERY
concept 3 HAD THE RULERS OF THIS AGE KNOWN, THEY WOULD NOT HAVE CRUCIFIED THE LORD OF GLORY.

seed 2 concept NOT RELIGION, NOT OUTWARD BEHAVIOR MODIFICATION THROUGH THE WORKS OF THE LAW OR FLESHLY EFFORT, BUT RATHER INWARD TRANSFORMATION THRU INTIMATE RELATIONSHIP WITH CHRIST BY BELIEVING, ABIDING AND YIELDING, MAKING MEDS A DISCIPLESHIP THAT IS...
seed 2 * CHRIST-CENTERED, GRACE-CENTERED, AND RELATIONSHIP-CENTERED

1st scripture ACTS 17:22, 30
concept 1 I PERCEIVE IN ALL THINGS YOU ARE VERY RELIGIOUS.
concept 2 THESE TIMES OF IGNORANCE GOD OVERLOOKED IN PART, BUT NOW HE COMMANDS ALL MEN TO REPENT *(FROM RELIGION)*.

2nd scripture 1JOHN 2:18, 4:3
concept 1 THE ANTICHRIST IS COMING, THERE ARE MANY ANTICHRISTS IN THE WORLD.
concept 2 EVERY SPIRIT THAT DOES NOT CONFESS THAT JESUS HAS COME IN THE FLESH IS NOT OF GOD. THIS IS THE SPIRIT OF ANTICHRIST WHICH IS ALREADY IN THE WORLD.

seed 3 concept NOT ROTE MEMORY, NOT PREACHY, BUT RATHER CONCEPTUALLY ENGRAVING GOD'S WORD IN THE HEART BY SPEAKING IT PROPHETICALLY AND POETICALLY, MAKING IT PERSONAL, POSITIVE AND PRESENT TENSE WHICH RESULTS IN...
seed 3 * PLANTING AND ENGRAFTING GOD'S WORD

1st scripture PROVERB 3:3
concept I BIND MERCY AND TRUTH AROUND MY NECK AND WRITE THEM ON MY HEART.

2nd scripture 1 CORINTHIANS 3:3
concept I AM AN EPISTLE, NOT WRITTEN ON STONE, BUT WRITTEN BY THE SPIRIT ON THE FLESHLY TABLETS OF THE HEART.

seed 4 concept FOCUS NOT ON PERSONAL STUDY, *(ALTHOUGH PERSONAL STUDY IS ENCOURAGED)* BUT RATHER SPIRIT-LED FELLOWSHIP WITH A VISION *(PLAN AND CURRICULUM)*. WE CALL THIS...
seed 4 * LEARNING THROUGH THE ENJOYMENT OF FELLOWSHIP

1st scripture ACTS 2:42
concept I AM STEADFAST IN THE APOSTLES' DOCTRINE AND FELLOWSHIP, THE BREAKING OF BREAD AND PRAYER.

2nd scripture PHILEMON 6
concept THE SHARING OF MY FAITH IS MADE EFFECTUAL BY THE ACKNOWLEDGING OF EVERY GOOD THING THAT IS IN ME THROUGH CHRIST JESUS.

seed 5 concept 1 NO PRACTICE OF RANK, STATUS, OR TITLES... NO LORDING OVER... NO EXALTATION OF MEN,
concept 2 BUT RATHER EACH DISCIPLE TAKING THE INITIATIVE TO REVIEW THE SEEDS LEARNED AND LEARNING A NEW SEED WHEN HE IS READY...
concept 3 BEING FULLY QUALIFIED TO TEACH *(PAY FORWARD)* EACH SEED LEARNED...
concept 4 TAKING THE INITIATIVE AS A SERVANT LEADER TO TEACH SEEDS TO OTHERS... WE CALL THIS ...
seed 5 * SHARED INITIATIVE AND SHARED LEADERSHIP

1st scripture 2 CORINTHIANS 8:3-5
concept 1 I AM WILLING TO GIVE BEYOND MY OWN ABILITY.
concept 2 I IMPLORE OTHERS TO RECEIVE THE GIFT OF MINISTERING TO OTHERS.
concept 3 I GIVE MYSELF FIRST TO THE LORD AND THEN TO OTHERS.

2nd scripture 1 CORINTHIANS 7:35
concept I TEACH YOU FOR YOUR PROFIT, NOT TO PUT YOU ON A LEASH, BUT SO THAT YOU CAN SERVE THE LORD WITHOUT DISTRACTION.

POD 2 - Structure *(SLow.FaSt)*

seed 1 * SEEDS
concept 1 A SEED IS A UNIT OF TRUTH AND REVELATION THAT INCREASES THE POWER AND PRESENCE OF GOD IN MY LIFE.

concept 2 MEDS BASIC CURRICULUM *(PHASE I)* HAS 100 SEEDS IN 22 PODS *(4 OR 5 SEEDS PER POD)* AND INCLUDES 100'S OF SCRIPTURE PASSAGES.

1st scripture MATTHEW 13:11
concept IT'S BEEN GIVEN TO US TO KNOW THE MYSTERIES OF THE KINGDOM BUT NOT TO THEM.

2nd scripture MARK 4:8
concept SEED THAT FELL ON GOOD SOIL PRODUCED 30, 60, AND 100 FOLD.

seed 2 * LEVELS
concept PHASE I OF MEDS SPIRITUALLY FACILITATES AND GUIDES EACH DISCIPLE THROUGH 3 YEARS' WORTH OF ORGANIZED, OBSERVABLE, MEASURABLE, AND ENJOYABLE CHRISTIAN GROWTH AND MATURITY.

1st scripture MARK 4:26-28
concept A MAN SOWS A SEED...
THE MAN SLEEPS BY NIGHT AND WAKES AT DAY... THE SEED SPROUTS BUT THE MAN KNOWS NOT HOW...
THE EARTH YIELDS FIRST THE BLADE, THEN THE HEAD, AFTER THAT THE FULL GRAIN IN THE HEAD.

2nd scripture JOHN 13:35
concept THEY WILL KNOW WE ARE HIS DISCIPLES BY OUR LOVE FOR ONE ANOTHER.

seed 3 * FORMAT
concept ALL SEEDS HAVE A SEED NAME, A CONCEPT OR CONCEPTS RELATED TO THE SEED NAME, A SCRIPTURE OR MULTIPLE SCRIPTURES, AND A SCRIPTURE CONCEPT OR CONCEPTS. ADDITIONALLY, A SEED MAY HAVE A PRINCIPLE OR PRINCIPLES, AND RELATED CLUES OR HINTS, AS WELL AS ACRONYMS USED AS LEARNING AIDS.

1st scripture ECCLESIASTES 12:9, 10
concept 1 THE TEACHER SEARCHED OUT, PONDERED, AND SET IN ORDER GOD'S WORD.
concept 2 THE TEACHER FOUND JUST THE RIGHT WORDS TO IMPART KNOWLEDGE TO THE PEOPLE.

concept 3 THE WORDS WERE LIKE NAILS USED BY THE MASTER CRAFTSMAN TO BUILD THE SPIRITUAL HOUSE.

2nd scripture ISAIAH 28:9, 10
concept 1 EACH DISCIPLE NEEDS TO BE WEANED FROM THE MILK.
concept 2 THE WORD INCREASES IN US LINE UPON LINE, PRECEPT ON PRECEPT, A LITTLE HERE A LITTLE THERE.

seed 4 * SPECIAL ADDENDUM PODS
concept ARE FOR THOSE WHO DESIRE FUTHER SPIRITUAL GROWTH AND MATURITY. CURRENTLY THERE ARE DOZENS OF PHASES, HUNDREDS OF PODS, AND THOUSANDS OF SEEDS AVAILABLE TO BE MASTERED.

1st scripture JEREMIAH 33:3
concept I CALL TO THE LORD AND HE ANSWERS ME AND HE SHOWS ME GREAT AND WONDERFUL THINGS THAT I DO NOT KNOW.

2nd scripture PHILIPPIANS 1:6
concept HE WHO BEGAN A GOOD IN ME WILL CARRY IT ON TO COMPLETION.

POD 3 - Process *(OBRE)*

seed 1 * ONE SEED...
concept AT A TIME PERMANENTLY MASTERED FOR ETERNAL WISDOM.

1st scripture PROVERBS 24:27
concept PLOW THE FIELD, THEN BUILD THE HOUSE. *(FIRST THINGS FIRST)*.

2nd scripture PROVERBS 24:3, 4
concept THROUGH WISDOM THE HOUSE IS BUILT. BY UNDERSTANDING IT IS ESTABLISHED. BY KNOWLEDGE THE ROOMS ARE FILLED WITH ALL PRECIOUS AND PLEASANT RICHES.

seed 2 * BALANCED CONVERSATIONAL FELLOWSHIP...
concept RELIES ON SPIRIT REGULATED CONVERSATION AND FELLOWSHIP THAT BENEFITS ALL PARTAKERS.

1st scripture PROVERBS 27:17
concept AS IRON SHARPENS IRON, SO ONE MAN SHARPENS ANOTHER.

2nd scripture EPHESIANS 4:29, 30
concept LET NO CORRUPT WORD PROCEED FROM YOUR MOUTH, BUT ONLY THAT WHICH IS USEFUL FOR BUILDING UP OTHERS. DON'T GRIEVE THE SPIRIT WHO HAS SEALED US.

seed 3 * REPETITIVE AND PERSISTENT MUTUAL FEEDING
concept BY THIS EACH DISCIPLE IS PROGRESSIVELY AND THOROUGHLY CONSTITUTED WITH GOD'S GRACE AND TRUTH.

1st scripture PHILIPPIANS 3:1
concept TO REPEAT THE SAME THINGS IS NOT TEDIOUS FOR ME AND IT KEEPS YOU SAFE.

2nd scripture PSALMS 119:11
concept I HAVE HIDDEN YOUR WORD IN MY HEART THAT I MIGHT NOT SIN AGAINST YOU.

seed 4 * EDIFICATION BY DISPENSATION
concept ACTIVE PARTICIPATION IN THE ECONOMY OF GOD ...
(GRK. OIKOSNOMOS) = LAW OF THE HOUSE = EACH BELIEVER BECOMES A TRUSTED STEWARD FOR DISPENSATION OF GOD'S WORD.

1st scripture EPHESIANS 3:2
concept THE DISPENSATION OF THE GRACE OF GOD WAS GIVEN TO ME FOR YOU.

2nd scripture GALATIANS 5: 7-9
concept 1 YOU RAN WELL, WHO HINDERED YOU.
concept 2 THIS PERSUASION DOES NOT COME FROM THE ONE WHO CALLED YOU.
concept 3 A LITTLE LEAVEN LEAVENS THE WHOLE LUMP.

POD 4 - Results *(UICI)*

seed 1 * UNDERSTANDING...
concept OF GOD'S WORD AND HOW TO RIGHTLY DIVIDE IT IS GREATLY INCREASED.

1st scripture PROVERBS 4:5
concept GET WISDOM, GET UNDERSTANDING AND DO NOT TURN FROM IT.

2nd scripture PROVERBS 10:4
concept A SLACK HAND MAKES ONE POOR, A DILIGENT HAND MAKES ONE RICH.

seed 2 * INTIMACY...
concept WITH CHRIST BY ONGOING REVELATION IS GREATLY INCREASED.

1st scripture GALATIANS 3:1-3
concept 1 WHO BEWITCHED YOU BEFORE WHOM CHRIST WAS CLEARLY PORTRAYED AS CRUCIFIED?
concept 2 DID YOU RECEIVE THE SPIRIT BY WORKS THE OF THE LAW OR BY THE HEARING OF FAITH?
concept 3 ARE YOU SO FOOLISH HAVING BEGUN IN THE SPIRIT YOU ARE NOW SEEKING PERFECTION BY THE FLESH?

2nd scripture EPHESIANS 3:12
concept IN CHRIST WE HAVE BOLDNESS AND ACCESS WITH CONFIDENCE THROUGH FAITH IN HIM.

seed 3 * CONFIDENCE...
concept TO EFFECTIVELY MINISTER GOD'S GRACE AND MERCY TO OTHERS IS GREATLY INCREASED.

1st scripture PROVERBS 14:26
concept IN THE FEAR OF THE LORD THERE IS STRONG CONFIDENCE, AND THE CHILDREN HAVE REFUGE.

2nd scripture 2 TIMOTHY 3:17
concept AS A MAN OF GOD I AM THOROUGHLY EQUIPPED FOR EVERY GOOD WORK.

seed 4 * INSIGHTFUL WISDOM
concept ABILITY TO APPLY, CONNECT, EXPLAIN AND EXPRESS THE MULTI-FACETED MYSTERIES OF GOD AND HIS WORD TO OTHERS GREATLY INCREASED.

1st scripture PROVERBS 18:16
concept A MAN'S GIFT MAKES ROOM FOR HIM,
AND BRINGS HIM BEFORE GREAT MEN.

2nd scripture DEUTERONOMY 29:29
concept THE SECRET THINGS BELONG TO THE LORD OUR GOD, BUT THOSE THINGS WHICH ARE REVEALED BELONG TO US AND OUR CHILDREN FOREVER.

3rd scripture PROVERBS 25:2
concept IT IS THE GLORY OF GOD TO CONCEAL A MATTER,
BUT IT IS THE GLORY OF KINGS TO SEARCH OUT A MATTER.

end of phase IV - Essential Elements of MEDS

Appendix 13

Most Effective Discipleship Seeds *(MEDS)*
(Promotional flyer)

What is faith-righteousness?
Is today's Bible reliable?

Can I know for sure my eternal destiny?
Is religion Antichrist?
What is the Kingdom of God?
What is "ungodly" obedience?
Can I have an intimate relationship with God?
Why praise and worship?
How can I know that I matter?
What is my spiritual gift?
What is the real meaning of the Sabbath?
How can I experience consistent triumph over sin?
Is "church" a building?
Is self-worth a Biblical teaching?
Does our tradition make God's Word of no effect?
What is an over-comer?
How does my unforgiveness of others affect me?
How do I "put on" the armor of God?
What is the hidden source of my pain and anguish?
Why is being a "doer of the Word" not what you think it is?

Is Jesus God?
Why is understanding the "kenosis" important?
Is God ever angry with me?
What is the "offense of the cross"?
What is the best way to pray?
What is the "works" of patience?
What is the "strength of sin"?
What is the power of the tongue?
What is the purpose of my life?
What are the 4 lives in me?
Is God 3 or 1?
What is true humility?
Is God ever the source of evil?
Is it important to love yourself first?
What is prayer ministry?
What is the root of righteousness?
What is the fruit of righteousness?
What is the unpardonable sin?
How do I gain a godly contentment?
What is the fallacy of "heavenly mansions"?

KNOW AND BE ABLE TO GIVE DEFINITE BIBLE ANSWERS TO THESE AND MANY OTHER IMPORTANT QUESTIONS.

BECOME ROOTED, GROUNDED, AND ESTABLISHED IN ESSENTIAL LIFE AND BIBLE TRUTHS.

MOST EFFECTIVE DISCIPLESHIP SEEDS *(MEDS)* IS A PRIORITIZED PATTERN OF 100 ORAL SEEDS OF TRUTH TO WRITE PROGRESSIVELY AND PERMANENTLY ON YOUR HEART FOR AN ABUNDANT LIFE ACCOMPLISHED THROUGH THE ENJOYMENT OF FELLOWSHIP!

Appendix 14

Grid for year 1 / Phase I grids *(pegboard)* pods 1-7

This page is for individual Disciples to study the Seeds on their own when there is no one to fellowship with. Use this chart along with the chapter overviews at the end of each chapter *(see key at end)*

KEY
Bold Capital letters to far left= symbol for Name of Seed
c = concept of Seed or Scripture
4c = 4th concept
S = scripture address
x = variable of formula
P = Principle
b = baptism

* grid pod 1
F c S c S c
A c S c
C c S c
C c S c S c

* grid for pod 2
B c S c S c
D c S c S c
S c S c c c S c
R c S c S c

* grid for pod.3
3 c c c S c
B c *(27x)*
2 c S c
K c c c c S c c c

* grid for pod 4
4 c c   S c   S c
c c
c c
c c

P c c   S c   S c   S c c c

K c   S c   S c
3 c c   S cc cccc cccc
c cccccc
K c   S c

* grid for pod 5
5 c c   S c   S c   S c
c c
c

P c c c   S c   S c   S c
c c

P c c   S c   S c
c c
c c

T c   S c   S c

* grid for pod 6
6   S c
  P c   P c   P c   P c
  P c   P c c c c

D c   S c

S c c   S c   S c   S c

P c   S c

grid for pod 7 *
7 bc bc bc bc   S c   S c   S c
bc bc bc

W x+x+x=x   S c c c c c c c c
c c c c

F 1c 2c 3c 4c   S c
5c 6c 7c

S c S c S c

F 1c 2c 3c 4c S c S c S c
5c 6c 7c

Appendix 15

grid for GALATIANS PHASE

This page is for individual Disciples to study the Seeds on their own when there is no one to fellowship with. Use this chart along with the chapter overviews at the end of each chapter *(see key at end)*

KEY
Cap letters to far left = symbol for Name of Seed
Indented Cap Letter = Special Seed Name
c = concept of Seed or Scripture
S = scripture address

Subject. c

* grid for chapter and...
Pod 1 Prin. c
D c
N c
R c
P c
no specials

grid for chapter and...

Pod 2 Prin. c
S c
R c
N c
M c
specials
C c
F c

grid for chapter and...
Pod 3 Prin. c
P c
S c
L c
C c
specials
B c
R c
F c

I c
F c
L c
C c
A c

G c
A c
A c

grid for chapter and...
Pod 4 Prin. c

No standard seeds for chapter 4
specials

H c
F c
S c
S c

B c
E c

Z c
L c

grid for chapter and...
Pod 5 Prin. c

S c
F c
C c
I c
specials
F c

H c
P c
L c
L c

O c
L c
W c
F c
C c

ABOUT THE AUTHOR

D.S. Foster, while incarcerated, received, pioneered, and developed the Most Effective Discipleship Seeds (MEDS) in response to his heart's desire to serve others effectively. He is living proof that God uses the humbled and broken to accomplish His Kingdom purposes. Through MEDS, Foster has significantly transformed many lives through this proven discipleship practiced in the enjoyment of fellowship and the Holy Spirit's power. His unique "conceptual learning" and "pay it forward" approach has benefitted multitudes of believers. Many have far surpassed their expectations by learning and writing on their hearts dozens (or hundreds or more) of essential scripture concepts and locations.

AUTHOR'S FINAL THOUGHTS

I have labored with great pleasure in this Discipleship for over 15 years. Through MEDS I have experienced tremendous growth in my spiritual life and witnessed the same in hundreds of others. I am delighted to help any church, small group, or individual implement this Discipleship in sphere of influence. My contact information is:

Davidforjesuschrist7@gmail.com
269-270-2811

www.ingramcontent.com/pod-product-compliance
Lightning Source LLC
LaVergne TN
LVHW011802060526
838200LV00053B/3655